PILGRIM IN THE LAND OF ALLIGATORS

Florida History and Culture

UNIVERSITY PRESS OF FLORIDA

Florida A&M University, Tallahassee
Florida Atlantic University, Boca Raton
Florida Gulf Coast University, Ft. Myers
Florida International University, Miami
Florida State University, Tallahassee
New College of Florida, Sarasota
University of Central Florida, Orlando
University of Florida, Gainesville
University of North Florida, Jacksonville
University of South Florida, Tampa
University of West Florida, Pensacola

University Press of Florida
Gainesville/Tallahassee/Tampa/Boca Raton
Pensacola/Orlando/Miami/Jacksonville/Ft. Myers/Sarasota

Pilgrim

IN THE

LAND OF

ALLIGATORS

More Stories about Real Florida

Jeff Klinkenberg

Foreword by Gary Mormino and Raymond Arsenault

For my always inspirational mentors,
Gary Mormino and Ray Arsenault

Copyright 2008 by the *St. Petersburg Times*, the Times Publishing Company
Printed in the United States of America on acid-free paper

16 15 14 13 12 11   6 5 4 3 2 1

First cloth printing, 2008
First paperback printing, 2011

Library of Congress Cataloging-in-Publication Data
Klinkenberg, Jeff.
Pilgrim in the land of alligators: more stories about real Florida / by Jeff
Klinkenberg; foreword by Gary Mormino and Raymond Arsenault.
p. cm.—(The Florida history and culture series)
ISBN 978-0-8130-3208-5 (cloth)
ISBN 978-0-8130-3694-6 (paperback)
1. Florida—Description and travel—Anecdotes. 2. Klinkenberg, Jeff—
Travel—Florida—Anecdotes. 3. Florida—Biography—Anecdotes.
4. Florida—Social life and customs—Anecdotes. I. Title.
F316.2.K565 2008
975.9—dc22   2007032163

The University Press of Florida is the scholarly publishing agency for the
State University System of Florida, comprising Florida A&M University,
Florida Atlantic University, Florida Gulf Coast University, Florida Interna-
tional University, Florida State University, New College of Florida, Univer-
sity of Central Florida, University of Florida, University of North Florida,
University of South Florida, and University of West Florida.

University Press of Florida
15 Northwest 15th Street
Gainesville, FL 32611-2079
http://www.upf.com

CONTENTS

Series foreword vii

Foreword by William McKeen ix

Preface xi

Acknowledgments xiii

MY FLORIDA

1. Big Cypress: Loop Road 3

2. Pass a Grille: The Beach 12

3. Corkscrew Swamp: Cypress Trees 15

4. De Leon Springs: Pancakes 20

5. St. Petersburg: Indian Mound 24

FLORIDA ICONS

6. Ocala: Coppertone Girl 31

7. Wakulla Springs: Return of the Gill Men 37

8. Miami Lakes: Skink 45

9. St. Augustine: Ponce de León 53

10. St. Petersburg: Babe Ruth 60

11. Winter Haven: Miz Marjorie's Mommy Dearest 68

12. Tallahassee: Lucy 75

13. Clearwater Beach: The Clearwater Monster 84

WORKING FLORIDA

14. Tarpon Springs: Sponge Diver 91

15. St. Petersburg: Folding the Map 96

16. Gibsonton: Making Biscuits 100

17. Ybor City: Coffee Talk with el Cafetero 104

18. Fort Green: Citrus Ladders 109

19. Lake Wales: Playing the Carillon 113

20. Tampa: Pop Overton 118

21. Okeechobee: Hog Catchers 123

22. Palmetto: Snead Island Boat Works   130

23. East Point: Highway Patrolman   134

DANGEROUS FLORIDA

24. Weeki Wachee: Cave Diving   141

25. Gainesville: Mojo   145

26. St. Petersburg: The 1935 Hurricane   150

27. St. Petersburg: Revenge of the Sandwich   156

28. Summerdale, Alabama: Bull Sharks   161

LIVING AND DYING

29. Arcadia: Al and Karen Smoke   173

30. Bradenton: Going Barefoot   180

31. St. Petersburg: Tommy   184

32. Ellenton: Freedom Riders   189

33. Tampa: The Bone Man   198

34. St. Petersburg: Plume Hunter   204

35. Gainesville: David Stevenson   209

36. Vero Beach: Mosquito Man   218

37. Anna Maria Island: Old Jack Gray   224

38. Weeki Wachee: Picture Man Tells His Story   226

39. St. Petersburg: Mother's Nature   230

SERIES FOREWORD

Pilgrim in the Land of Alligators: More Stories about Real Florida is the latest volume of a series devoted to the study of Florida history and culture. During the past half century, the burgeoning population and increased national and international visibility of Florida have sparked a great deal of popular interest in the state's past, present, and future. As a favorite destination of countless tourists and as the new home for millions of retirees and transplants, modern Florida has become a demographic, political, and cultural bellwether. Florida has also emerged as a popular subject and setting for scholars and writers. The Florida History and Culture Series provides an attractive and accessible format for Florida-related books. From killer hurricanes to disputed elections, from tales of the Everglades to profiles of Sun Belt cities, Florida is simply irresistible.

The University Press of Florida is committed to the creation of an eclectic but carefully crafted set of books that will provide the field of Florida studies with a new focus that will encourage Florida writers to consider the broader implications and context of their work. The series includes standard academic monographs, as well as works of synthesis, memoirs, and anthologies. And, while the series features books of historical interest, authors researching Florida's environment, politics, literature, and popular or material culture are encouraged to submit their manuscripts as well. Each book offers a distinct personality and voice, but the ultimate goal of the series is to foster a broad sense of community and collaboration among Florida scholars.

The publication of *Pilgrim in the Land of Alligators* provides a welcome addition. Jeff Klinkenberg knows the bayous and backwoods of the Loxahatchee and Corkscrew Swamp, but he also can hold court in a debate about the perfection of the Cuban sandwich or the intricacies of a citrus ladder. For over three decades, he has studied and written about Florida. Amid a vanishing Florida rushing toward modernity, Klinkenberg represents a vanishing breed of Florida journalist. The award-winning *St. Petersburg Times* reporter prowls for authentic and eccentric characters and places that make the state both precious and slightly wacky.

Jeff Klinkenberg is a Florida treasure. He reminds Floridians that the paradise that drew generations of New Englanders and Ohioans to the Sunshine State can still be found. He takes readers on a tour of his boyhood stomping grounds, the Everglades Loop Road. He also takes them cave diving and biscuit making. He introduces readers to Florida icons: Lucy Morgan, the Clearwater monster, a Freedom Rider, hog catchers, the state highway patrolman warning motorists of the perils of not paying for gasoline, and artisans who craft citrus ladders, giant biscuits, and ethereal pancakes. But mostly, *Pilgrim in the Land of Alligators* is about the "real Florida."

Gary R. Mormino and Raymond Arsenault
Series Coeditors

FOREWORD

A few years back—in better budget times—I hired Jeff Klinkenberg to teach our feature writing course at the University of Florida. Whenever possible, we try to bring in working reporters to teach in the Department of Journalism. Gainesville's talent pool is shallow and it's sometimes hard for a measly university paycheck to lure journalists from Jacksonville, Orlando, or Tampa Bay. Getting a star columnist from the *St. Petersburg Times* was a coup.

Though it meant a higher rate than we usually pay ("The Klinkenberg Bonus," he insisted we call it) and a dull Interstate drive from St. Petersburg, Jeff was willing to make the sacrifice—as long as we also paid for a specified number of nights' lodging at the Herlong Mansion in Micanopy. (He hopes one day to wake up face-to-face with one of the Herlong's ghosts.)

The second week of that semester, a young woman showed up at my door, looking for her feature-writing class. She had missed the first week.

"It's meeting at Paynes Prairie today," I told her.

"Uh, *yeah*," she snorted. "No, I mean, like *really* . . . where is it?"

"It's meeting at Paynes Prairie," I repeated. "For real."

The student rolled her eyes and slouched out of my office. *I wonder how long she'll last?* I thought.

But that's Klinkenberg. Like all great teachers, he knows that writing can't be taught—it can only be learned—and that chances are you won't learn much of anything sitting in a classroom. Jeff insisted that his students see the world up close and personal, in all of its weirdness and splendor.

I've always thought that Jeff had the best job in Florida: *Have Radials, Will Travel.* He drives the county roads and blue highways of this wacky state and gets to meet the sort of people you'll never see on the network news. Lots of journalists have followed this sort of path. Before the Second World War, Ernie Pyle drove around the country, finding common-man stories that were syndicated by the Scripps Howard News Service. In the midst of the bad craziness of the 1960s, CBS News correspondent Charles Kuralt delivered literate and soothing fables of off-the-beaten-path America.

Both of those journalists were poet laureates of the road and I bet they wouldn't mind scooting over to give Jeff the shotgun seat. Like them, Jeff is a true believer in the idea of wonderment around the next bend. For thirty years, he has turned his eye on all of Florida's creatures—great and small, sacred and profane, human and otherwise. As the state becomes ever more "pallid and boring" (Jeff's phrase), he still manages to crawl into the corners to find the rare, precious, beautiful, and odd.

There's a lot of debate in the journalism business about the future of newspapers. Most academic chin-scratchers seem to think it's bleak and that only aging dilettantes and technological dinosaurs still read newspapers. But I've always believed that the future of print journalism is in its past—in great stories, well told. Television, radio, and the Internet long ago swiped the real news from newspapers and left us with big, wide-open spaces to do what newspapers do best: tell stories. Since humans first gathered around a campfire, we wanted stories. When we crawled into daddy's lap at bedtime, we just wanted stories. When we trudge to the end of the driveway at the crack of dawn, it's stories that we want to find when we rip open the newspaper. I've always thought it the height of arrogance that this generation thinks it will preside over the death of something that's been around, in some form or another, since 59 B.C. As long as newspapers print great stories, they will have an audience.

Jeff Klinkenberg is a masterful storyteller. It's a pleasure to open up the paper and be drawn into one of his great tales. It's an even greater pleasure—a weenie roast, even—to have his works collected in this wonderful volume.

William McKeen

PREFACE

Like William Bartram, who visited Florida in the eighteenth century, I am a pilgrim in the land of alligators. Bartram toured the South between 1774 and 1776, paddled a canoe, caught bass, chatted with Seminoles, drew pictures of plants and animals, and was terrified the gators were going to eat him.

A lot of folks who should know better tell me the real Florida, the authentic Florida, is gone. Kaput. But I'll tell you something. What Bartram experienced in his time, a Floridian can easily experience in the twenty-first century. I do. Anyone who holds this book in his or her hand can do the same.

Of course, much has changed in the last couple of centuries. I live on Florida's west coast, in Pinellas, the most urban county in the state. Often the traffic and the congestion and the noise get me down. At the same time, I can walk from my house in downtown St. Petersburg five blocks and attend a major league baseball game at Tropicana Field. I can walk to the St. Petersburg Museum of Fine Arts and admire a painting of primitive Florida by my favorite nineteenth-century landscape artist, Martin Johnson Heade. Last time I fell off my bicycle and bashed open my face, I was transported by ambulance to a wonderful, modern hospital, Bayfront Medical Center. The ER doctor didn't make me pretty, but at least she stitched my lip and nose back together so I wouldn't scare my grandkids.

I guess I am a civilized wild man. As a city rat, I am glad Florida is a modern place. I love to drink Cuban coffee in Ybor City in Tampa. I love a restaurant that serves good biscuits. As a country mouse, I am even happier a good deal of my state remains primitive. I like going barefoot. I like cypress swamps. I am thrilled when I encounter an alligator. You can be devoured by alligators in Florida. You can step on stingrays and rattlesnakes. A friend of mine lost his arm to a bull shark. And you know what? You'll read about this later, but I'll tell you right now that my friend didn't blame the shark for what happened. When you dip your toes in the water here, when you push your kayak off the bank in the Ten Thousand Islands of the Everglades, you're in the wilderness. What a marvelous place to visit, to live, and to die.

Bartram, whose book *Travels* has been in glorious print since 1791, understood the unusual culture of Florida. So did Harriet Beecher Stowe, who moved here to escape the hoohaw after *Uncle Tom's Cabin* and ended up writing a beautiful book about her St. Johns River home in *Palmetto Leaves*.

This book is a collection of essays I wrote about Florida culture at the beginning of the twenty-first century. Some of the essays look back, but most of my stories are rooted in the present. This book is about Florida people, living and dead. It is about Florida places, some battered and some bruised, but still holding on.

Holding on like those alligators. They'll be here when the pilgrims are gone.

ACKNOWLEDGMENTS

I want to thank the following people for their love, friendship, or encouragement: Mimi Andelman, Ray Arsenault, Kathy Arsenault, Caryn Baird, Andy Barnes, John Barry, Kelley Benham, Richard Bockman, Heath Bowman, Neil Brown, Stephen Buckley, Dawn Cate, Joe Childs, Roy Peter Clark, Deborah Curtiss, Sean Daly, Eric Deggans, Lane Degregory, Bob Devin-Jones, John Fleming, Michael Foley, Tom French, James Gibson, Bob Graham, Jeanne Grinstead, John Hires, Scott Keeler, Frank King, Lori King, Steve Klemawesch, Heather Klinkenberg, Kyle Kreiger, Bill Maxwell, Bill McKeen, John Moran, Gary Mormino, Lynne Mormino, Meredith Morris-Babb, Beth Navage, Wilma Norton, Eugene Patterson, Marty Petty, Howell Raines, Dorothy Shea, Paul Shea, Jack Stephenson, John Stewart, Sheila Stewart, Christopher Still, Charlotte Sutton, Howard Troxler, Susan Giles-Wantuck, Randy Wayne White, and my editor, Mike Wilson.

Love and happiness to my astonishing wife, Susan King, and to our lovely adult children, Kristin, Peter, Katie, and Lindsay, and to our grandkids, Jakob and Mary Jane Bowman.

MY FLORIDA

I

BIG CYPRESS

Loop Road

First I tapped the brake. Then I stepped hard. The 11-foot alligator, sprawled across Loop Road in South Florida, stayed put. With no room to turn around and no desire to drive in reverse, I honked.

The gator, insolent creature, ignored me. Fighting road rage, I inched closer, almost nudging the beast with my front tires. Nothing. I had no intention of leaving my truck, but I swung open the door to see what would happen. The ka-chunk must have made the vehicle seem menacing. Hissing like a dragon, the great reptile lumbered into the swamp.

As the bubbles dissipated, the swamp once again became placid, and for an instant I was tempted to visit the shoreline for a better look. Then I remembered the late Clara McKay, the woman everybody called the "Beer-Worm Lady" because that's what she sold at her little store. She knew the Big Cypress, knew the ways of critters, but one day she let her guard down. To hear her tell it, she was dipping water for her beloved pet cats when a big alligator lunged up and tore off her right arm.

I remained securely behind the wheel, nudged the gas pedal, and continued my journey down the Loop Road and into my past.

When I was a teenager, the Loop Road was the real Mister Toad's Wild Ride. It was the most untamed place I knew, the most remote, smoke-'em-if-you-got-'em, people-unfriendly byway in Florida. It was 26 hellish miles of moon-crater potholes, gape-jawed alligators, choleric cottonmouths, and swamp men who would just as soon spit on your tennies as say hello. In the twenty-first century, the federal government owns 700,000 acres of the Big Cypress National Preserve. The potholes are

The Loop Road. Photo by Jeff Klinkenberg.

gone and laws are now occasionally enforced, but otherwise the Loop Road remains a marathon of crushed gravel, reptiles, and watch-your-back roughnecks.

It begins at Monroe Station on the Tamiami Trail in Collier County, meanders south for a spell, then snakes back northeast toward the Tamiami Trail at the Miccosukee Indian Reservation in Miami-Dade County. Construction crews built the road in the 1920s but forgot to add civilization.

The uncivilized nature of the Loop Road made it attractive to nature lovers, but also to plume hunters, gator poachers, orchid thieves, moonshiners, pot growers, and nonconformists. Many settled along the Loop where it dips, briefly, into Monroe County. The nearest Monroe County sheriff's substation is about 80 miles away, by road, in the Florida Keys.

An hour east of the Loop Road is Florida's gritty urban center, Miami. An hour west is conservative and wealthy Naples. On certain places on the Loop Road, it feels like the nineteenth century.

When Hurricane Wilma shut down coastal South Florida in 2005, the dozen or so full-time residents of the Loop felt only mildly inconvenienced. They are accustomed to wind and flood. They know how to patch a roof and remove a fallen tree from the porch. They are smart enough to store drinking water and to keep their matches dry. About the time Neil Armstrong walked on the moon, the Loop Road got electricity. A few residents still think fondly of the days before electricity.

In modern Florida, wardens from the National Park Service patrol Loop Road. But it is still the wrong place to lock your keys in the car, run out of gas, or suffer a dead battery. Cell phones seldom pick up a signal on the Loop Road, but mosquitoes and horseflies work overtime even on a mild February day. Never leave your vehicle without first checking for snakes.

I saw no reptiles when I stopped the truck, and when I stepped onto the road, the swamp grew immediately silent. The crickets, first to recover their wits, commenced chirping. Then the red-winged blackbirds peppered me with sardonic screeches. The pig frogs added hearty grunts to the Loop Road cacophony.

I snapped photos of the cypress trees, the ferns, the lily pads. I snapped a photo of the lonely road. Years ago, everybody felt the need to be armed, but nowadays we tourists toted cameras in case we encountered a panther, bear, or swamp nymphet.

The Loop Road is Florida's Garden of Eden—before the serpent tempted Adam and Eve and God shamed them into wearing clothes. I wouldn't be the first to see somebody sauntering the Loop fashionably naked.

When I was a kid, my dad and I fished on the Tamiami Trail, mostly in the Everglades, though sometimes farther out in the Big Cypress. In 1965, my friends and I began visiting Loop Road on our own. We'd fish for bass at dawn and look for snakes after the sun got up. My friends and I were more comfortable among cold-blooded reptiles than warm-blooded girls. One of us would drive. The others would sit on the hood armed with pillowcases. Spotting a snake, we would leap from the hood, catch the snake with a bare hand, and stuff it into the pillowcase. I wish I could say we were gathering snakes for the good of science, but we weren't. We were catching and later releasing them for the sheer thrill of messing with something that would bite if given a chance.

After a scintillating morning with the snakes, we'd stop at a place called Monroe Station on the intersection of Loop Road and the Tamiami Trail. Built in 1928, it was originally a gas station and convenience store. By the time I discovered it, Monroe Station was the redneck capital of South Florida.

Big Joe Lord ran the place, helped by his wife, Sweet Sue. Big Joe was always angry, usually at the government, which was poised at the time to buy the Big Cypress Swamp and possibly put him out of business. He was also angry about Vietnam War protesters, men with long hair, pot smokers, forced busing, and maybe the direction of the wind. I kept my long hair and opinions under my hat, sat at the counter, and ate Sweet Sue's ham steak with red-eye gravy.

Whenever I'm in the Big Cypress, I stop at Monroe Station for old time's sake. It closed in 1987 and is one good hurricane from falling down. Under the dust, among the cobwebs, one old business card clung to the dining room wall. "T. K. Riggs," it said. "Unemployed." I punched the telephone number on the card into my cell phone. The woman who answered said "Nobody here by that name." Exploring the place, I saw rusty cans and whiskey bottles through yawning holes in the floorboards. Roach droppings, looking like coffee grounds, blanketed Sweet Sue's old luncheon counter.

The park service plans to spend $500,000 to restore the old building. Rangers may use it as an office, a visitor center, or a museum. If Big Joe Lord's ghost haunts Monroe Station, maybe he'll stop cussing the government. But probably not.

When I was a kid, another place to eat on Loop Road was the Gator Hook Lodge in the tiny community of Pinecrest. A sign outside the door warned, "No Guns or Knives Allowed Inside" and was roundly ignored. A guy named Jack Knight ran Gator Hook. I remember him being rough around the edges, but an okay guy. On Saturday nights, he always hired a band. The fiddler in the Gator Hook band was Ervin Rouse, who had written "Orange Blossom Special" back in the 1930s. I never heard him play, but he lived out there with his dogs, Butterball and Curly.

Even at lunchtime the Gator Hook Lodge was an uninviting place, which made it attractive to teenage boys hoping for adventure. When the screen door banged shut behind you, every head in the tavern turned to see who had entered. At midmorning, many patrons already staggered around drunk.

Peter Matthiessen set his novel *Lost Man's River* in the Everglades. Perhaps the most menacing scene takes place in the Gator Hook, when a drunk, one-armed gator poacher explains his relationship with park rangers.

"Now I ain't got nothin personal against the ranger," the poacher said. "Might could be a real likable young feller, just a-tryin to get by, same as what I'm doin. Might got him a sweet lovin wife and a couple real cute li'l fellers back home waiting on him, or maybe just the sweetest baby girl—same as what I got! Ain't no difference between him and me at all!

"But if'n that boy tries to take my gators, well, I got my duty to my people, ain't that right? Got my duty to take care of my little girl back home that's waitin on me to put bread on the table! Ain't that only natural? So all I'm sayin—and it would be pathetical, and I am the first one to admit it—all I'm sayin, now, if any such a feller, and I don't care who, tries to keep me from my hard-earned livin I surely would be sorry. 'Cause I reckon I would have to leave him out there."

One time my dad asked how the fishing and snaking had gone. I gave him a report and casually mentioned the interesting eatery on Loop Road. He turned pale. "Not a place for you," he said.

The Gator Hook is gone now, torn down except for steps I have heard about but never can find. Jack Knight is dead. Ervin Rouse is dead. Whenever I drive the Loop Road I adjust my iPod to the playlist I call "Country Blues." Sooner or later, "Orange Blossom Special" comes on.

Years ago, it took three hours to drive the Loop Road because of potholes. Now it takes about an hour, depending on gator traffic. In some places, the road is straight as a rifle barrel; in other places, it curves through the swamp like a Miccosukee's bow. The road is about 12 feet across, narrower at bridges, which, by the way, lack railings.

The Florida panther is the rarest large animal in North America, but I know a guy who has seen three over the years on Loop Road. I know people who have encountered bears. Gators are as common as the lizards in your backyard.

Gator in the road! It crashed like a falling piano into the black water. Bromeliad air plants on the high branches dripped like icing from a cake. Pretty white ibises hopped from log to log. The old-timers ate them. Now the white ibis is threatened and most of the old-timers are extinct.

As I approached Pinecrest, I noticed evidence of human habitation. Old cars. Fences. Threatening signs. "My dogs can make it to the fence in three seconds. Can you?"

I pulled up to a fence and waited. A woman ambled out, gave me the eye. I told her about my appointment with Sandy Dayhoff.

Sandy Dayhoff, a park ranger for thirty-five years, represents the only official law and order on the Loop Road. The year she turned seventeen—1962—she dropped out of Miami High School and married "one of those swamp boys," Fred Dayhoff. They moved to Loop Road.

"We didn't have electricity, running water, phones, or even a car for years," she told me. "We didn't need it or want it." Twice a month her mother drove from Miami with staples. Otherwise the young couple was self-sufficient. Sandy grew vegetables and raised ducks and chickens. Fred was an accomplished hunter, killing deer, hogs, and turkeys. On the Loop, he is called "the Invisible Man" because of his shy ways. Sandy is a private person, too. I asked what she did to pass the time. "I stay busy." Read? "Yes." What do you read? "All kinds of things." Listen to music? "I love music." What kind? "All kinds."

She had curly brown hair and eyes like dark pools. She looked sturdy enough to skin a hog, drag a gator out of a hole, and put a curious reporter in his place.

"I've never wanted to leave here," she said. "The nights are so beautiful. Years ago the stars were so bright you couldn't believe it. The stars are still pretty, but if you look east now you see this big dome of light coming from Miami. Miami seems to get closer every year."

During rainy season, mosquitoes are fierce. Bobcats eat chickens. One time Sandy's foot encountered the fangs of a snake.

"Pygmy rattler," she said. "I was wearing flip-flops. Somebody should have written D-U-M-B on my forehead."

Was the bite painful?

"Yes."

Go to the hospital in Miami?

"Naw."

Back on the Loop Road, I stopped my car next to a neat grave. "RIP," the tombstone read. Somebody had placed fresh flowers. Across from the grave was what looked like a fort. A sign on the 8-foot wall said "Lucky's Place." Lucky turned out to be the irrepressible Lucky Cole, age sixty-three, a 250-pounder who wore a cowboy hat and a bandanna. His hair and beard were dyed black. The mat of hair on his muscular arms was so thick it took a moment to identify a tattoo as a bald eagle.

Lucky grew up in Miami but spent boyhood weekends hunting along Loop Road. After a career in construction, he retired here in 1990. He started out with a modest trailer, then built a house and decks and a greenhouse and bathrooms and even a pool.

Lucky told me he considered the Loop Road pretty close to heaven. He loved nothing more than sitting on his deck at sundown, talking to Wife No. 3, watching the birds and smoking a big cigar.

He told me he felt happy whenever a thirsty tourist stopped and asked for beer. Lucky didn't run a store, but he'll provide beer, or a chaw of tobacco, or fuel for an airboat, in exchange for a donation to his retirement fund.

As the tourist sips his beer and chews the fat, he might ask Lucky about the grave. If the tourist is from Michigan, Lucky might announce that he killed and buried an obnoxious tourist from Michigan. "Actually, nobody's in the grave," he confessed to me. "It's just a conversation piece. I like to have a laugh."

Lucky told me he disliked rude people. If he asks, "Do you have some time?" be prepared to stay a spell. He showed me his antique barber chair, his Coke machine, his neon Budweiser sign, his other doodads and geegaws. "Come over here and check out my bathroom," he called. I followed him to a door with a sign above that said "The Cat House."

I gulped. A long-dead house cat, stuffed by a hasty taxidermist, deco-

Lucky Cole of the Loop Road. Photo by Jeff Klinkenberg.

rated the counter by the sink. I was unable to focus on the unfortunate cat because every inch of wall and ceiling was covered by photographs of women—but not the kind I expected to encounter on the Loop Road.

Turned out Lucky was a commercial photographer as well as swamp man. His photos of sunsets and swamps were graced by models who may or may not have remembered to wear a bikini top. "They pay me to make their pictures, that's right," he said. "I give them their pictures, they use them in portfolios or just keep them to remember what they once looked like."

At Lucky's urging I perused photos of women straddling motorcycles, women leaning provocatively against the mailbox out on the Loop Road, women wearing cowboy hats and six-shooters and little else. I felt fifteen again, sneaking a peak at the centerfold in *Cavalier* magazine at Park Shore Pharmacy in Miami. If Howard the druggist catches me, he'll tell my mother.

Back on the Loop Road, I headed toward the Tamiami Trail, toward civilization. Most people hate driving on the Loop at night, but I have never minded, never had an emergency out there. A couple of times I shut down the engine and listened to frogs. A couple of times I stopped and called for owls. Alas, they snubbed me.

Near the bridge across Sweetwater Strand, red eyes glowed in my headlights on the road ahead. I was hoping for a panther, or a bear, or one of Lucky's swamp nymphets.

But it was just an opossum. Dragging its tail on the dusty road, it vanished into the trees.

February 12, 2006

2

PASS A GRILLE

The Beach

I like to go to the beach in a storm. I like to go to the beach nearest to my home in St. Petersburg when lightning bolts are crashing down like pitchforks thrown by Zeus from Mount Olympus. I like having to fight the wind to open the door to my truck, and feeling the sting of sand against my skin. Finally, I like the solitude of the beach, the utter loneliness of the beach. If you live in crowded coastal Florida, it is the only time you have the beach, and the wilderness the beach represents, to yourself.

Boom! That was close. I stay in my truck, windshield wipers keeping time with my beating heart. Australian pines, bobbing and weaving in the squall, evade no punches. Laughing gulls know enough not to laugh. They hunker in the dunes.

My years of sitting on a towel and basting for hours are behind me. I hate the hustle and bustle of finding a parking place, putting money in a meter, and listening to loud music or intrusive conversation. I am tired of hearing my dermatologist cluck with disapproval as she whittles away strategic patches of a once handsome forehead.

As a beach consumer, I am looking for open spaces and room to think. Such beaches exist in the Florida Panhandle; a few months ago, as I hiked such a beach near Apalachicola on an overcast day, a family of deer traipsed across a vast sand dune. Where I live in west central Florida, I don't count on seeing deer. But if I want the beach to myself, I go in the rain. Better yet, I wait for a storm.

Clogs of dead sea oats fly down the beach like tumbleweed. I wear glasses to protect my eyes against the blasts of sand. The rain beats down so hard the surf seems bruised and bleeding. But rain is rain and sea is sea; if the surf were King Kong, it would be beating its chest in triumph. As a teenager, I loved to surf in heavy weather. As a gray-haired adult, mortality no longer an abstract, I am less inclined to get my feet wet. I know if I tried to wade out in this surf, I'd be swept to my doom.

For some of us, perhaps that is the appeal of the beach in a storm. It's a wild place, a dangerous place, utterly indifferent to humanity. "The sea speaks a language polite people never repeat," wrote Carl Sandburg. Man, it can knock you for a loop.

In interior Florida, the great predators, Florida panthers and black bears and Eastern diamondback rattlesnakes, are quickly vanishing as forests are laid bare. Dip your toe into the surf at even an urban beach and you've entered a wilderness ruled by sharks that will eat you if they are hungry enough. "The sea—this truth must be confessed—has no generosity," wrote Joseph Conrad.

The squall passes, the lightning calls a truce. In the lull I walk the deserted beach toward the jetty. When a flock of black skimmers whips by, I am the audience. Farther offshore a pair of dolphins reveal their dorsal fins. Closer in, a school of cownose rays flaps majestically past.

I prefer terra firma. A pitiful sailor, I can get seasick staring at a glass of water. Watching a roiled sea from the beach on a stormy day is like having a ringside seat at a prizefight. The excitement is not necessarily accompanied by a bloody nose. I take a moment to sit in the sand and read my worn copy of *The Sea and the Jungle*, H. M. Tomlinson's account of a voyage across the Atlantic to the Amazon in a tramp steamer in 1909. "I had never seen so much lively water so close," he wrote of his trip aboard the *Capella*. "She wallowed, she plunged, she rolled, she sank heavily to its level. I looked out from the round window of the Chief's cabin, and when she inclined those green mounds of swell swinging under us and away were superior, in apparition, to my outlook."

Fighting mal de mer, and also concerned about the arrival of the latest squall, I retire to my pickup truck. Here comes the rain. Here comes a wind even more powerful than the wind before. As my truck rocks, I pretend I'm on the crew of the *Capella* or, even better, I am standing on the deck of the *Pequod*, with my harpoon-toting friend Queequeg, waiting for Ahab to issue the order to lower the boats. Call me Ishmael.

July 7, 2003

3

CORKSCREW SWAMP

Cypress Trees

Sometimes I go to Corkscrew Swamp Sanctuary in southwest Florida to watch birds and butterflies, alligators and snakes, turtles and newts. I always look for black bears and panthers, all the while knowing I would have to be very lucky to see one. Usually I am satisfied to encounter Spanish moss, old man's beard lichen, resurrection fern, pond apple, and, inevitably, pond scum.

But mainly I go for the cypress trees. Corkscrew Swamp Sanctuary, operated by the National Audubon Society, is the Land of the Giants. The 11,000-acre swamp contains the oldest and largest living things remaining in our state. Whenever I feel an attack of narcissism, when I have spent a little too much time shadow-boxing in the mirror, Corkscrew is my antidote. It is a splendid place to discover humility.

The titans in the deepest section of the swamp, accessible by a 2.2-mile boardwalk, never experienced a logger's saw. Some trees reach 130 feet into the sky. Four tall men, if they were comfortable enough with their masculinity to grasp hands, might be able to wrap their arms around the trunks of the largest trees. But maybe not. In the Land of the Giants, even a macho man is right puny.

"There is no other place in Florida like this." Ed Carlson, the Paul Bunyan of swamp men, was bragging to me. He's 6 feet 5, wore size 13 boots, and weighed—well, never mind the claims of untrustworthy scales. When he wades through muck he is heavy enough to worry about sinking. Yet even he was a twig in the swamp. Craning his neck to gaze at the treetops, he almost grew dizzy.

Boardwalk at Corkscrew Swamp. Photo by Jeff Klinkenberg.

Carlson, fifty-four at the time of my visit, discovered Corkscrew as a teenager. A summer job resulted, then a science education at the University of South Florida, followed by full-time employment in the Land of Giants. In the twenty-first century, he was running the joint. When he ambled the long boardwalks of the sanctuary, talking a mile a minute, the thrill for him was not gone.

"Hear that? A red-shouldered hawk. Oh, listen: a pileated woodpecker. Oh, snowy egret. See the plume feathers? Breeding season is here. Wow: Check out that banded water snake! It's HUGE. One time I was wading through the swamp and suddenly a cottonmouth was lying in a clump of water lettuce that was building up INCHES in front of me in deep water and I swear that cottonmouth was looking me straight in the eye . . ."

Ed Carlson was the kind of swampman who took joy in a close encounter with a venomous serpent. Fortunately, visitors need not play chicken with moccasins to enjoy Corkscrew. They can saunter along a sturdy boardwalk and chat with park rangers situated every hundred yards or so. The lazy can even watch a movie in the spectacular visitor center and call it quits. Or take home one of those cool, colorful inexpensive guides from the bookstore.

But I travel the boardwalk, which twists through the trees like one of the Swampman's snakes. Carlson was so loath to harm certain trees he changed the route of the boardwalk or left gaps so trees could sprout through the slats.

At Corkscrew, the celebrities are pond cypress and bald cypress trees, so named because they lose their needles in winter. At first, a visitor encounters pond cypress. They're modest in size—think of them as the wooden matches of the forest. Deeper in the swamp, a visitor encounters the first bald cypress trees. They're larger than the pond cypress—a

Ed Carlson of Corkscrew Swamp. Photo by Jeff Klinkenberg.

cigarette to a wooden match. Keep walking until you reach the heart of the swamp, the dwelling place for the grandfather trees. Compared to those matches and cigarettes, they're Cuban cigars.

When the Spaniards first explored La Florida, those trees were already a century old. By all rights, they should be gone. Loggers harvested virtually every ancient cypress tree from Florida in the early twentieth century. In 1954, Audubon acquired Corkscrew, named after a twisty river that flows into the Gulf of Mexico. Now we can experience a true primeval forest. Now we can stand on the boardwalk and stare slack-jawed at the old ones.

If these trees could talk, they might tell of Calusa warriors and Spanish conquistadors—as well as the space age.

Spring is a wonderful time to visit Corkscrew, if bittersweet, sort of like fall in the North. Yes, weather is comfortable, flowers are in bloom, and baby birds are atwitter. But before long I know I will be wishing I bought hurricane shutters.

Corkscrew, east of Bonita Springs, was spared a direct hit from Charley in 2004. But winds still sheared off tops of a few stately trees. Hurricanes and fire are among the only things that can hurt the grandfather trees. Even so, they have endured all manner of insult during the last six centuries and are still standing tall. If they can avoid bad luck, they have another good four hundred years of life in them.

"What I worry about most is fire," Ed Carlson told me. In a severe drought, even swamps catch fire. "We believe there was a catastrophic drought about six hundred years ago that was followed by a catastrophic wildfire. I hope I never live to see such a fire in my lifetime."

Corkscrew Swamp looks like it was here at the dawn of creation. On an overcast day, it feels like a black-and-white movie; you almost expect King Kong to burst through the trees. Night herons call, even during the day, and frogs respond with frantic grunting and creaking. In the wet season, amorous alligators join the concert with their bellowing.

Carlson, hardly timid about abandoning the boardwalk, watches his step during alligator mating season. More than once he has been chased through the water, through the ferns, and over the muck by testy saurians. Even a large man can move fast in the Land of Giants when he has a mind to.

An alligator bellow—what the late herpetologist Archie Carr called a song from the Mesozoic—is a warning to stay on the boardwalk. Fortunately, visitors can stay out of harm's way when admiring a cypress knee, which is something like a root that pokes out of the water next to the trunk of a tree. A cypress knee, by the way, looks like the cap worn by Merlin in *The Sorcerer's Apprentice*. Nobody has quite figured out their purpose, though Ed Carlson has a theory: Muck collects between the knees. Muck eventually rises above the water. Voila! Land ahoy. Cypress trees don't mind dry feet once in a while.

"Hey, look over there! See them?" We know spring has arrived when the wood storks return to Corkscrew. An endangered species, wood storks—a tall wading bird with a featherless black head—are already building nests in the tops of cypress trees. In April, Corkscrew is a nursery to five hundred pairs or more. In the old days, of course, Corkscrew boasted five thousand nests and fifteen thousand chicks. Those days are gone, not because Corkscrew has changed, but because surrounding land, where parent wood storks once hunted food for their offspring, is now tomato farms, citrus groves, and strip shopping centers.

When I visit the Land of the Giants, strolling a boardwalk perched over prehistoric reptiles, as herons cry and leopard frogs croak from the foliage, I find it easy to pretend that Florida is still an ancient place, untouched by modernity.

On the way home, stuck in the interstate traffic, honking at the idiot who keeps changing lanes, I know the truth of the matter.

I will try to hang on to my memories.

March 10, 2005

4

DE LEON SPRINGS

Pancakes

Whenever I get depressed about modern Florida, about the traffic, the road rage, the roadkill—when I find myself fretting about mosquitoes, sweat, and tropical winds—I come down with a hankering to eat pancakes.

The best place to eat pancakes in Florida, if not the world, is at the Old Spanish Sugar Mill and Griddle House in De Leon Springs State Park in northeast Florida. When I eat pancakes at the old restaurant, I try to sit near a window and look out at the spring and its gin-clear water, corpulent largemouth bass, prehistoric alligators, and mischievous otters. Such a view whets the appetite for a plate of piping-hot flapjacks. But the main appeal of the rural restaurant is the cooking. I go because I have complete confidence in the culinary talents of the cook.

Forgive the bragging, but the cook is a fascinating middle-aged man with green eyes and a pleasant smile.

"Honey, you ever eat here before?" asked the blond waitress. I confessed that I had.

"Then you know it's time for you to plug in your griddle and get going."

I plugged in the griddle. Soon I could feel it heating up. In fact, the whole room was growing warmer by the moment. That was because every table in the place featured a griddle. The restaurant is the only cook-your-own-pancake eatery in Florida.

My server, Peggy O'Neill, returned. She placed on the table pitchers of batter, containers of syrup, butter, cooking oil, and a spatula. "Have you ever cooked pancakes before?" asked the take-charge gal. I was pretty sure I had.

"Okay. Then you know you have to use a little oil or else your pancakes are going to burn. Don't be afraid of using a lot of batter. Lumps are good. People tell me, 'My pancakes turn out too thin.' They are afraid of lumps. Lumps give body. But here's the secret: If you want to make perfect pancakes, honey, let 'em bubble before you flip."

Hungry as a bear, I couldn't wait to start cooking. I had earned my meal by jogging the park's 5-mile Wild Persimmon Trail. I had hopped cypress knees, stumbled over oak roots, and gotten my feet wet in a swamp. I had followed the tracks of deer, raccoons, and bobcat. In fact, I had looked for bears.

Ursus americanus floridanus, omnivores, eat mostly vegetable matter, though slow-witted armadillos occasionally show up on the menu. Black bears often are spotted by hikers on the Wild Persimmon Trail, but I wasn't worried. The only time my heart went pitty-pat was when I trotted through the web of an impressively muscular golden-orb weaver spider.

Not exactly Davy Crockett, I screamed and flailed at my clothing in panic. Of course, I neglected to mention my girlish shrieks to the server.

I poured white batter onto the griddle and watched the young pancake take the form of a sweet potato. As I poked, as I prodded, the pancake evolved into something that resembled a manatee calf.

I am one of those people who considers cooking an art, so I next doled out a mixture of five-grain batter—wheat, buckwheat, rye, rice, and corn—and got to work. The new creation changed quickly from round to oval and then to something that reminded me, vaguely, of a side view of a human face. Hmmmm. Something familiar. I manipulated the sizzling batter a bit and leaned back. As the self-portrait emerged, I looked forward to eating my own nose.

"People are really artistic when it comes to cooking pancakes," explained my server. "They create alligators, otters, even Mickey Mouse."

Mickey Mouse discovered Florida in 1971, but Floridians have breakfasted at the springs for ages. Five thousand years ago, aboriginal people camped on the water, according to archaeologists who excavated artifacts that included dugout canoes. In 1779, British explorers traded with Seminoles at the spring; later, white settlers built a mill and farmed cotton, corn, and sugarcane. Seminoles burned down the mill during their war with federal troops in 1835. Federal troops burned it to the ground during the Civil War.

The mill, and the spring, refused to accept defeat. In the early twentieth century, both became a tourist attraction and, later, the winter home for the Clyde Beatty Circus. A fifth-generation miller from Ohio, Peter Schwarze, bought the mill and started a bakery at the site in 1961. An entrepreneur, he was sure he'd improve business by opening a cook-your-own pancake restaurant. Turned out he knew his onions.

In the winter, when tourists are thicker than sand flies in Florida, some hungry patrons wait two hours to pay good money for the privilege of cooking their own pancakes. On a busy weekend, the Old Spanish Sugar Mill Grill and Griddle House goes through 800 pounds of batter. Many customers take seriously the "all you can eat" promise on the menu.

My first two pancakes, more cooked than raw, went down easy as pie, prompting me to pour another round. I made smaller pancakes this time, silver dollar pancakes, and was vigilant about flipping them the instant they bubbled. I sampled them with honey, though I preferred the maple syrup and molasses. I was tempted to ask the waitress for blueberries, but the addition of fruit would have added a whole dollar to my bill.

My third round of pancakes was as delicious, but fearing I might explode, I didn't go for a personal-best fourth round. Servers remembered the time a single diner, a bearish-looking male, polished off twenty large pancakes in a sitting. I am confident he went home happy.

My depression about the state of Florida had vanished along with my appetite. I sauntered outside and opted to take a dip in that refreshing spring. First I tried to remember my late mother's rules for swimming. Can one eat pancakes and go swimming immediately without risking fatal cramps? Or should the concerned Floridian wait a half hour or so before going in? I compromised. I entered the spring without waiting, but remained in the shallows. Hate to ruin a good breakfast by drowning.

June 7, 2004

5

ST. PETERSBURG

Indian Mound

When I want to be alone, I go to an Indian mound in Boca Ciega Bay not far from where I live in west central Florida. It's quiet up there, except for the rustle of the breeze in the treetops, a good place to think. In cool weather I need not worry about mosquitoes, though sometimes I crave solitude so much I endure bug bites even in the heart of summer. Hidden among the oaks, my mound is a few hundred feet from a popular restaurant on Park Street. Sometimes as I hunker on the mound I can smell the restaurant's celebrated jerked chicken on the wind. Of course, the people who built the mound knew nothing about jerked chicken. Their menu was heavy on clams, oysters, and mullet.

They were known as the Tocobaga. Over centuries, they built giant mounds out of discarded shells throughout west central Florida. Some mounds were simple dumps for garbage. Others were places to bury their dead or to worship. I like to think that some folks sat on the mounds to think or for the view or for the joy of it.

When I visit the mound, I also try to imagine what it must have been like on that spring day in 1528 when a Spanish ship showed up in Boca Ciega Bay. Was somebody at that moment shucking oysters on the top of the mound or biting mullet flesh off a smoking backbone? Perhaps somebody wading in the marl, collecting blue crabs in a pine needle basket, yelled an alert.

Until that moment, the Tocobaga were masters of their world. But Pánfilo de Narváez, the notoriously cruel conquistador, was on the way.

I like the bacon, lettuce, and tomato sandwiches from Williams Sub Shop five minutes away over on Tyrone Boulevard. The BLTs aren't on the menu, but they will make one for you if you ask nice. I like the way the Williams women who run the restaurant cut the tomatoes into small cubes and are generous with the bacon. I am pretty sure I could be a vegetarian if it weren't for those BLTs.

The Indian mound is a good place for a picnic. There are no tables, but if you don't mind sitting on the grass, or leaning against an oak limb, you can be comfortable. Sometimes I read a book with my lunch, maybe poetry by Peter Meinke or Mary Oliver, or some Florida history. Recently I was up there with Raymond Arsenault's *St. Petersburg and the Florida Dream*. His book includes what happened to the poor Tocobaga.

We actually know quite a bit about them. Narváez brought a secretary, Cabeza de Vaca, who wrote everything down. The Tocobaga were healthy and strong. About twenty thousand of them lived in a series of villages and towns that stretched from Tampa Bay to the north side of Charlotte Harbor. They slept in palm-thatched huts, built temples dozens of feet high, and crafted elaborate jewelry.

Their "religion sought to explain and enhance a recurrent pattern of birth, life, death and renewal," writes Arsenault. "The Tocobaga . . . lived in a world of cyclical equilibrium and subtle adaptation, a world where there was little need for a linear sense of time or development."

What exactly does that mean? It means they paid attention to the seasons. In the winter, mullet were fat with roe and schooled by the millions. They must have been easy pickings for a good man with a spear. In the spring, scallops hid in the turtle grass. In the summer, blue crabs scurried through the shallows. In the late fall, some pretty plump oysters and clams must have been gathered in the clear water near today's Bay Pines VA Medical Center. The mosquitoes in the mangroves, the little biting flies that emerge from the sand at dusk, would drive most of us mad. Not the thick-skinned Tocobagas. They learned to endure. The Tocobaga disdained clothing, for the most part, instead covering their bodies with elaborate tattoos—probably stuff that would impress the kids who roam nearby Tyrone Square Mall in the twenty-first century.

How many oyster shells did it take to build mounds 100 feet long and 20 feet high? Mounds that have survived going on five centuries? I guess somebody good at math could figure it out, but I am going to guess countless generations of Tocobaga had to eat millions of oysters to produce those mounds.

In west central Florida, their history is under our feet, at Safety Harbor, at Pinellas Point, at Terra Ceia, at Tierra Verde, on the eastern shores of Tampa Bay—their history is under our parking lots and under our buildings.

I live within walking distance of Bayfront Medical Center in downtown St. Petersburg. Night and day I hear the wail of ambulance sirens and the roar of emergency helicopters landing and taking off. On the quieter south side of the complex is the remainder of what must have been a mighty Tocobaga mound. Many old-time St. Petersburg residents remember when Bayfront was called Mound Park Hospital.

My favorite Tocobaga mounds are scattered along Park Street between Tyrone and Central Avenue. Once the site of a huge village, the area is now a wealthy neighborhood where landscapers huff and puff while pushing mowers up modest hills that once were Tocobaga mounds. At nearby Abercrombie Park, you can leave your car and stroll to the bay across a former Tocobaga terrace that is now a place where residents walk their dogs.

Near Saffron's, the Caribbean restaurant on Park Street, I take possession of my mound. Oaks and cabbage palms and black earth hide the oyster shells, but there's no mistaking that you are at the top of the mound. I hear a motorcycle in the distance, followed by the cry of an osprey. I try to answer the osprey but break into a wracking cough. My weak lungs, damaged long ago by an immune disorder, remind me once again of mortality.

Narváez once was described by the historian Samuel Eliot Morison as "both cruel and stupid." He was "the most incompetent of all who sailed for Spain in this era."

No matter. The Crown valued ruthlessness. Ruthless, Narváez wanted gold. The conquistadors, according to some historians, marched east across Pinellas to what we now call Safety Harbor, where Narváez met a Tocobaga chief, Hirrihigua. A fight broke out, and a soldier wounded

Hirrihigua. When his mother intervened, she was hacked to death. Narváez fed pieces of her body to his pet greyhounds.

It was the beginning of the end. Within a century, all the Tocobaga were gone, vanished from the face of the earth, victims of war and diseases for which they had no immunities. Of course, the stars kept on shining and the mullet kept on leaping. And here we are now.

So I finish my lunch and put the leftovers into a paper sack as the cardinals twitter and the blue jays scold. I stop for a moment to admire a collection of laughing gull feathers a previous visitor hung from the branches, perhaps to honor the memory of a lost tribe.

Not everybody visits the Tocobaga mounds for spiritual sustenance, however. Dangling from another branch like a big lavender flower is a more earthly souvenir of contemporary society, a pair of women's very skimpy underpants.

Hope she didn't catch cold.

January 19, 2004

FLORIDA ICONS

6

OCALA

Coppertone Girl

When I was a boy, growing up in Miami, we drove across MacArthur Causeway on our way to the beach. Near Biscayne Boulevard, on the side of a downtown building, was the biggest billboard I had ever seen. On the billboard, a dog was pulling down the bathing trunks of a little girl in pigtails. Eisenhower was still president, and everybody was repressed except maybe those finger-snapping, reefer-smoking, free-sex beatniks in Greenwich Village, so it was shocking to be able to look out the window of our Nash Rambler and see an innocent little girl's butt cheeks being exposed by a rude dog for all the world to see.

"Don't be a pale face," said the letters on the sign. "Use Coppertone."

That ad for suntan lotion was perhaps the most memorable come-on in the golden age of advertising. You could see the ad on street corners in San Francisco and in Manhattan, on the blue highways of the Great Plains and here and there throughout the Wheat Belt. The Coppertone Girl was as American as a Moon Pie. But if you lived in the Sunshine State then, if you lived anywhere near a beach, you considered her as quintessential Florida. She was a postcard of sorts that celebrated the sand and the sun and our state as a place where anything could happen.

Recently, I made a telephone call to a woman named Cheri Brand to ask if I could drive up to Ocala and talk to her about the Coppertone ad. There was silence on the phone; reporters learn to dread silence. Finally she said, "Oh, no. Not that. It's so old. You don't want to write about that. Really. Nobody cares." The Coppertone Girl with the bare cheeks, forty-eight when I spoke to her, was in no mood to bare her soul.

"You know," she said, "you don't want to talk to me. You want to talk to my mother. My mother is much more interesting than I'll ever be. Mother is the real story." Usually, when somebody says don't talk to me, talk to my mother instead, a reporter comes down with the willies. The gray-haired mother produced by the reluctant interviewee turns out to be a saint who whips up apple butter by the gallon, or a kindly grandma who knits smiley faces on feathery quilts for shivering orphans, or a reincarnated Elizabeth Browning who minutes ago finished writing an 800-line poem about her cat, Slinky, and is looking for a publisher. Not that there is anything regrettable about quilts, apple butter, and cat poetry that always rhymes moon with spoon.

Joyce Ballantyne Brand, eighty-six that year, was the opposite of an apple-butter gal. I did not bring a martini shaker with me to Ocala, but I should have.

"Mind if I smoke?" she asked in a nicotine voice. "My whole house is my ashtray."

"Mother," said her daughter, the reluctant Coppertone Girl, "be careful of what you say to a reporter. They're always looking for something to make the story better."

Joyce Ballantyne Brand, a commercial artist who gave the world the Coppertone Girl, the Pampers Baby, and countless half-dressed women who posed on many a risqué calendar, gazed across the table at me through giant pink eyeglasses and the haze of cigarette smoke. I got the feeling she knew how to handle hayseed reporters. "So whattya want to know?" she growled.

I wanted to know everything, I confessed, from the beginning to now, but especially about the Coppertone Girl that had titillated me as a young boy.

"Be careful, Mother," said her daughter from across the table. "Don't use any swear words."

"Ah, I won't," she said. "But you know, I get tired of talking about the Coppertone Girl. Yeah, it was a good billboard, but it was hardly the only art I ever produced. But that's what everybody remembers. That's what everybody wants to talk about. The Coppertone Girl."

I felt my face grow hot.

"Hey," she said. "Go use the bathroom."

Coppertone Lady. Photo by Stephen Coddington.

Blushing even more, I glanced at my fly. Zipper closed, thank God. But I had drunk a quart of coffee on my drive north, so I did as ordered. In the bathroom I was admired by a life-sized mermaid sprawled in the tub. The sculpture had fine, shapely hips and more than ample breasts.

"Well," Joyce Ballantyne Brand said when I emerged, "at least I didn't make her face very pretty. Otherwise she'd be obscene."

So the mother of the reluctant Coppertone Girl told me her story. She said she was born in Nebraska near the end of World War I and liked drawing and making paper dolls; during the Depression she sold paper dolls for a buck apiece. She said she habitually entered art contests and won a scholarship to Disney's School for Animation in California.

She remembered the day when the Disney representative heard her girlish, teenage voice over the phone and rescinded the scholarship. Women married and had babies and gave up careers, she was informed. A woman was a poor investment.

"Not the last time I heard that," Joyce growled. She spent two years at the University of Nebraska and two years at the American Academy of Art in Chicago. She met and married her first husband, artist Eddie Augustiny. She said she drew pictures for dictionaries, did maps for Rand McNally, painted murals for movie theaters, and learned to fly a plane. She was barely twenty-five. "This is what you want to hear about?" she asked. "Boring."

World War II began, and even male artists got drafted. Doors opened to women, and her old college professor, the famous pinup artist Gil Elvgren, got her a job at a studio known for churning out the sexiest calendars on earth. Even closing in on ninety, Joyce is an attractive woman. As a young woman, she resembled the Donna Reed in *From Here to Eternity*, only earthier. Often she used herself as a model, gazing into the mirror while painting a buxom doll who later would be admired in a greasy garage by drooling auto mechanics. Today, her pinups are collector items.

She showed me a few. They weren't naked. "Mine always had some clothes on or at least a towel on," she said in that smoky voice. "I didn't go in for dirty stuff like they do today."

My face grew hot again.

"Mother," said her daughter, the reluctant Coppertone Girl, "tell him your philosophy about pinups."

"The trick is to make a pinup flirtatious," Joyce said. "But you don't do dirty. You want the girl to look a little like your sister, or maybe your girlfriend, or just the girl next door. She's a nice girl, she's innocent, but maybe she got caught in an awkward situation that's a little sexy." Joyce and her husband divorced. She married a TV executive, Jack Brand, and they had lots of laughs together. He was creative; she was creative. They had their own lives and interests and always supported each other and avoided jealousy. She used him as a model for a famous ad for Schlitz beer. She did portraits of the well-known and the little-known. Sometimes, when subjects wouldn't relax, Joyce threatened to get them drunk. Whiskey worked wonders.

In 1947, she began a long association with *Sports Afield*, the outdoors magazine. Her illustrations accompanied the stories. One time she painted a mermaid on the cover. Full of mischief, the mermaid hung boots and tires on the hooks of oblivious anglers. The mermaid—Joyce again had used her comely self as a model—was quite provocative. Some readers objected: How dare she lead men and boys astray in a magazine devoted to an innocent pursuit like fishing? Joyce lost no sleep about the complaints.

Interesting, but I brought up Coppertone to Joyce. Tell me about Coppertone. Well, okay, Joyce said. The boring Coppertone story. In 1959, Coppertone solicited drawings from prominent commercial artists for a new ad campaign. She was given a few examples, produced by other artists, to go by. Using her daughter, then three, as a model, she tried a few sketches.

"I made Cheri look a little older and gave her shorter legs. They liked my paintings, and I got the job."

Joyce received $2,500, a good day's work. "Just another ad," she said. "Just another baby ad. Boring."

Joyce did not do boredom well. The Brands moved to Ocala in the mid 1970s so Joyce could be near her parents, but she hated Ocala. She was used to Chicago. She was used to a penthouse in Manhattan and artsy friends who smoked pipes and drank martinis. It was hot and buggy in Florida. Frogs grunted and alligators roared. People ate grits, for heaven's sake. They ate fried catfish. "Backward. Not even a Federal Express office. I'd go to a paint store for supplies and would literally find a sign on the door that said, 'Gone Fishing.' I didn't think I'd be here long."

She and Jack took possession of a grand old three-story building in downtown Ocala. In 1985, Jack developed a cough that was diagnosed as lung cancer. "I could kill him for dying," Joyce told people at the funeral. Recently she gave her sprawling third-floor studio to her daughter, Cheri, and to Cheri's husband, for living quarters. Now Joyce lives on the second floor, which is filled with her art and her memories.

Her daughter helps out when she is not working at the YMCA, where she is a personal trainer. Cheri still has blond hair like she did when she was the Coppertone Girl but doesn't braid it into pigtails. She has a good tan, and I was tempted to ask about her tan line but lost my nerve.

"People can be incredibly boring about the Coppertone Girl," she said. "Sometimes they ask to see my tan line. It's irritating."

I felt my face grow hot.

"People seem very excited to learn that I was the Coppertone baby, and they share stories of how the billboard was a landmark in their memories. In 1993, there seemed to be a renewed interest. I was invited to appear on the *Sally Jessy [Raphael] Show* and *Entertainment Tonight.* Anyway, that's about it."

The Coppertone Girl's mother told me to follow her. As she showed me stuff, Joyce used her walker to get around her home. She showed me her paintings of circus clowns. She showed me her painting of an alligator. She is painting a portrait of a friend ill with Lou Gehrig's disease and wants to capture the woman's impish personality. She doesn't want a sad painting. "Too much sadness in the world already." She will take her time finishing the portrait. When you are eighty-six, and you need a walker and have arthritis in your hands, you take your time even if you are twenty-six in your heart.

In the morning, she drinks Ovaltine, a habit she picked up when she illustrated an Ovaltine ad in the 1940s. In the afternoon she sips Yoo-Hoo. In the evening—Joyce was always an evening person—she will not turn down a stiff martini. "I've had my chance to remarry," she said, leaning close and igniting another Benson and Hedges. "Men with money, too. I like men, I value their companionship, but I don't want to get married again."

September 5, 2004

7

WAKULLA SPRINGS

Return of the Gill Men

There should be a sound track for this terrifying tale about the Gill Man. The sound track should be scary and dramatic—maybe with a creaky theremin oooweeeooooweeing in the background only to be replaced, at the unbearably tense moments, by braying trumpets. Well, if not trumpets, something really loud, a chorus of out-of-tune violins, a kettle drum, and perhaps a threatening oboe.

When *Creature from the Black Lagoon* was filmed in North Florida a half century ago, Hollywood took its horror movies seriously. Color? Who needed color? The cigar-chomping moguls knew cheap black-and-white would suffice. They knew a good story when they heard one, maybe a story about an expedition gone awry, with idealistic scientists butting heads with a venal businessman who wants to exploit the exciting discovery. Of course, there had to be a beautiful swimsuit-clad woman in peril—in peril not from some computer-generated yawner of a monster like in horror films today, but a flesh-and-blood creature in a sturdy rubber suit that looked half human, half ugly toad. And, for heaven's sake, the monster had gills. Terrible, slimy, pulsating gills!

BAH BAH BAAAH!

What you just heard were violins and kettle drums and oboes and theremins tuning up. It's the cue that Ricou Browning is emerging from the water.

Ricou Browning was seventy-three when I met him but still looked scary. He had dark, penetrating eyes and big arms and shoulders. He didn't smile much. In fact, when he dislikes a question he'll tell you. If he takes an instant dislike to you—that can happen—he will not spare your feelings.

BAH BAH BAAAH!

Ricou Browning played the Creature fifty years ago in the fall of 1953. That is, he performed as the Creature when the Creature was swimming underwater at Wakulla Springs, a few minutes from Tallahassee. There was another actor who played the Creature during out-of-the-water scenes filmed in Hollywood. We will explain the two-Creature controversy a little later. For now, let us concentrate on Ricou.

While I watched nervously, a little afraid of Ricou's reputation as a no-nonsense guy, his head popped out of the water in the swimming area at Wakulla Springs State Park. His broad shoulders followed. Then his goose-bumped torso—the water was 72 degrees, after all—emerged all covered by goose bumps. The Gill Man! And he was coming my way.

BAH BAH BAAAH!

"Water's cold," he said amicably. "But it feels refreshing."

What a relief. A good mood.

"This place, it's still beautiful," he said. Behind him, the crystal-clear water boiled out of the deepest, most powerful spring in North America. "I don't think it's changed since we made the movie."

Dan Wester, director of the Tallahassee Film Society, conducts what he calls the Creaturefest at the park every fall. At thirty-nine, Wester wasn't born when *Creature from the Black Lagoon* was made, but it remains among his favorite horror films, up there with those other (and more famous) Universal International Picture offerings, *Dracula*, *Frankenstein*, and *The Wolfman*.

"*Creature* was the last of the great monster pics," Wester told me. "It really holds up as a film."

In the twenty-first century, *Creature* enjoyed a large cult following among fans of the genre. Internet pages were devoted to it. Grown men and women, including some who appeared perfectly normal, collected *Creature* movie posters. A few brave souls managed to make a living selling *Creature* toys and photographs.

Several hundred had descended on Wakulla Springs for the annual Creaturefest weekend when I was there. They came to meet kindred souls and to visit the Florida shrine where the coolest scenes in the movie were filmed. Of course, they hoped to meet movie stars, at least the ones who were still breathing.

Ben Chapman, who played the monster out of the water, never missed one. He was seventy-five, lived in Hawaii, and relished telling people he was the Gill Man, his most famous role. He had his own Web page—it included a photo of his Universal contract and his life's daily minutiae—and liked to brag that he, and nobody else, deserved to be called the "original Creature." He was a staple at autograph shows all over the country.

Julia Adams, who played the beautiful scientist Kay Lawrence, was a good sport, too. She remained poised and attractive at age seventy-three. In the old days, as a publicity stunt, her studio insured her long legs for $500,000. Alas, they were hidden by slacks whenever she emerged to sign autographs when I was around. The still athletic Ginger Stanley, seventy-two, who doubled for Adams in the spectacular under-water scenes filmed at Wakulla Springs, was a regular at Creaturefest, too. It was she who had persuaded the last holdout, her old friend Ricou Browning, to give it a try.

Browning, who lives near Fort Lauderdale, had never attended a Creaturefest before. Oh, he wasn't embarrassed about making a horror movie—he made an honest $500 a week as Ben Chapman's double. It's just that he was bewildered by the Cult of the Gill Man: all those fans who argued the merits of a horror movie in Internet chat rooms and who took sides about which actor, Browning or Chapman, should be credited as the "ultimate Gill Man."

As fans stepped forward to take his photograph, he told me, "I'm not sure why I'm even here. Maybe it'll be fun. Maybe it won't."

Another reason for his indifference, I thought, might be his personality—a little prickly—and his own rich resumé.

In the 1940s, Browning helped start the tourist attraction and starred as a "merman" at Weeki Wachee. During its 1950s heyday he was public relations director at Silver Springs, where he also performed as the underwater Gill Man in the movie sequels *Revenge of the Creature* and *The Creature Walks Among Us*. In Walt Disney's *20,000 Leagues Under the Sea*, he played an anonymous diver in Nemo's crew. In Miami, he invented *Flipper*, writing the movie screenplay and directing the popular television show. He directed the underwater scenes in the films *Never Say Never Again* and *Thunderball*. "Only Sean Connery can be James Bond to me," he said. "He's a very nice man, and he became a very good diver."

Yet it was his role as the Gill Man that seemed to fascinate most people. I asked him why he thought the movie remained so popular. "I have no idea," he said.

Perhaps it's the "Beauty and the Beast" angle, I suggested. You know, like in *King Kong*.

He was tired of the conversation.

"Could be," he said. "Well, listen, I need to go take a shower."

BAH BAH BAAAH!

Before he could escape, a couple of slick guys approached him. The slick guys introduced themselves to the Gill Man as important documentary filmmakers. From New York. Got it? From New York. If you were making a movie, and looking for actors to play the roles of New York filmmakers, they'd have been perfect. They were tough-talking let's-show-the-southern-country-bumpkins-what-we're-all-about-in-your-face kind of guys. In the Florida heat, one even wore a leather jacket.

They told Ricou Browning they wanted to do him the favor of letting him appear in what would surely become a documentary masterpiece: *Fifty Years of the Creature*.

"Get out of my face with your [censored] New York ways," hissed Ricou Browning.

BAH BAH BAAAH!

The censored word wasn't obscene. It was just the kind of unpleasant description, applied to Italian men, you might hear in *The Sopranos*.

"I KNOW somebody in the Mafia," one of the trembling-with-rage New Yorkers told me a little later. "If Ricou Browning said that to him, Ricou would be dead right now."

BAH BAH BAAAH!

Ricou Browning was born in Fort Pierce, grew up in Jensen Beach, and went to Florida State University. He got a job lifeguarding at nearby Wakulla Springs, which was managed by a Florida legend named Newt Perry, who taught everybody who was anybody how to swim and dive and breathe air through a hose.

Later, on Perry's behalf, Browning scouted out a pond on U.S. 19 in Hernando County. "I dove in and it was full of abandoned cars and refrigerators," he said, "but we cleaned it up." Mermaids soon were wowing tourists at Weeki Wachee. As a merman, Browning helped train them to breathe out of hoses and dive deep without breaking their eardrums. One pretty blond girl, just out of high school, hated the part of the show when she had to dive to an underwater cave. That's because a huge catfish lurked inside the mouth, looking menacing.

"One day the catfish just disappeared," the girl—*Creature from the Black Lagoon*'s underwater love interest, Ginger Stanley—told me five decades later. "Ricou took care of it. Ricou was the kind of guy who took care of problems."

When Hollywood scouts came to Florida in 1953 to look for an underwater location for an upcoming horror movie, Ricou was hired to show them around. He took them to Wakulla Springs, where the Hollywood big shots fell in love with the primeval forest and river. They wanted to test their underwater cameras and asked him to go for a swim. They were so impressed with his prowess they offered him the role as Ben Chapman's underwater Gill Man double. Browning got them to hire his mermaid pal, Ginger Stanley.

They did two memorable scenes. In one, Kay Lawrence (Julia Adams) dives into the river for a dip. Of course, it's Ginger Stanley who actually is doing the swimming. Stanley performs a beautiful underwater ballet, her standard Weeki Wachee act. Unknown to her character, a few feet below lurks the Gill Man. Browning mimics her every graceful move.

It wasn't easy. Browning's costume, which cost $18,000, was heavy and cumbersome. "Like swimming in an overcoat," Browning told me. He wore no goggles or mask, yet he had to look through the eyeholes of the costume. "It was like peeking through a keyhole, only everything was blurred."

At least he didn't worry about drowning during the ballet sequence. In another scene, the Gill Man tucks the terrified Stanley under his arm and dives for a cave 50 feet below. "We had to hold our breaths and clear our ears without letting the audience know we were clearing our ears while I swam straight down," Browning said. "When we got into the cave, two assistants swam over with air hoses."

"We did it in one take," Stanley said, "didn't we, Ricou?"

"One take," he said. "Thank God. We could have drowned."

BAH BAH BAAAH!

Ken Ratliff told me that he never missed a Creaturefest. He'd driven all night from Kentucky. "I loved the Creature movies," he said. He had also figured how to make a buck out of his passion. He sold monster toys at festivals and mall shows throughout the South. "I've got boxes and boxes of monsters all over my house," he said. "My wife said, 'Please, at least don't store them in the bedroom.' It's an antiaphrodisiac."

Fans flocked to his booth while we chatted. They flocked to booths selling old horror movie posters (*Invasion of the Saucer Men*) and vintage magazines (*Fangora*). Most fans, everyday folk, could have been your next-door neighbors, maybe even your kindly aunt and uncle. Others could have been cast members from *Night of the Living Dead*. They wore black clothing, leather especially, and sported tattoos and body piercings. "I came all the way from Gulfport, Mississippi," declared Nick Leon, pierced eyebrows undulating like an eel. "I loved the *Creature*. It's a pure horror movie. Good monster."

Johnny Gilbert, thirty-eight, was a titan in the Cult of the Creature. The Arizona resident made his living managing parks. But his passion was the Gill Man. "I was one of those kids who put together those plastic models of movie monsters," he said. "I never missed the midnight horror movies on television. Those old monsters were our Pokemon. I grew up, but now I'm having my second childhood."

He called himself "The Arizona Gill Man." He bought, traded, and sold Gill Man items, everything from photographs to copies of the screenplay. In his spare time, he sculpted statues of the Gill Man and sold them for $85 a pop.

As he sold his statues, photographs, and candles, Ben Chapman— the fellow who jealously guarded his reputation as "the original Gill Man"—was developing a cramp in his writing hand signing autographs. He had stacks of his own photograph and stacks of old posters. As he signed, light glinted off his pinky ring and its creepy Gill Man face.

"When the picture was finished," Chapman told me, "the studio asked the major stars to pose for publicity photos. I was the one who posed as the Gill Man. Just me. If you have a photograph signed by someone else it is of no value."

Ricou Browning was nearby, signing his own Gill Man photographs. They may not have been the official studio version, but they were from the movie, the underwater scenes. He also was selling personal photos of himself posed in his costume, the monster's head under his arm. He signed those.

"Uh, Mr. Browning, I loved you in the movie," an awe-struck fan told him. "I'd love to buy a couple of photographs and get your autograph."

"Sure," Browning said. "They're $20 each."

BAH BAH BAAAH!

Ben Chapman was a tall guy with a rubbery face. Born in California, he grew up in Tahiti before moving back to San Francisco after high school. Dark, handsome, and athletic, he found work as a nightclub dancer. One day he dropped by Universal Studio in Hollywood to say hello.

"Somebody told me to stand up so I stood up. They told me to turn around and I turned around. The next day they called me and offered me the job of the Gill Man. I said, 'What Gill Man?'"

Made in nineteen days, the film was released in early 1954. It garnered good reviews, though the *New York Times* sniffed, "It's a fishing expedition that is necessary only if a viewer has lost his comic books."

But it was popular with audiences. *Creature from the Black Lagoon*, made on a $600,000 budget, grossed $2 million by year's end. "They just don't make movies like that anymore," Chapman lamented. "It was a scary picture, but it was wholesome and there was a real story. Not like the garbage today. You know, I just canceled my *People* magazine. It's full of the same no-talent celebrities every issue. And you know what? Actors today look like hoboes. Actresses look like hookers. You want to ask them, 'Don't you have a bleeping mirror?'"

Contemporary popular culture disgusted the old Gill Man. "Who are those two you can't escape? Jen? Ben?"

He was talking about Jennifer Lopez and Ben Affleck.

"In fifteen years nobody will remember them," Chapman predicted. "But after fifty years, *Creature from the Black Lagoon* still rocks."

BAH BAH BAAAH!

Ben Chapman and Ricou Browning met for the first time when their costumes were being developed in California a half century ago. They hadn't seen each other since.

Dan Wester, the director of the sponsoring Tallahassee Film Festival, watched them nervously. "Given all that talk on the Internet about who's the real Creature, we don't know if we're going to have a fistfight," he said.

Unfortunately, no punches were thrown. The two old monsters greeted each other, shook hands, maybe not warmly, but politely. Not even Chapman brought up the sensitive topic of "who's the real Creature."

"I think a lot of that talk has been stirred up by the Swimming Creature versus the Walking Creature fans," Wester whispered to me. "All I can say is some fans take this stuff very seriously."

Late in the day a commercial photographer showed up to make a picture for posterity, the first photo of the two Gill Men together. Neither Gill Man looked enthused to me, but they followed the photographer outside anyway.

They ambled to the spring, where the camera man had erected a life-sized cardboard cutout of the Gill Man. The camera man wanted his guys to pose next to it, maybe shake hands or peer around it.

Ben Chapman, natural ham, got into this new role with a mighty grin. Ricou Browning? Well, Ricou Browning was Ricou Browning.

"You want us to do what? Pose with that cardboard cutout?" he asked. "You must be into hokey stuff."

Heh, heh. The photographer chuckled nervously.

Browning posed grudgingly.

"If that picture appears in the paper I'll eat my hat," he said.

BAH BAH BAAAH!

November 23, 2003

8

MIAMI LAKES

Skink

Where was Skink when you needed him? Where was Skink when the roadkill on the Palmetto Expressway in Miami was piled as high as an alligator's eye with pancaked raccoons, armadillos, rat snakes, doggies, and kitties, ad nauseam? You hungry, Skink?

Skink at the moment was not hungry. He had enjoyed orange juice and eaten raisin bran for breakfast. He was behind the wheel of a shiny Acura with leather seats and headed for an appointment. Did Skink have appointments? In those wonderfully lurid Carl Hiaasen novels, Skink was a spontaneous guy.

In the novels, Skink was the former environmentalist governor of Florida, Clinton Tyree, who went mad after years of dealing with mendacious politicians and pond-scum developers. Known only as Skink, he escaped to the Everglades and subsisted mostly on roadkill, emerging only to discipline a disgusting villain or slip steel into the backbone of a pusillanimous hero. "I remember the first time I ever heard about Skink," said the man behind the steering wheel. "I was in the airport and a friend walked up with a Carl Hiaasen novel called *Double Whammy* and said, 'You are in this novel.' I held my ego in check and did not run over right away and buy the book to see if I was mentioned. But I read it eventually and discovered Skink."

South Florida did strange things to a man, even one as centered as two-time governor and three-time U.S senator Bob Graham. "I do not think I am Skink," he said as we got on the interstate. "But every once in a while I will see a dead possum on the side of the road and wonder if I should pull over."

The big man leapt from the cab and dashed back into the road. . . . Decker saw him snatch something off the center line and toss it onto the shoulder. . . . Decker saw it was a dead opossum. Skink ran a hand across its furry belly. "Still warm," he reported. Decker said nothing. "Road kill," Skink said, by way of explanation. He took a knife out of his belt. "You hungry, Miami?"—From *Double Whammy*

It may sound strange, but at the beginning of the twenty-first century possibly the two most popular politicians in Florida were Bob Graham and Skink. It was even stranger that the very proper Bob Graham, who was born in Miami in 1936, and the magnificently misanthropic Skink, born in a writer's imagination in 1987, shared commonalities that had nothing to do with flattened possums or skinning knives.

Both were passionate protectors of the Everglades, valued Florida's culture, loved its history, had eccentric senses of humor, and leaned to the populist side. Skink showed up on the best-seller list, and Graham never lost a political race. Both Democrats had legions of fans in a state that voted Republican. To walk around Miami Lakes with Graham, even months after his retirement from politics, was to accompany the Bishop of Rome through St. Peter's Square. Nobody kissed his ring, but they would have if he had offered. There were no hands he failed to shake nor cheeks he forgot to kiss.

"We wish you were still in Washington," said a former constituent outside the country club.

"If you'd been on the ticket, John Kerry would have been elected president," declared a diner at a local restaurant.

As for Skink, all you had to do was type his name and the name Carl Hiaasen into your Web browser and watch the references pop up. Lots of folks, it turned out, wished Skink were real. They thought Florida needed somebody like Skink to keep the jerks in line. "We've all been mad enough at politicians to imagine some form of vengeance that Skink would approve of," wrote Erik Ness in the Internet magazine *Grist*.

Skink, after all, never hesitated to shoot the tires out of dirt bikes that terrorized wildlife in otherwise peaceful forests. To Skink, a bad hurricane was a growth-management tool. "An eviction notice from God," he roared, lashed to a bridge as a catastrophic hurricane bore down at the beginning of *Stormy Weather*. On second glance, Skink and Graham hardly looked like seeds from the same guava. Graham not only avoided supping on roadkill, he worked to avoid fainting at the sight of blood. Skink's everyday wardrobe included a shower cap on his bald pate, a necklace made of human teeth, and a kilt held together with safety pins; some people wondered if the always formal Graham wore a blue suit, with a matching palm tree tie, to bed.

Graham fought his weight and had a moon-shaped, baby face. Skink was lean as a panther, lost an eye in a fight, and clamped the twin tendrils of his crazed beard in place with vulture beaks. Skink lived on the edge of lunacy among crocodiles and mosquitoes; Graham was famous for writing the minutiae of his day into color-coded notebooks. He could recite what he had for breakfast on Mother's Day 1978. Skink was comfortable with guns and could build a fire without matches. Graham was clumsy with his cell phone, couldn't figure out the garage door opener, and asked me to help him open a jar of mustard at lunch.

"I seem to have erroneous directions," Graham said politely into his cell phone when he got lost on his way to a TV station for an interview. "Erroneous" instead of "wrong." If Skink ever needed to communicate the incompleteness of an idea he would avoid using the word "inchoate," though it popped up in the senator's conversation when I was with him. But no matter. After four decades in politics, he had returned to the South Florida of his birth, where crocodiles traipsed in golf course sand traps and dealers employed man-eating pythons to guard their stashes of illegal narcotics.

Bob Graham had retired. Although Carl Hiaasen told me he didn't have Bob Graham in mind when he created Skink, I wondered if Graham might surprise him.

I wondered if the senator was going to discover his inner Skink any day.

"I am glad to be out of Washington," Graham told me. "I have not had one day of buyer regrets. I am very glad to be home."

When he was a boy, home was literally the Everglades. His dad, Ernest Graham, arrived in Florida in 1920 to manage a farm for the Pennsylvania Sugar Co. Ernest Graham's nickname was "Cap." One time a University of Florida historian asked Bob Graham the origin of his father's nickname. "I do not know what the basis of carrying that nickname was," Graham was quoted, "but it was the most prevalent way by which he was addressed."

Talk about Skink: Cap Graham, before moving to Florida, was an amateur boxer, mined gold in Montana, and managed a gold mine in, of all places, Deadwood, South Dakota, the rip-roaring western town where Wild Bill Hickock got shot in the head by the coward Jack McCall. Wild Bill never got to play what seemed like a decent poker hand, two black eights, two black aces, and the jack of diamonds. Good luck, however, followed Cap Graham. When the sugar company failed, he was able to buy 7,000 acres at fire-sale prices on the edge of the saw grass. He raised dairy cows, potatoes, and a family. Bob's two older brothers lived in a houseboat for a spell. One of them, Bill, who was fighting cancer the year I visited Bob, remembered picking up water moccasins and gathering alligator eggs.

Cap Graham's wife, Florence, died in 1934. He married Hilda Simmons the next year. Then came Bob. He was so much younger than his siblings that he felt like an only child. He acted like one, too. By some accounts he was the terror of any number of day-care centers. His Skink-like habits included expectorating on the unsuspecting.

In 1962, two years before Graham entered politics, his family turned their land into houses. A diamond in the middle of an otherwise industrial area, Miami Lakes in 2005 was spiffy with million-dollar homes, curving streets, bass-infested lakes, and thick canopies of oaks and mahoganies.

"We did not know much about development, but we knew how to plant things," Graham said. He enjoyed showing off those trees. Shade—real shade provided by tall, native trees—was less common in modern Florida than Skink would have liked. Outside the Miami Lakes city limits, visitors were more likely to encounter spindly trees and toothy animals from alien lands. Alligators dined on 12-foot pythons from Burma and armored catfish from the Amazon. Modern Miami was a far piece from Graham's quieter Miami, the place where he caught native garfish and learned how to milk cows.

He hadn't milked a cow in a coon's age, though his family still maintained 300 acres in the middle of Miami Lakes. The Graham Dairy closed eons ago, but Holstein cows came with the landscape. In his townhouse, art sculptures included wood cutouts of classic black-and-white cows. When he needed surgery in 2004, Graham was pleased that his doctor used a bovine valve to repair his heart. Later, he was thrilled to learn that the lifesaving bovine was a Holstein. From his home, Graham can easily amble over and see his cows. He and Adele, his still glamorous wife of forty-seven years, waked at 7 each morning. Bob sauntered to a convenience store for the newspaper, shaking his head as he read headlines about what those wild and crazy Republicans were up to in Washington and in Tallahassee.

Skink would have had fun with them. Many readers maintain that Hiaasen's *Sick Puppy* contains the most satisfying moment in all of modern literature, the moment when Skink seizes the new crooked, development-loving Republican governor, pulls down his pants, and etches the word "Shame" onto the derriere of the shocked pol with a turkey vulture's beak.

Graham has a real fondness for vultures, the sentinels of the Everglades; he is also too smart to actually want to handle one, even to acquire a beak. Among other things, vultures discourage theft of their beaks and further invasion of their private space by projectile vomiting, a talent Skink had yet to cultivate.

After breakfast—cereal, muffin, or heart-healthy fruit—Graham ambled three blocks to the family company's office. Although he was promoting his most recent book, *Intelligence Matters*, his account of America's failure to deal with terrorism in time, he had started a new volume he planned to call *What Every Citizen Needs to Know to Make Democracy Work for Them*. As he typed, he listened to Jimmy Buffett on the stereo.

In the novels, Skink preferred the psychedelic Moody Blues, though readers suspected he must certainly find inspiration in Warren Zevon, "Excitable Boy," perhaps, or even "Rottweiler Blues," a song about modern Miami life that Zevon had written with the help of Carl Hiaasen.

My favorite part of the song was the chorus, when a paranoid Miamian warns the man on his porch about knocking on the door if he didn't know the name of his rottweiler's name.

Folks with delicate sensibilities seemed to move out of Miami sooner or later, troubled by crime and traffic and suburban sprawl. Graham, a

Southern-Gentleman-of-the-Old-School variety, who still called Miami "Miam-ma" and hurricanes "hurra-cans," had no plans to rent a moving van.

Perhaps it was his inner Skink that gave him the bark to want to stay in the tough city. Once he had been known as Governor Jell-O. But in the Senate, at least toward the end of his career, when he ran as a Democratic candidate for president, he became as scrappy as a snapping turtle. Known for the temperance of his remarks, Graham suddenly enjoyed shooting out dirt-bike tires, at least symbolically. He complained about the sitting president's oil-drilling energy policy and tax cuts. He was among the very few senators who publicly opposed the war in Iraq.

Still, you could almost hear Carl Hiaasen, who finally escaped Miami for the Keys, chuckling as he tapped out an e-mail comparing his beloved Skink with Bob Graham. "Bob Graham's dapper grooming and chipper loquaciousness automatically disqualify him as the inspiration for Skink," he wrote me, "though I'm delighted to know that he occasionally fantasizes about warm road kill stew. Although Bob and Skink share the same passion for the state," continued the author, who had grown up fishing and snaking in the Everglades, "I can't picture the senator taking target practice on tourists' rental cars, as Skink sometimes does. Nor can I picture Skink on Capitol Hill, except perhaps in a straitjacket."

Bob Graham drove his Acura through Miami Lakes, found the expressway, headed west, left the expressway, got lost in a crummy neighborhood, returned to the expressway, then abandoned the expressway at the proper exit. The road was lined by industrial buildings whose windows were guarded by bars or razor wire. The road was lined with cement factories and high-tension wires, pines from Australia and pepper trees from Brazil. Empty beer cans and cups skidded across the road like tumbleweeds in Cap Graham's Deadwood.

Once this had been the Everglades. Republicans occasionally liked to point out that the Graham family had helped author the destruction of the Glades with their sugar farming, dairy operations, and developments. While such accusations were unfair—environmentalists were rare in 1930—there was truth to the charge.

Graham stopped in front of a lonely field and a lonely house built from coral. "My bedroom was on the other side," he said. "We had no air-conditioning, and it was always so humid at night. I remember looking out the window at the Everglades. You could see the fires burning."

The Everglades inevitably burned during dry season when he was a boy. Because of inadequate flood-control measures, the Everglades was often dry when it should have been wet and wet when it was supposed to be dry. As governor, Graham made fixing the Everglades a priority. As a senator, he helped make the Everglades an international cause. Even his toughest critic, the author of *Everglades: River of Grass*, appreciated him. The Grande Dame of the Glades, Marjory Stoneman Douglas, called him "my Everglades boy." He was an Everglades boy as much as anybody, even Skink.

"Over on the other side of the trees was the canal we swam in," he said. "I do not remember catching bass, but I do recall catching garfish. Over there was a dairy barn. I had my own horse, Tony, a fine Arabian who never once bit me. I learned to drive when we lived here. I drove a milk truck to Miami High School before I finally got a 1949 black Ford coupe. Near our back door was a swing. We had citrus trees. In the winter, their blossoms had a most pleasant fragrance. It is funny how one can remember those details."

His mood darkened. "You know, I do not drive out here often. I have wonderful childhood memories. It is sad to see the changes that have occurred."

He stepped away from the car, leaned against the fence, gazed long and hard at the old house. Someone he had never met owned it now. A coral house would last forever. Skink could tie himself to it in the next big blow. Or blow it up for that matter and declare the explosion a victory for the lost Everglades. Chickens clucked across the yard. In the distance, hound dogs lay in the shade. Graham was downwind, and they failed to smell him. Otherwise their ears would stand up, and they would give chase with a howl. The senator, so far away from Washington and his youth, would have to outrun the dogs to his car.

"In the summer, it rained so much our property was an island. There were so many frogs. The frogs were very loud. We boys would go out with our Red Ryder BB guns and shoot frogs. You know, you cannot just shoot a frog with a BB gun because the pellet will bounce off the head.

You have to wait for them to croak. When they croak, they look up and expose the soft flesh on their throats."

Back behind the wheel, air-conditioning on, modern Florida only inches away, he said, "It was not exactly Huckleberry Finn. But it was close."

Skink might have rebuked the boys for shooting at frogs for no good reason. On the other hand, he might have told them, "Hey, boys, you're in for a treat. Put those BB guns down for a sec. Want to try some of this roasted possum?"

May 8, 2005

9

ST. AUGUSTINE

Ponce de León

Oh, Juan Ponce de León. What have you wrought? We can understand your generation's desire for gold. Everybody wants to get rich, the quicker the better, even now. But we who settled the New World are even more interested in the legend that says you were searching for invigorating waters, a fountain of sorts that would return even wrinkled conquistadors to their salad days. Oh, Juan Ponce! When you caught sight of the new land on April 2, 1513, you named it La Florida because it was the Feast of Flowers. But if you could only see La Florida now.

Nobody is allowed to look older than forty, your excellency. Everybody is required to be on a first-name basis with a plastic surgeon or the neighborhood artisan who will tattoo a youthful rose just above the crack on their perfectly proportioned rumps. The prematurely gray are expected to color their hair or cover it with a ball cap, worn, of course, backward. There is no reason to offend more attractive younger people with unsightly yellow teeth. Dentists can make even old people presentable.

In modern Florida, your worship, nobody who wants to be considered young is allowed to drive a Pontiac or a Lincoln Town Car. Youthful older people drive Jeeps and Hummers. They instinctively avoid meatloaf at the early bird. Instead they drink martinis and eat sushi at midnight bistros. Nobody is impotent in La Florida, if you don't mind such a saucy word. Thank you, Viagra.

Oh, Señor! You ought to see the tight butts and perky breasts on any of our fine beaches on a sunny weekend morning. You ought to see the earrings and the pierced belly buttons and the ponytails. And that's just the older men. One more thing, your highness. Sorry about those

Calusa aboriginals and their poisoned arrows. In La Florida, we like to believe we will live forever.

Listen, your holiness: Florida has always been a place for starting anew. Its first people trooped onto the emerging Peninsula about twelve thousand years ago. The native people managed quite well until the arrival of the first European tourist. Oh, Ponce de León! Five centuries after your first beach walk, your presence is everywhere in our state. It is almost impossible to find a town in our midst that lacks at least one street named after you. In St. Augustine, America's oldest city, turn off Ponce de Leon Boulevard onto Old Mission Avenue, and then take Magnolia east. You will discover Fountain of Youth National Archaeological Park.

In St. Augustine, founded in 1565, folks take their legends seriously. "This is the original Fountain of Youth," declared the woman who issued my admission ticket as jasmine blossoms perfumed the air. Wiseacre historians elsewhere, your greatness, contend that you probably never set foot in what became St. Augustine, and that you never put quill to paper your thoughts regarding a fountain of youth.

Historians think you first came to the New World with Columbus, helped settle Hispaniola, and discovered for Spain the island later known as Puerto Rico. They say you ruthlessly governed the Carib aboriginals, sometimes letting loose greyhounds against the unruly who objected to being treated as slaves. When slaves died, you sailed to the Bahamas and captured more.

The islands under your rule apparently provided little material treasure other than aboriginal flesh and bone, which only whetted appetites for more ambitious exploration. Carib Indians, according to legend, talked about magic springs in Bimini and a magic river west of Bimini that rejuvenated old men. Perhaps the Caribs believed the legend, or perhaps they were trying to get you Spaniards out of their hair. In 1512, at any rate, you sailed north from Puerto Rico hoping to find Bimini. Instead, in the spring of the following year, west of Bimini, you came across a lush, tropical land that also had nice beaches. Where you landed precisely is open to disagreement. Your navigators, after all, lacked the GPS devices that today are routine accessories even on our Hummers. Historians say you made landfall somewhere between Cape

Canaveral and St. Augustine and encountered native people known as the Timucuan. Covered with tattoos, Timucuans were apparently taller and longer-lived than you sickly Spaniards. So perhaps there was something special about the water in La Florida after all.

"It is not preposterous to imagine the Spanish being utterly captivated by the magical natural discoveries of the New World: snakes with rattles, eels that sent currents through tropical waters, birds with indescribably beautiful colors and awkward shapes, new beverages and foodstuffs and breathtaking scenery," University of South Florida historian Gary Mormino told me. "Considering the mysterious new worlds unfolding, is not a Fountain of Youth possible?"

Oh, Ponce! Did you not find anything liquid worth drinking? Did you not write anything down? Did you mean to help future tourist attractions compete for the title "Fountain of Youth?" Some say you sailed from today's Jacksonville up the St. Johns River to what is now called De Leon Springs State Park in Volusia County. A century ago, an enthusiastic chamber of commerce fellow, his typewriter on fire with muse, touted the spring because the water "reinvigorates the frame exhausted by fatigue, weakness or heat, hardens the flesh and leaves the skin smooth and unctuous. The liver and kidneys are stimulated to greater activity and relieved of congestion and many cases of wonderful cures of kidney disease, catarrh, fever sores, rheumatism, boils, crysipelas, jaundice, asthma, nervous depression, etc. are known."

Despite stories of smooth, boilless epidermi, not to mention the rheumatism- and jaundice-free lifestyles of De Leon Springs bathers, others were convinced that Warm Mineral Springs had to be the real fountain. Just off U.S. 41 between Venice and North Port in southwest Florida, the spring attracts tourists by the hundreds to this day. Filled with minerals and perpetual 80-degree water, the spring feels like a hot tub to the youngish old folks who swear by the place. Oh, Ponce! Even St. Petersburg, once known cruelly as "death's waiting room," has a Fountain of Youth. Built in 1901, it lies a few hundred feet beyond the right-field fence of Progress Energy Park on Fourth Avenue South. It is a peaceful garden spot, hidden among lush shrubbery and shade trees. You can sit there for hours and have the place to yourself.

Years ago, the fountain was a mecca for tourists and residents who filled jugs with the magical water. Casey Stengel, who played for the Boston Braves when they trained in St. Petersburg in the 1920s, delighted in posing for chamber of commerce photographs while swilling the fountain's sulphur-tasting potion. Of course, Casey still got old. By the time he was managing the Yankees in the 1950s, his face was wrinkled and his earlobes sagged to his spikes. Still, he did make it to eighty-five.

At St. Augustine's Fountain of Youth, hope springs eternal. There are beautiful gardens, histrionic peacocks, and historical exhibits to get the blood boiling. Fine and dandy, but most folks want to glimpse the storied fountain and perhaps drink deeply. "I'm 123 years old," chortled the guide, Joe Kobza, though he looked more like sixty.

He led his flock into a dark room. Inside, water trickled from a fountain. Cameras flashed; video cameras hummed. Kobza poured water into paper cups and handed them out like communion chalices. Everybody drank eagerly and everybody made a face. The water had the distinct taste of rotten eggs. Nobody turned young right away.

Listen, Ponce: Deborah Olivieri told me she relates completely to the ancient Timucuans of your day. She eats fish; they ate fish. They shot arrows with bows; as a youth she accompanied her dad to his archery range. Also, she liked tattoos. She owns Ms. Deborah's Fountain of Youth Tattoo Studio Inc. at 78 Lemon St. in St. Augustine. Many of Ms. Deborah's patrons looked like they stumbled in from a cast party for *The Pirates of the Caribbean*. But more and more youthful old people, looking for a different kind of Fountain of Youth, were dropping by for tattoos.

"We've done eighty-year-olds," Ms. Deborah said. "I did a seventy-eight-year-old not long ago. I did a butterfly on her right forearm. Older people are a real challenge because their skin is very thin and elastic. But she really wanted it. She works in a cafeteria at a nursing home and wanted everybody to see her tattoo when she served food."

Ms. Deborah was poised to hit the half-century mark on her next birthday. But she had coal black hair, perfect white teeth, and three rings in her nose. She had the lovely, smooth skin of a teenager. Her youthful skin was also swarming with tattoos. Her last tattoo had been permanent blue eyeliner. Her first tattoo, a unicorn on her buttocks, was inked more than two decades ago by husband No. 1. "It's a little lower than it used to be," she said with false modesty.

Between her first and last tattoos were a hundred others. They included flowers, vines, animal horns, a mermaid, a heart, and lady luck. She had a tattoo that said "Mom" and a tattoo that celebrated a former boyfriend, "Richie." She had tattoos on her breasts, hips, and arms, legs, hands, and feet. She had traveled all over the world for tattoos, though she had inked a few herself. "This skull and marionette strings I did myself," she said. "It's a self-portrait. I guess I was having a bad day."

Sometime in the future, Ms. Deborah told me, she intended to open another business, a bed-and-breakfast in Yucatan for tattoo artists, a place where they could kick back and relax, eat organic food, look at the clouds and blue water, and maybe not get stared at disapprovingly by old fogies who don't understand what being young is all about. Perhaps the real Fountain of Youth is in the Yucatan.

In the youth business of modern Florida, Ponce, there is some argument regarding tattoos. You have the young people, and the young old people, who value them. The competing view comes from another corner of the market.

"I do not like dealing with tattoos."

Mila Mician was talking. Over in Tampa, a block or so off Dale Mabry, was her business, Body by Mician. A former army plastic surgeon, Mician specialized in making aging people look younger. She did breast augmentations and butt lifts, fixed eyes and noses, and even improved calves and tummies. But she drew the line at removing that "I'm out spending my children's inheritance" tattoo from your upper back.

"Tattoos are nonpredictable. To remove them is time-consuming and expensive," she said. "It costs ten times more to remove a tattoo than it costs to get one. If it's a small tattoo, or if it's the name of an ex-husband and you hate him, I might be able to excise it. If it's a big tattoo and you liked it at one time, I say keep it. Stand behind your decision."

Mician had been born in Prague, Czechoslovakia, and spoke with a charming accent. She became a U.S. citizen in 1967, got her medical degree from the University of Florida, and retired from the army as a lieutenant colonel more than a decade ago. In the bright lights of her office, she appeared to have striking purple hair. "I lie about my age," Mician revealed. Oh, we could have found out, Ponce, but why bother in a story about the Fountain of Youth?

"Who wants to be old these days?" Mician continued. "Who wants to have gray hair these days? I have older women patients who now date much younger men because they look so good. This one woman complained to me about her boyfriend's immaturity. I said, 'Well, at least he's not eighteen.' She said, 'He's twenty-two!'"

The doctor tucked their tummies and gave them cleavage Charo would envy. "Sometimes I say no. I say, 'You would be better off getting a new boyfriend than having surgery. You look fabulous.' But if you are a dancer or you work at that restaurant—what is it called? The Hooters?—I understand that your breasts are your livelihood. They tell me, 'I know they will be heavy and make me miserable later. But I'll be able to get my breasts fixed again after my career is over.'"

What about those butts?

"For a while, everybody wanted to be Jennifer Lopez," the doctor answered. "They wanted a J.Lo butt. Of course, I did some J.Lo butts. With the butt, you want to make the incision in the crack so your patient can wear a T-back. What I like about what I do is it marries medicine with art."

She had a Web site. Most every plastic surgeon in Florida does, Ponce. The Fountain of Youth Institute—you would love it, Ponce—had one of the grandest. The Web site told the story of C. Randall Harrell, M.D., who was practicing on U.S. 19 in Pinellas County's Palm Harbor when I made my pilgrimage. He was born in Georgia, canoed in the Okefenokee, and spent happy times in Florida with his Jacksonville grandparents when he was a boy. Jacksonville is an hour's drive from St. Augustine and the Fountain of Youth National Archaeological Park. Harrell, who had wavy red hair and a devil-may-care mustache, loved the park. He loved the possibility of immortality.

The desire for immortality, for resisting aging with all your might, was right out in the open at the beginning of the twenty-first century. Those makeover television shows, Ponce! Those aging movie starlets! The trophy girlfriends of wealthy lawyers! "People used to sneak into town with bags over their heads to have cosmetic surgery," Harrell said. "Now they are very proud of their surgery. It's a celebrity thing."

Photos of celebrities he had improved hung in his office, including singer Judy Collins and former Dallas Cowboy quarterback Roger Staubach. Harrell's office workers, it turned out, were attractive enough to be TV anchorwomen. One of them, Marissa Morris, the office spokeswoman and the doctor's wife, once had anchored the newscast of a Tampa station.

"I still do some trauma surgery," Harrell went on. "But mostly, I do this now. It's a very exciting time to be a plastic surgeon. At one time, after you reproduced, it was time to go to the grave. Now we live another fifty years beyond having children. We don't want to age like our parents. We don't want to look like our parents. And we don't have to. I have done breast reductions for women in their eighties. Vanity doesn't go away with age."

We all want to live forever, Ponce. You wanted immortality and fame. That is why you returned to Florida in 1521 even though you were sixty-one, old for a European. This time you sailed up the west coast and made landfall somewhere in today's Lee County, perhaps Estero Bay.

The Spanish Crown would have appreciated your ambition to establish another colonial outpost. You would have been the toast of Madrid! Think of all the young senoritas who would have wanted to dance with you!

Unfortunately, you picked the headquarters of Florida's fiercest aboriginals, the Calusas. They had encountered Spaniards before and knew what to do. Ponce, you arrived with two hundred soldiers, Catholic priests, horses, livestock, seeds, and building material, but the Calusa warriors did not meet you with applause or flowers or the keys to their cities. Fox News was not around to show it, but we know from historians that they threw spears and fired arrows in your direction. One arrow embedded in your thigh. Historians think you were carried to the ship immediately.

Historians don't know if you died on the ship, or if you died of infection in Cuba, the ship's destination. They just know you died, as all men and women must do, later or sooner, no matter what.

June 27, 2004

10

ST. PETERSBURG

Babe Ruth

Babe Ruth's ghost jaywalked across Central Avenue one spring afternoon in the twenty-first century just in time for cocktail hour. He strolled into the Pink Elephant and ordered a boilermaker. The young bartender announced, "On the house. I want it said that I bought a drink for the Babe."

It was dusk when Babe stepped outside with a whiskey glow on that famous moon-shaped face. His eyes darted toward a tall platinum blonde who sashayed past in a slinky red dress. You could tell Babe wanted to say something snappy, but he let her pass without a come-on. Instead, he climbed into his big black limousine and was gone. The limo must have been a ghost, too.

When major league baseball's Grapefruit League season commences every March, the ghost of Babe Ruth still haunts the streets of my hometown, St. Petersburg. And why not? He spent ten springs there beginning in 1925, when he was the most famous baseball player in the land and possibly the best-known athlete in the world.

In the twenty-first century, it would be like having Lance Armstrong living in our midst for a couple of months. The difference is that Ruth was that rare celebrity comfortable among ordinary folks. He needed no bodyguards. He was friendly with the press. Joe Blow could buy him a drink. He showed up at a downtown barber shop every morning for a shave and a few jokes. He visited sick kids in the hospital. At the dog track, where he was a regular, he'd freely dispense gambling tips. You wanted an autograph, he gave you an autograph or posed for a photograph or let you use his name in your local-yokel advertisement.

St. Petersburg was a small town, but by staying here he helped make it important to the rest of the world. He was part of the boom that happened after the 1921 hurricane and before the Depression. As money discovered St. Petersburg, developers built grand hotels and spectacular golf courses. At the sparkling new Coliseum, international stars Rudy Vallee and Benny Goodman entertained. Over at Waterfront Park, near today's Bayfront Center downtown, Ruth drew huge crowds.

He loved it. He loved the Florida weather, especially when it was sunny, when he could sneak out in the morning before practice and play golf. He loved our courses, especially the wide fairways that could contain his mighty drives. He was a lousy putter; the man didn't know his strength and sometimes threw his club in disgust when the ball rolled past the cup. But he laughed afterward.

He loved the fishing, especially chasing grouper in bucking seas with stout tackle. Perhaps grouper reminded him of himself, corpulent, a little homely, yet athletic and appealing. He'd bring them in and have a cook at the hotel fix them for supper. No gourmet, he was as happy wolfing down a half dozen ball-park hot dogs or pickled eggs.

By all accounts, Ruth worked hard during spring training, but he played just as hard away from the field. He was one of those people who didn't consider beer an alcoholic beverage. Alcohol meant whiskey. He drank a lot of beer and whiskey. He was married twice, though hardly a fanatic about his wedding vows, and usually found women willing to share his bed whether it was in the house he rented in the Old Northeast or rooms at the Don CeSar, the Flori-de-Leon, the Princess Martha, or the Hotel Dennis, where he supposedly enjoyed staying in Room 310 because it was big enough to throw a party. In the morning, recovering from the bacchanalia, he swigged bicarbonate of soda, then drove over to the New York Yankees' training facility, which is now called Huggins-Stengel Field, named after the club's two most famous managers. The Devil Rays practice there in modern times. It's a green pool table of a park just west of Fourth Street N next to Crescent Lake. It's a good place to look for the ghost of Babe Ruth.

It's modern these days, but when Ruth was a Yankee the park lacked even an outfield fence. During one practice in 1925, Ruth unaccountably abandoned his right-field position near the lake and retired to the dugout.

"What's going on?" roared Miller Huggins, the Yankee manager who treated Ruth as an incorrigible kid.

"I ain't going out there anymore," Ruth answered. "There's an alligator."

Somebody chased the gator back into the lake. Otherwise Ruth might have become a ghost even earlier.

Before I tell you more about Ruth's notorious womanizing, his affection for strong drink, his gluttony, the spring-training battles with Yankees management, the off-hours high jinks involving smelly mackerel and snappish alligators—before we chase Ruth's ghost another iota—perhaps a little history of his youth is in order.

George Herman Ruth was born in Baltimore in 1894. He once told a biographer, "I was a bum when I was a kid." A habitual truant, he learned to cuss, drink, and steal at an early age. His parents sent him to the Catholic brothers of St. Mary's Industrial School to straighten him out. Maybe they did and maybe they didn't. What is clear is that the troubled youth learned to play baseball very well.

He signed a professional contract with the minor league Orioles in 1914. Before the season was over, he was a member of the major league Boston Red Sox, a pitcher initially, but a budding slugger-outfielder. Teammates called him "Babe" because of his naiveté off the field. On the field, there was nothing childish about him. He was hitting home runs by the tubful. In the dumbest deal of all time, the Red Sox sold him to the Yankees in 1920.

New York was Babe's kind of town. He wore flamboyant camel hair coats and drove a convertible. He was a big tipper, a bigger celebrity, a man-boy who was likely to say anything to anyone without much thought. On the steamy afternoon he met President Warren G. Harding, he felt the need to comment about the weather. "Hot as hell, ain't it, Prez?"

Squirming at a formal dinner party, he stood up and gravely announced to the rest of the table: "I have to piss." When he returned, a friend quietly admonished him. Embarrassed, Babe apologized to dining companions.

"I'm sorry I said piss."

People who knew him claimed he was the slugger of all time when it came to flatulence. He actually won a trophy for an especially sterling performance. His hearty belches could rattle the bats stacked in the dugout. The sportswriter Frank Graham once wrote: "He was a very simple man, in some ways a primitive man. He had little education, and little need for what he had."

One ritual of the St. Petersburg spring was the contract negotiation between the Yankees' skinflint owner, Col. Jacob Ruppert, and his star. In 1929, Ruth hit forty-six home runs and batted .345. He wanted a $100,000 salary. Outraged, Ruppert battled Ruth through the press. After all, Lou Gehrig, who had hit thirty-five home runs and was nothing but well-behaved—he was so good to his mother!—was only making $8,000. Ruth threatened to quit. Then he signed for $80,000. A reporter pointed out that Ruth was now making a higher salary than President Herbert Hoover. "I had a better year," Ruth sniffed.

The late sportswriter Red Smith always doubted the veracity of Ruth's snappy reply. "The Babe was not that well-informed on national affairs," he wrote.

Nor was Ruth a man of letters. One spring, the poet Carl Sandburg conducted a St. Petersburg interview with the most famous man in America. "At least a million hot ball fans in this country, admirers of yours, believe in the Bible and Shakespeare as the two greatest books ever written," said Sandburg, "and some of them would like to know if there are any special parts of those books that are favorites of yours."

Babe Ruth didn't have to think long. "A ballplayer don't have time to read," he declared. Sportswriters of his era usually hid character flaws from the public. In one spring-training story told now, but not then, Babe ran naked through a railroad car while being chased by a woman with a butcher's knife. Bigger than life, Ruth inspired tall tales. Some of them may have been true.

Ruth's first spring training as a Yankee was in 1925. With his first marriage failing, he was drinking, eating, and chasing women in a Ruthian manner, too. Finally, spring ended. The Yankees headed north by train. By North Carolina, Babe was deathly ill and was taken off the train. He spent weeks in the hospital. Sportswriters called his illness "the bellyache heard around the world" and blamed one too many hot dogs. But some suspected the Bambino actually was suffering from a terrible case of the clap.

So a couple of little people, who were then called midgets, show up at Waterfront Park. Of course the Yankees put them in uniform. Guess who poses with them for the photographers? At a nursing home, a woman known as Grandma Fenton celebrates her 104th birthday. Guess who shows up with roses? He attends weekly boxing matches and volunteers to referee. In the middle of baseball practice, representatives of the St. Petersburg Order of the Elks present him with his very own baby alligator. He lets it loose and players spill out of the dugout.

In a different time and in a different place, Babe Ruth could have gone for Ardith Rutland in a big way. Like him, she enjoyed hunting and fishing, laughing, and having a good time. But, alas, she was a babe herself when she met the Babe. She was five when she sold him orange juice and peanut butter cookies.

As Ardith told me the story in her Snell Isle home, Babe's ghost was sitting next to her on the couch. Rutland's family lived in Clearwater, within walking distance of the famous Belleview Biltmore Resort golf course. She and her older brother set up their juice stand on the edge of the fairway. Every time Ruth played by, and he played by quite a bit, he stopped for refreshments.

"You know who I am?" he asked.

She had never heard of Babe Ruth, but she had heard of Baby Ruth candy bars. Did he have anything to do with candy? Actually, the candy bars had been named after President Grover Cleveland's daughter. Ruth found it all hilarious; next time he played golf, he had a Baby Ruth in his pocket for the little girl.

"My uncle always brings me two," the sassy little girl pouted. Next time he brought a pair. Eventually, he was courting the child's favor with a box of Baby Ruths. The last time she saw him he paid his 25-cent juice-and-cookie bill with a $10 bill, no change required.

"He was always nice as can be," said Mrs. Rutland seven decades later. "Whenever I read something off-color about him, I always felt bad. He was so nice to kids. People around here really enjoyed him."

He had a deep voice with a hint of a Baltimore accent, which sounded southern, which must have endeared him to locals. And like many of them, he couldn't get enough of fishing. Spring training often coincided with a run of migrating king mackerel in the gulf. After one trip, Ruth left a dead mackerel on the lawn of a house rented by a colorful Yankee pitcher, Vernon Gomez.

Ruth was incapable of remembering names so he relied on nicknames based on physical characteristics. Gomez threw the ball with his left hand, and so he was forever Lefty." The chunky pitcher Urban Shocker was "Rubber Belly." The sharp-featured catcher Pat Collins was better remembered as "Horse Nose." Everyone else he called "kid."

Mike Mastry, one of those kids, was eighty-four when I talked to him about the Babe.

As he scooped live shrimp from the tank at Mastry's Bait and Tackle on Fourth Street S, his eyes lit up when he thought of 1933 and the Babe. He'd skip school and pedal his bike over to Kress, the dime store on Central Avenue, and buy a dozen baseballs for a quarter each. He'd ride his bike to the ballpark, wait for his chance and approach Ruth for autographs.

"He signed my baseballs and after the game I'd sell them for a dollar each. That was a fortune back them. I thought I was rich."

It became a daily ritual. "He never turned me down, not even once. Oh, he knew exactly what I was doing. But you know, I think he got a kick out of a kid who was willing to hustle for a buck. He even posed for a picture signing an autograph so I could use it for a prop when I sold the balls."

Baseballs autographed by Babe Ruth are worth a fortune these days. "I wish I had kept one," Mike Mastry said sheepishly. "But wait a minute, I want to show you something."

Limping from arthritis, Mastry hobbled behind a counter covered by hooks and lures and line and reels and fished an old photo out of a drawer. In the photo the Babe is standing next to a handsome, athletic kid.

"Can you believe it's me with Babe Ruth?"

Babe Ruth smoked, chewed tobacco, and dipped snuff. He died in his sleep of throat cancer on August 16, 1948. He was only fifty-four. No wonder his ghost is restless. Baseball fans should pay attention, keep their eyes peeled. Liable to see him anywhere.

He slept at 346 Sixteenth Ave. NE in St. Petersburg, in a fine house that sold for $350,000 in 2003. He slept at the Princess Martha, the hotel built at 401 First Ave. N in 1924. He stayed at the Don CeSar, on the beach, and at the Jungle Country Club Hotel, now gone, on Park Street. He stayed at the Hotel Dennis, built in 1925 at 326 First Ave. N, across the street from Williams Park.

He loved the Dennis, especially Room 310, which was customized for parties and practical jokes. There was a skeleton in the bathtub. One chair was rigged to collapse. Another zapped sitters with electricity. It was the Babe's idea of a great hotel. In the twenty-first century it was called Kelly's, and rooms rented for $150 a week.

Ruth often rented a penthouse at the Flori-de-Leon, built in 1925, at 130 Fourth Ave. N. He stayed one season in Apartment 701, though he preferred 702. Teammate Lou Gehrig often took 701. A reserved man, Gehrig prized the private elevator. It didn't matter to Ruth. He wasn't afraid of encountering a fan.

"Gehrig was supposedly very quiet," said Ron Adams, who lived at the apartment complex seven decades later. "Ruth was boisterous. His neighbors complained about the smell of hot dogs and sauerkraut." Richard and Eleanor Simmons were living in Ruth's old apartment when I knocked on the door. In their sixties, they had moved here from New York in 2002. They didn't follow baseball, but they liked the idea of living in Babe's old place. It no longer smelled of hot dogs and sauerkraut.

It had one of the grandest views in the city. It had fine hardwood floors. It had a nifty fireplace. Above the fireplace hung a painting of a naked woman. The Babe would have approved.

He was known as a tireless sexual athlete. One night, according to a story I read in Robert Creamer's *Babe: The Legend Comes To Life*, Ruth brought a woman into the hotel suite he shared with the outfielder Bob Meusel. Meusel, half-asleep in his own room, tried to ignore the great commotion coming from Babe's room. Finally it stopped. Then Meusel smelled cigar smoke. Minutes later, the yells and cries returned, followed minutes later by more cigar smoke. Between noise and cigar smoke, Meusel slept badly that night.

In the morning, Meusel asked his roommate how many times he had been romantic.

"Count the cigars," Ruth said.

Seven butts lay in the ash tray.

March 21, 2004

11

WINTER HAVEN

Miz Marjorie's Mommy Dearest

As I was reading the newly discovered and darkly revealing "lost" novel by Marjorie Kinnan Rawlings called *Blood of My Blood*, I kept thinking about the first time I came under the spell of Mrs. Rawlings, who lived and wrote for so many years at Cross Creek.

I was twelve when I encountered *The Yearling*, the Pulitzer Prize–winning novel she published in 1938. There was no better read for a boy who hated school and shoes and lived only for fishing and poking around the Everglades with his dad. At night, as the crickets sang outside the open window, I lay in bed, under the covers, with my flashlight trained on Mrs. Rawlings's words: "Sound filled the swamp. Saplings crashed. The bear was a black hurricane, mowing down obstructions . . ." Penny Baxter, his boy, Jody, and their dogs, Rip and Julia, were on the trail of the notorious rogue bruin Old Slewfoot.

I still read *The Yearling* every five years or so, though no longer by flashlight. I now see that its underlying themes make *The Yearling* more of an adult novel than a child's book. It is the complicated portrait Rawlings drew of Jody's mother, Ma Baxter, who is homely and heavy and bitter about life. Penny Baxter tries to inspire his son. Ma Baxter, afraid to love too deeply, takes the wind out of her little boy's sails as if she is preparing him for a long life of defeat.

Why? Why such a harsh portrait of a mother?

Now we may have the answer.

"The physical ugliness of my mother was the bitter drop that tainted the fluid of her life."

That's how Rawlings began *Blood of My Blood*, which she called fiction but wrote as autobiography. It's about her family's history, from her grandparents to when she marries and leaves home. It's about her loving father and his passion for country living and beauty. But the central character is her domineering mother, who manipulates and schemes and tries to run her daughter's life to a point where only a nervous breakdown or rebellion can result.

In Marjorie's case, it was rebellion.

"It's sort of Marjorie's version of *Mommie Dearest*," explained Rawlings scholar and actor Betty Jean Steinshouer, who has portrayed the author in one-person dramas for more than a decade.

Mommie Dearest, written by Joan Crawford's daughter, Christina Crawford, was a harrowing account of child abuse. So is *Blood of My Blood*, though Ida Kinnan somewhat redeemed herself at the very end of her life. But it is clear her daughter never got over a traumatic youth. Although Rawlings continues to be hailed by her most innocent fans as an Earth Mother and Maria von Trapp rolled into one, she was in fact an unhappy woman who struggled with depression and alcoholism for most of her life.

"Ida laid the foundation of her child's life on personal appearance," Rawlings wrote of her mother and herself in *Blood of My Blood*. "She remedied the lank thinness of its hair by curling it with hot irons. When it was necessary to take it out in public on a rainy day, she lamented bitterly. She swathed its head in veils, and unwrapped it like some fragile trophy, peering anxiously for vestiges of the curl. Her first anger at the child burst out when, crisp in white organdie and a small pink sash, it waddled away and sat down in a mud puddle. She shook it viciously. She so impressed it with the enormity of this offense that the girl reached full maturity before she was able to shake off a tense stiffness when in fresh clothes."

In 1928 Marjorie Rawlings moved to Florida after a brief stint as a northern newspaper reporter. She was thirty-two when she and her first husband, Charles, bought a farm at Cross Creek with the intention of growing oranges and writing up a storm. He wanted to write adventure stories for magazines, and she dreamed of being the next Jane Austen.

In 1929, she submitted *Blood of My Blood* to Atlantic Monthly Press and received a polite rejection. Most authors would have immediately sent the manuscript to another publisher, but she put it away and went on with her life.

What a life it turned out to be. She managed to get the attention of Maxwell Perkins, the famous editor of Ernest Hemingway, F. Scott Fitzgerald, and Thomas Wolfe. He rejected her attempts to become Jane Austen but was captivated by her letters about the hardscrabble lives of rural Floridians. Perkins advised Rawlings to write about them. And so she did.

She became one of America's most beloved, and respected, authors over the next dozen years. But as depression and alcoholism took over, she seldom published. Instead, she devoted ten years to what she hoped would be her masterpiece. That novel, *The Sojourner*, published in January 1953, was widely considered a failure. Eleven months later she suffered a fatal stroke. Only fifty-seven, she died a disappointed woman.

In 1988, when Anne Blythe Meriwether was thirty-nine, she was working on her doctorate about southern women and literature at the University of South Carolina when a New York book dealer who knew of her interests sent her a mysterious box of old papers. She almost fell down when she started reading.

"I spread them out on my kitchen and couldn't believe it," Meriwether told me when I telephoned her in 2002. "Supper came and went. I kept reading until I was through."

She was reading letters Marjorie Rawlings had written to Julia Scribner, the young daughter of her publisher. The letters offered advice to a troubled teen. Rawlings told Scribner, kindly, that it was time to grow up. She praised Julia's talent and spirit, and said she needed to buckle down and work. Quit the partying!

She knew Julia struggled with a difficult parent.

"It is possible," Rawlings wrote, "that in your case, as it was in mine, only your mother's death will liberate you, and that is a price one would wish not to pay for liberation."

At the bottom of the box lay eighty typewritten pages.

Meriwether started reading. It was *Blood of My Blood*. Why had she given it to Julia Scribner? Nobody knew, but perhaps she wanted to inspire a younger woman about what was possible even if you had grown up dysfunctional.

After Julia Scribner's death, the manuscript and the letters lay in a box stored in an attic until Meriwether got them.

"Nobody but Rawlings and her first husband and Julia had known about *Blood of My Blood*," Meriwether told me. "All of them were dead. It just came into my hands."

In 1988, Meriwether attended a meeting of Rawlings fans to share her discovery. Many were delighted, but some were shocked, none more than Rawlings's widower, her second husband, Norton Baskin. He claimed Meriwether's manuscript was a fake. When it was authenticated by experts, Baskin filed suit, saying his wife's writings belonged to him. It took four years for the court to decide in Meriwether's favor.

Finally she could edit the work. "Every time I read it, and every time I read it now, I'm stunned," Meriwether said when I called. "I'm stunned by the brutal honesty of it. She's harsh not only on her mother but on herself. But her mother, oh my: the tug of war between mother and daughter, the mother's desire to shape a child in her own image, and almost being able to do it. It's scary and heartbreaking. You almost can't sit down and read it for pleasure. It's too painful."

At Cross Creek, a tiny village in rural, conservative north Florida, Rawlings was considered a live wire. It wasn't only that she had divorced her first husband, almost unheard of in the God-fearing community, but it was also the fact she chain-smoked in public and didn't hide her love for liquor and guns.

She feuded with neighbors but had their respect, because she wasn't afraid of them one bit. And she loved their kids, especially boys. Her neighbors were the Glissons, and their boy Jake, a blond dreamer. One day Mrs. Rawlings found him lying next to the creek watching a little water mill he'd constructed out of palm fronds. He became one of the models Rawlings used for the wide-eyed boy in *The Yearling*.

Some neighbors feared Rawlings's sharp tongue, but Jake was too innocent to be scared, he once told me. Afraid he was failing high school, he asked a teacher what would happen if he could convince the famous Marjorie Kinnan Rawlings to talk to the senior class. "You'll graduate," said the teacher, who had no idea that Jake knew the author. The next day Jake showed up at school with his neighbor, who agreed to address the whole school. "If I do this," Mrs. Rawlings said to the principal, "Jake passes. Right?"

Jake passed. When we spoke last, he was in his seventies. He still flinched when people talked bad about his Miz Rawlings. I also interviewed Idella Parker several times in the 1990s. She's mentioned in Rawlings's *Cross Creek* as "the perfect maid." An African-American in Cracker Florida during its most racist period, she had a complicated relationship with her employer. Rawlings was a liberal who sometimes used the "n" word.

Parker hated and feared Rawlings, but also loved and protected her. Sometimes she tried to grab away the car keys after Rawlings had spent a drunken afternoon at her typewriter. Rawlings once turned her car over on a slippery road, breaking Parker's ribs.

Toward the end, Parker could no longer tolerate working with Rawlings and had to leave. In her eighties, ailing herself, Parker loved visiting the old farmhouse, now the Marjorie Kinnan Rawlings State Historic Site, and talking about the times the two of them cooked up a storm and gossiped.

Dessie Prescott died in 2002 at ninety-five, near Crystal River. When I interviewed her in 1996, Dessie and I had a grand time swilling beer and talking about hunting and fishing. Prescott taught Rawlings how to survive in the woods and appears in a chapter of *Cross Creek*. She was an old-time Cracker woman who slept with a shotgun at her bedside and was delightfully familiar with the phrase "son of a bitch." Though younger than Rawlings, she was in some ways a mother figure for her friend, whom she called "Young 'un."

Rawlings loved people like Prescott. But she also enjoyed the company of Hemingway, Fitzgerald, Wolfe, Margaret Mitchell, and Robert Frost, the poet, who often stayed with her at Cross Creek. Rawlings liked to say those other authors suffered greatly from "cosmic despair." Of course, she did, too.

Whenever I wanted a few goose bumps, I went to watch Betty Jean Steinshouer. In college, she was the oratory champion of Missouri and later got a master's degree in literature from Madison University in Virginia.

Acting was her passion. After meeting Hal Holbrook, who did thousands of one-man shows as Mark Twain, she decided she might be able to combine her flair for the dramatic with her love of literature. She performed all over the country as Willa Cather, Gertrude Stein, and Marjorie Kinnan Rawlings. She lived in St. Petersburg.

I drove to Winter Haven and watched one of her performances as my favorite Florida author.

"I'm in dire need of drink," were her first Marjorie words to the audience. She claimed her husband had hidden the Bacardi from her. Then she got out her Lucky Strikes; Rawlings was a five-pack-a-day smoker.

When Betty Jean performed as Rawlings she almost became Rawlings. I've heard tapes of Rawlings speaking, and so had Steinshouer. Rawlings's voice was a little nasal, a little snotty, a little snobby. She'd say "ad-VER-tiz-ment" instead of "ad-ver-TISE-ment."

"Does my voice bother you?" Steinshouer's Rawlings asked the audience. "I'm afraid I'm sounding more and more like my mother. That's very disturbing. I was talking to Hemingway once. He hated his mother as much as I hated mine . . ."

My hair stood on end.

Rawlings always told people how she longed for a child. She never conceived and considered that still another failure in a life filled with failure. Once she wrote the young Julia Scribner: "How I wish you were my daughter! I would be the right sort of mother for one like you."

A few years before her death, she wrote another friend: "I have been in such anguish. I came closer to killing myself than ever before. . . . I have always felt that without my writing, I was nothing. . . . Sexual failure, lack of happiness, none of it matters if I can say the things I want to say."

At the time she was working on what would be her last book. *The Sojourner* is fiction, but it's the story of her family. It is *Blood of My Blood*, written not by a young writer, but by a polished novelist who knew how to hide the personal in a story that seemed made up. Again, the central character is a manipulative mother who damages her child.

Oh, Marjorie.

"*Blood of My Blood* and *The Sojourner* turn out to be bookends," Anne Blythe Meriwether told me. "At the end of her life she was still trying to work out her relationship with her mother."

May 2, 2002

12

TALLAHASSEE

Lucy

"Hey, Lucy!"

A lobbyist driving on College Avenue shouted at her from his Jeep.

"You doing something bad?" she hollered back.

"No, ma'am!"

"Tell me something I'm not supposed to know."

"Not me, Lucy."

In Tallahassee, nobody called her Ms. Morgan, or Mrs. Morgan, or even "that Lucy Morgan," though she knew some folks described her as "The Bitch."

She was just plain Lucy. Perhaps it was the spectacular drawl that went back to her Mississippi roots that invited informality. Or the fact she sometimes was observed knitting doll clothes for her grandchildren as she listened to testimony at a murder trial. Anyway, she never objected to "Lucy." Nor did she protest "darlin'," "sweetie," or "honey."

"Ah have always liked to be unner-ahstimated," she explained in a raspy voice that sounded like she had been munching pecans. Subtitle: Lucy was happy when somebody important underestimated her, when somebody thought she was not as smart as she actually was. "To be a southern woman in a cap'll full of good ole boys is an advantage. When they fand ayout A'hm serious it's too late."

If Lucy had been a character in a Puccini opera it would have to be Turandot. Lucy loved opera, Puccini especially. Frankly, Turandot was her kind of gal. Turandot was a fetching though calculating princess who over the years has lured many a prince to his doom.

Lots of princes tried to win Turandot's favor. But the femme fatale enjoyed toying with her suitors. She told her latest beau she would marry him if he could provide the answer to three trick questions. A prince who answered wrong was not sent packing—he was beheaded.

I was dispatched to Tallahassee in 2006 to write about Lucy when she was poised to retire after nearly four decades of reporting for Florida's largest newspaper, the *St. Petersburg Times.*

For decades politicians, lobbyists, and sheriffs had nervously massaged their throats the instant Lucy started asking questions. They knew Lucy's pen, indeed, was mightier than the sword.

Lucy's basket was filled with dozens of heads. In 1982 she was a Pulitzer Prize finalist for exposing a drug-smuggling ring in Dixie and Taylor counties that resulted in 250 people going to jail, including government officials. In 1985 she and another reporter, Jack Reed, won the big enchilada for investigating problems in the Pasco County Sheriff's Office. Her Pulitzer hung on an office wall.

For two decades, she headed her paper's Tallahassee bureau, covering governors, legislators, judges, sheriffs, and lobbyists, including some who actually intended to make the state a better place. Not many of them, of course. Frequently she caught a dunderhead doing something stupid, embarrassing, or illegal and felt the need to tell her readers about it.

She probably listened to *Turandot* on her stereo as she removed their heads.

"I would rather have an enema than be interviewed by you," Jack Latvala, former Republican senator from Pinellas County, once barked after a trying day when Lucy had many questions.

"There was once a great Green Bay Packer offensive guard named Jerry Kramer," said Democrat Bob Graham, the former governor and U.S. senator, when I called. "He was asked about his coach, Vince Lombardi. Kramer said, 'Coach Lombardi treated all his players democratically. He treated us all like dogs.' I would say Lucy was a very democratic reporter."

A scary quote. And Lucy always *liked* Graham. She thought he was that rare, honest public servant.

I was almost afraid to tell Graham not to relax; Lucy's retirement wasn't going to be a traditional retirement. She intended to work part-time for her paper, maybe do some investigative work, nothing terribly big, through heaven knew what she might turn up. Perhaps she would get the chance to put the famously straight-laced Graham on the hot seat one last time.

Hell's bells. She wasn't dead yet—she was still in her prime, only sixty-five. A few drops of poison surely remained in her trusty old pen.

"Hey, Alan," she shouted at an insurance lobbyist whose ear was glued to his cell phone. "You doin' somethin' bad?"

He grinned and nodded in the affirmative.

"You want to confess?"

He grinned and nodded no.

"Nothing ventured, nothing gained," Lucy muttered, ambling away.

A walking contradiction, was this Lucy woman. She was the wife of an old-fashioned guy who owned what might have been the last perfect flat-top haircut in the state. Mother of four grown children, grandmother of eight with one great-grandchild, she could cuss like a cowboy with hemorrhoids, then quietly get back to her knitting.

She had wept through operas all over the world. Pavarotti was her favorite. Loved ballet, too. She was glad that she had seen Baryshnikov, during his glory days, when he was especially appealing while wearing tights. "Nice tush," she said with affection.

She was a wine connoisseur who ate with elbows on the table. She liked to be the center of attention and frequently interrupted whoever else had forgotten his manners and grabbed the spotlight. "Lucy, let me finish," her husband said calmly when I joined them for supper.

A shopaholic, she loved buying new clothes when her husband wasn't watching, though she inevitably dressed casually, part of her "go ahead and underestimate me" philosophy. She often arrived at work in a modest blouse and stretch pants tugged over her farm woman's sturdy frame. No heels, just sneakers. Walking with a limp, surrounded by an intoxicating cloud of Estée Lauder, she was breathless while hobbling up the hill toward the Statehouse and the people's business.

So innocent and huggable! Lucy, why aren't you home baking an apple pie?

Duck! For God's sake, duck!

"Look," she was known to advise a self-important rookie senator. "You don't have to be a horse's ayass. You can be straight with me."

Perhaps he was too shocked to reply just then. No matter. Sooner or later he would learn his responsibilities, his reason for being, and answer Lucy.

"Lucy was relentless," said Rob Hooker, a *Times* deputy managing editor who worked with Lucy on her celebrated stories in west central Florida in the 1980s. "She has wonderful people skills, the uncanny ability to get people to talk to her and tell her things they shouldn't have."

Nervous evildoers tapped her phone and pawed through her garbage looking for dirt while she investigated them. They followed her car and threatened her—anonymously, of course—over the phone at midnight. They scared her children and grandchildren. They put out a bumper sticker: "Screw Lucy Morgan." They menaced her sources; sometimes Lucy felt compelled to meet sources in a Belk Lindsey department store in New Port Richey. While Lucy tried on clothes in a changing room they'd pass crucial information about the Pasco County Sheriff's Office under the door.

In 1973 an ambitious district attorney wondered where she was getting information about corruption in Dade City and dropped a subpoena on her lap. "I would go to jail rather than reveal a source" was Lucy's credo. A judge sentenced her to eight months because she wouldn't tell.

"I was prepared to go to jail," she told people years later. "I thought I might finally get some serious reading done."

At the bookstore she purchased the complete works of Lord Alfred Tennyson, the Victorian poet best known for *The Charge of the Light Brigade*.

"Just always wanted to read him," she said.

Alas, the Florida Supreme Court ruined her chance for absorbing reading. Overturning her sentence, the court also granted reporters at least a limited right to protect sources.

She was born on October 11, 1940, in Memphis but moved to Hattiesburg, Mississippi, before blowing out even a single birthday candle. Her mother, Lucile, divorced her father, Thomas Alin Keen, an alcoholic, when she was a baby. Lucy always credited her personality, and her success, on being raised by a strong mother, grandmother, and aunt.

"Mother never remarried," Lucy said. "She had a serious suitor once, but she always said she had never met a man to whom she would cede her closet space."

Her mother ran a pharmacy, listened to opera, sang in the choir, once chased a purse snatcher, and regularly booked passage on tramp steamers bound for the South Pacific. She took pride in her two smart daughters, Kay and Lucy.

Kay got a doctorate in psychology from Harvard. Lucy graduated from high school.

"Mother was disappointed when I got pregnant and got married at seventeen," said Lucy, who never finished college.

She married a coach and moved to Crystal River. The marriage failed after nine years and three children.

"It wasn't a good situation," Lucy said. "I was a single, stay-at-home mom with three kids under the age of six and negligible work experience."

One day an editor from the *Ocala Star-Banner* called. He was looking for someone to cover news in Citrus County.

"She was looking for a part-time reporter and got my name from the local librarian who told her I read more books than just about anyone else. The editor figured that a good reader might be able to write."

She could. Sometimes, at a midnight fire, Lucy showed up accompanied by her three toddlers. Lucy loved firefighters. She loved cops. They were sweet on her, too.

"It wasn't like it is today," Lucy told me. "I'd be at the scene of an arrest and a cop would yell, 'Lucy, grab the handcuffs and give 'em to me.'"

Occasionally a male officer asked her to check on a female inmate lying passed out in a pool of vomit in the drunk tank.

"It was actually a lot of fun."

Lucy was hired at the *St. Petersburg Times* in 1967. Her first boss was an old-fashioned guy who wore his hair in a flat top. He was Richard

Morgan, perhaps the most detail-minded editor in the history of the company—the kind of manager who handed an anxious reporter three excruciating pages of instructions on her first day of employment. Instructions typically might cover the 480 official minutes in the workday and suggest the reporter sleep close to the phone in case she was needed to cover a fire.

Their marriage, in 1968, had to be kismet. She thrives in chaos. He was all about order and stability. "Lucy has the patience of a lit firecracker," he told me on his way to making the bed while wearing pajamas that looked suspiciously like he might have ironed them.

In 1979, when her teenage son Al was killed in an auto accident, Richard was a comforting presence. After all, one of his children from a previous marriage had been killed in an accident, too.

In 2005, when I visited, they lived in a sprawling five-bedroom, north Tallahassee home surrounded by pine trees, camellias, and azaleas. Lucy, who had learned many lessons from her mother, allowed her husband one little closet.

"You ought to look in her closets," he told me quietly. "She's like Imelda Marcos. I've never seen so many shoes. What does she have, seventy-five pairs? One day I'm going to count those shoes."

"We will stop talking about my shoes and my closets this minute," Lucy ordered from across the room.

At seventy-four, Richard was retired and looking forward to Lucy staying home, if only because he needed help with the housework. He was among the few people on earth who regularly had the courage to tell Lucy things she wished not to hear. A few days before I interviewed them he was pleased to send her an e-mail pointing out an embarrassing spelling error in one of her stories.

They shared their bed with two Siamese cats, Lewis and Clark. Shell-shocked lobbyists who had been grilled by Lucy ought to have listened as she baby-talked those spoiled cats. On the den wall hung thirty photographs, paintings, and weavings portraying felines.

Patrolling the state Capitol, visiting offices, Lucy knew who was a cat person and who was not.

"Jeb sleeps with a Siamese," Lucy purred, though hopefully she only had the governor's word for it.

Even though Gov. Bush was kind to cats, she said she was frequently disappointed by his tendency to conduct the people's business outside the presence of reporters, namely her.

"I felt like you put me over your knee and spanked me," he complained after an especially critical story. Sounding exasperated when I talked to him, he said, "We still haven't figured out where she gets all her sources."

One time Lucy cooked him supper at her house. She had a good recipe for chicken amandine.

With her retirement close, she told me of her worries about the future of journalism. In her opinion, reporters were often too quick to confront, too quick to chase the "gotcha" story. Lucy preferred quiet investigations. She preferred to examine public records and read the fine print—before dropping the guillotine blade. "You don't want to shoot rubber bands," she said. "When the time comes you want a loaded gun."

She told young reporters to value a good source more than a good story. One of her favorite sources of all time was an alcoholic named George who mopped floors at the Pasco County jail. He liked Lucy because she always stopped to chew the fat. "You treat me like a human being," he told her. He often called her with tips he had gleaned from eavesdropping at the sheriff's office.

"The sheriff one time got tired of the leaks and made everybody on his staff take a lie detector test," Lucy said. "Everybody but George."

One Christmas George knocked on her door carrying a jar of his grandmother's jelly. George had long hair and a rough demeanor, but Lucy wasn't afraid to welcome him into her home.

"The trouble with reporters today is they avoid people like George," Lucy said. "A good reporter should be comfortable with all kinds of people—not just people exactly like them. If you don't want to talk to someone like George you might as well be an editor."

In the fall of 2006, Lucy officially yielded her job as Tallahassee bureau chief to Steve Bousquet, a veteran political writer. He told me about his anxiety regarding replacing a legend. She was nervous about it, too, though not for the same reason. She said she wouldn't miss counting paper clips, but feared being out of the loop.

The press gallery in the Florida Senate is named after her. She told me she couldn't imagine not sitting in her regular chair when the Senate was in session. How could state government go on without her?

Well, she had a few days left before retirement day. I was sitting at a desk outside her office working on my story while she listened to a selection from a Verdi opera, "Libiamo, ne lieti calici," the drinking song from *La Traviata*. Anna Moffo and Richard Tucker had such beautiful voices! As she listened, head bobbing, she quietly was investigating the lives of lobbyists for a future story.

Lobbyists apparently liked her—"I have some good friends who are lobbyists"—but mostly they feared her. The late Dempsey Barron, a hard-drinking senator, enjoyed telephoning Lucy whenever his office was overflowing with lobbyists. "Come on over for a chat," he'd say. When Lucy arrived, lobbyists scurried out of the office like cockroaches fleeing the bathroom light.

In 2000 she shattered her right ankle in a fall. After her official retirement, she planned to submit to surgery No. 8, this time at the Mayo Clinic. And when her bones knitted, she intended to do a little part-time work. There were a few people who needed investigating. She also wanted to write a memoir.

She and her husband owned a lovely cabin on a mountain in North Carolina. Their mountain cabin was an isolated place. It was a good place to think and to listen to opera and to pet cats and to knit doll clothes and to drink wine and to write memoirs. Of course, a mountain cabin was a perfect place for serious reading.

Lucy still had that Tennyson collection she had hoped to read the time she was sentenced to jail for not revealing sources. One of his famous poems was "A Farewell."

Flow down, cold rivulet, to the sea
Thy tribute wave deliver:
No more by thee my steps shall be,
For ever and for ever.

Flow, softly flow, by lawn and lea,
A rivulet then a river:

Nowhere by thee my steps shall be,
For ever and for ever.

But here will sigh thine alder tree,
And here thine aspen shiver;
And here by thee will hum the bee,
For ever and for ever.

A thousand suns will stream on thee,
A thousand moons will quiver;
But not by thee my steps shall be,
For ever and for ever.

September 16, 2006

13

CLEARWATER BEACH

The Clearwater Monster

Something scary happened on Clearwater Beach in west central Florida in the summer of 1946. A monster emerged from the Gulf of Mexico and wandered around knocking things down in the dark. The Clearwater Monster didn't hurt anyone, but left tracks, lots of them, which were discovered the next morning on the sand.

The tracks looked like nothing anyone had ever seen. They weren't the kind of tracks left by dinosaurs, but they were large, about 14 inches long and 11 inches wide. They featured a narrow heel and three long toes. The tracks were more birdlike than reptilian, though not entirely birdlike. They were a dispatch from an unknown world.

The news made the papers. The news made the radio. The monster was the talk of Clearwater. A few citizens stepped forward to announce they had seen something mysterious on the beach that night, something alien, and if you didn't believe them, why, you could jump in a lake.

Clearwater was modest town of fifteen thousand. The war was over. Yankees who had discovered Florida during military training lived in little bungalows and started having kids. Only the very rich had air-conditioning. But anybody could chill for a few hours at the picture show while enjoying *The Big Sleep* starring Bogey and Bacall.

Pinellas County was the grapefruit capital of the world. Mom-and-pop motels were scattered here and there up and down the coast, but it was hard to find parking meters. There were a few bridges, though many rowed their boats across Clearwater Harbor to the barrier island. Light pollution had not been invented. In the summer, teenage couples could neck on the beach and almost touch the Milky Way. Loggerhead turtles crawled up in the dark to lay eggs near the sand dunes.

Clearwater was a sleepy place, something right off a postcard—the perfect stomping ground for the monster.

The Clearwater Monster was clever. The fiend left tracks, inflamed imaginations, then vanished. Just when people had stopped thinking about him, he crept out of the surf again. This time he knocked over a lifeguard stand and left hair or feathers or something unearthly on wooden pilings.

He went on a rampage. The Clearwater Monster showed about 5 miles south on Indian Rocks. He visited the Sarasota waterfront 50 miles farther south. He looped back into Pinellas County, traveled along the St. Petersburg waterfront, and kept going until he found a place to leave tracks on the sand next to the Courtney Campbell Causeway in Clearwater.

Once he got the rampaging out of his system, he laid low for a few years.

In 1948, the creature showed up again, this time about 100 miles north of Pinellas County. A beachcomber found tracks near the mouth of the Suwannee River. "He's loose again!!" wrote *St. Petersburg Times* columnist Dick Bothwell, never afraid to employ an exclamation point in a good story.

Scientists were interrogated about the monster. One said, "It couldn't be real." Another thought the tracks might have been left by a giant salamander. "Plaster casts were made of some of the tracks," Bothwell wrote, "and it was estimated by some that the beast—if beast it was—might have weighed some 2,000 pounds."

It was left to Ivan Sanderson, a self-taught zoologist, author and WNBC radio commentator, to render the definitive opinion. As the flashbulbs popped, he studied the tracks, furrowed his brow, did some measuring. He was photogenic, a Douglas Fairbanks for the beach set, with slicked-back hair, a pencil-thin mustache, and a wardrobe that all but announced "Adventure!" Only an ascot could have improved his look.

Florida had a real monster on its hands!

"Definitely not a hoax," Sanderson announced. The tracks were so deep and wide, he opined, that only something heavy and tall could have made them.

"A giant penguin," was his theory.

On a June afternoon in 2006, on the sixtieth anniversary of the Clearwater Monster, a man named Tony Signorini answered the door of his house on S Prescott Avenue in Clearwater when I knocked. A rosary rattled in the pocket of his slacks.

"Come in," he said. "Make yourself comfortable."

He led the way to the kitchen table.

"What can I tell you?"

Something about yourself.

"I'm eighty-five years old. I was born in Pennsylvania, not far from Pittsburgh. I was in the air force. I worked on B-17s, B-24s and B-29s during the war. Then Elsie and I came to Clearwater to visit her folks. I remember it was December. It was snowing back in Pennsylvania! I said to Elsie, 'Do you want to go back?' She didn't, and I didn't either."

They stayed in Clearwater.

"I went to work at a place called Auto Electric. It was on Greenwood and Pierce. The guy who owned it was Al Williams. A lot of people thought Al Williams was kind of crabby. He actually had a good sense of humor. He was a real practical joker. I was never a practical joker. People thought I was real serious, but I had my fun side when I was around Al. One time, he put a horse in a jail cell in Clearwater!"

A horse?

"Yes, somebody let him in to do it as a joke on the police chief. That's the way it was back then. Everybody had fun with everybody. Another time we hung a weather balloon from the fire station. We put this electronic device in the balloon to make it explode on command. It sounded like a bomb going off! Lucky the war was over!"

The fire chief must have been a basket case.

"He knew it was Al. The fire chief called me up one night, said, 'We want you to call Al at home and tell him his shop is on fire.' I didn't want to do it, but I did. Al drove over there right away pretty scared. He said, 'You're in on this?' I said, 'I'm sorry, Al. They held a gun to my head.'"

Al must have had a little devil in him.

"He always had something going. One time, downtown, at the band shell, there was some kind of event happening. Cars were a lot different back then from today. You could take a hood right off a car! We went through the parking lot taking hoods off of cars! Then we put a yellow hood on a blue car and a blue hood on a red car and so on. It was lots of fun."

Sounds like it.

"Back in, I want to say 1946, though it could have been '47, Al gets his hands on a *National Geographic*. There was a picture of dinosaur tracks. Al said, 'You know, we could have fun with this.'"

You made a dinosaur track?

"It wasn't exactly a dinosaur track."

Do you still have it?

"Sure, it's in the garage."

Tony's son, who had been sitting by his dad, disappeared into the garage. He returned carrying something heavy.

"We made them in the shop," Tony said, looking at the weird boots his son lay on the table. "They were plaster at first, but you couldn't make a good track with plaster. It just didn't sink in the sand deep enough to look authentic. We went to this blacksmith shop and poured lead in our molds. Each track weighed 30 pounds. We bolted black high-top gym shoes to each track."

Then what?

"Al and I rowed out to the beach. I put on the shoes. I jumped out of the boat in shallow water. I was young then, about twenty-five or so, and much stronger than I am now, an old man. I had to kind of swing my legs out to the side and then forward to get going. Somehow I didn't break my legs. I left deep tracks about 6 feet apart. I made this big loop from the surf, up the beach, and then back into the water to the boat."

So Tony Signorini was the famous Clearwater Monster?

"Yes. We were surprised to read in the papers that people had seen the monster because nobody was on the beach that night. We got a kick out of that."

Did anybody ever tell on you?

"Not that I know of. I'm sure the police chief knew it was us, but he never said anything. My wife, Elsie, knew, because I'd go out about

10 o'clock at night and come back around 2 o'clock in the morning all covered with sand. She thought it was funny. And she knew there were worse things a man could be doing than making monster tracks."

Talk about the rest of your life.

"Well, Al died in 1969. I took over Auto Electric. Elsie and I had four kids, they grew up, they're all good kids. My Elsie died a few years ago on account of her lungs. I've had two heart surgeries, but I'm okay now, just a little slower. I stay busy. I volunteer at Morton Plant Hospital twice a week. I have volunteered three thousand hours at the hospital over the years."

Do they know at the hospital that you're the Clearwater Monster?

"I don't think so. They probably never heard of him."

Do they know about the monster at your church, St. Cecelia's?

"I doubt it. They just know me as the guy who's an usher at the 9:30 Mass on Sunday morning and the guy who hands out Holy Communion at the 5:30 Mass on Saturday afternoon."

Would the Eucharistic minister from St. Cecelia's like to leave some new monster tracks on Clearwater Beach?

"Sure, I'll go, though somebody will have to carry the monster shoes. They're too heavy for me now that I'm an old man. We'll go to Sand Key, but I have to tell you, it's not like it used to be. There's lots of people and buildings now."

June 26, 2006

WORKING FLORIDA

14

TARPON SPRINGS

Sponge Diver

The old man still dreamed about the bottom of the sea. He dreamed about sponges, about tiger sharks, about big-hearted men he thought would live forever but were now gone. "It is hard getting old," the old man said. Of course it was. You outlive your friends. Your body rebels. Your short-term memory fails. And yet you can't forget.

He had not forgotten the time he found a body. He had pulled on his helmet, descended to the bottom, and lumbered against the tide to look for a sponge diver who had become incommunicado. The other diver lay on the bottom, his neck black, his tongue protruding a good foot. At least that is how the tongue looked through the glass of the diving helmet when Phil Fatolitis saw him.

What had happened? Fatolitis couldn't be sure. He tugged his safety rope, and his crew topside hauled him up. "Drowned man," he announced.

Maybe other divers would have chosen that minute to try another profession. But Fatolitis loved everything about the sea, from the wind on his sunburned skin to the danger. Diving for sponges was in his blood: Back in Greece, his diver grandfather had jumped overboard while grasping a boulder that carried him into the depths.

One day in 2006 I paid him a visit. Soon he was talking about diving as we sat at the dinner table of his little bungalow on Read Street in Tarpon Springs. Actually, he was talking about his sadness about not diving. "My doctor doesn't want me to even scuba," he complained.

If it had been possible, he would have put together a crew one last time. They'd take the boat way out into the gulf, perhaps as far as the Middle Grounds, and for the last time he would haul on the suit, and his crew would bolt the heavy brass helmet to the breastplate, and he would slip overboard and wait for the satisfying moment his heavy boots touched rock bottom. He would rake in the sponges.

But why talk foolishness? He was eighty-two at the time of the interview. He had a bad heart and bad bowels.

"Ah, you couldn't put together a crew like that anymore anyway," he said. "All those guys I knew, guys who really knew what they were doing, are dead."

He was among the last of his kind, a diver from the glory days of Tarpon Springs who had worn the classic heavy gear, the iron boots, the old-fashioned helmet, equipment found in maritime museums in the twenty-first century.

"It's just me and one other diver from the old days who is still alive," Fatolitis told me. "He's in a nursing home here in Tarpon. He can't speak. I went to see him yesterday."

Fatolitis expected to receive an unhappy phone call soon. "I know his family will want me to be a pallbearer," he said. "But I don't know if I'll be able to bring myself to do it. It would be too sad."

For a man with his ailments, he looked surprisingly healthy to me. He had good skin despite all those years in the sun. He had lively brown eyes and a thicket of white hair on his head and eyebrows, and on his chest and his back. Macho lived.

He had come into this world on December 16, 1923, in Indiana, a fact he could only blame on his parents. During the Depression, they moved to Tarpon at the invitation of Uncle Petros Fatolitis, a sponge diver who promised employment.

Once Phil completed sixth grade, he was finished with formal schooling. "I become a sponger when I was twelve," he said. They'd go out on the *Demetra*, Uncle Petros's boat, for three weeks at a time. The boy helped with the lines, scraped sponges, hung them to dry, and dreamed of the day he might be allowed to dive.

He was not discouraged by his father's unfortunate accident. His father had developed the bends on his first and only dive. The decompression sickness damaged his brain, and he never walked again without dragging his leg. He died at thirty-five.

"Ready to dive?" Uncle Petros asked one day in the Gulf of Mexico.

The energetic boy was sixteen and immortal. On the rocky bottom, he located many fine sponges. Uncle Petros was proud. The crew was proud. They let him take home $1,200 of profit to give to his mother, a small fortune in 1939.

In the twenty-first century, the sponge was still important in Tarpon Springs. High school students, after all, called themselves "the Spongers," and tourists still purchased sponges in the gift shops along Dodecanese Boulevard. A couple of boats left the docks on the Anclote River every week or so.

But it wasn't the same. There were only about a half-dozen sponge boats; once there had been three hundred boats and about one thousand divers. "It is hard for me to visit the docks now," the old man said. "It's pitiful."

When he was a young man, a deep-sea diver was a hairy-chested hero, the most macho of men. "Tarpon was like the Old West. And we were like cowboys." After unloading sponges, the divers headed for the cafes to eat lamb and stuffed grape leaves and to drink and smoke and sing.

They talked, argued about women, fought with their fists, bled, spat out teeth, threatened murder, shook hands, said, "No hard feelings. See you tomorrow."

Soon he had his own boat, *Melba*, named after the first of many wives. How many wives? It was a sore subject. He counted his marriages on the fingers of more than one hand. Sponge divers seldom made the best husbands. They were away too often and too long. Ashore, they felt restless, dreamed of the sea.

A blight in the late 1930s killed sponges. Spongers left for the steel mills in the Midwest. Fatolitis dived deep, found enough sponges to get by because he was willing to go anywhere in the gulf, even the deep water. Not everyone could dive in deep water in those days, when the technology was relatively crude. They lacked stamina. Some divers landed on the bottom, harvested a bag or two, and surfaced right immediately to avoid the bends. In deep water, 120 feet or more, Fatolitis could stay down an astonishing twenty-five minutes if necessary without getting the bends. In shallow water, he could remain on the bottom for hours.

Hit the bottom, lean against the tide, lean so far forward your helmet almost scrapes bottom. Rake up the sponges, hopefully the valuable wool sponges, stuff them into a bag. Signal the boat. The crew hauls up the bag and sends another. Fill it again.

Mind what you're doing.

Pay attention to your air hose.

Shark!

Hammerheads swam close. Tiger sharks. Both man-eaters.

Phil Fatolitis wasn't afraid of tiger and hammerhead sharks. Oh, but the bull sharks. "Cotton-pickin' bull sharks. They were real aggressive."

Face them while retreating slowly. If they swim out of sight, tug the line five times, sponger talk for "Shark! Haul me up quick!"

Another blight struck in the 1940s. More spongers dropped out, tried other lines of work, or died, not so much from broken bodies but alcoholism.

Fatolitis rigged his boat to catch snapper and grouper when the sponges were in short supply. He worked construction, building useful houses that stand today. When the sponges returned, he returned to the bottom.

Technology changed. Nobody had to wear the heavy dive suits anymore. Instead divers wore lighter, less expensive equipment, including modern face masks modified with breathing hoses. The new equipment worked well, though some old-timers disdained the new. Once they had navigated by the stars and located prime bottom not with electronics but with rope and weights tossed overboard.

The oldest of Fatolitis's six children was fifty-nine in 2006. The youngest, a high school freshman, was fourteen. When I was there, Fatolitis suddenly called for Shelly, who was in her bedroom doing schoolwork. "Can you help me with the DVD player?" he hollered.

Flustered, she bustled into the living room and helped her dad start the DVD machine. He wanted to show me something.

The old man and I watched a documentary made in Tarpon Springs almost a half century ago. As it begins, a group of men are bidding, in Greek, for sponges at the auction house. The winner fills his truck with sponges. Then the action shifts to a boat heading down the river toward the gulf. Crewmen work on rigging, getting ready for life at sea. The handsome captain smiles into the camera with huge white teeth. He must have wowed the ladies.

The captain in the movie is Phil Fatolitis. He climbs into the dive suit and disappears over the side. The water is a murky green gray. He creeps along the bottom like a knuckle-dragging Neanderthal because of the current. So many sponges, and he probably felt he could harvest them all.

"It was very good work," Fatolitis said quietly when the movie was over.

Everybody on his boat knew how to work hard. Nobody got drunk at sea, at least when he was captain. Nobody went hungry. The cook was known for his fine beef stew and the way he leaned over the pot as the growing ash at the end of his cigarette defied gravity.

They went to sleep when the sun did, though sometimes a man wanted to talk, maybe about problems with his woman back on shore, and of course he always found a sympathetic ear.

"I miss the old days," Fatolitis said. "When I watch this movie, I remember them and I feel good."

It was Hemingway who said that all good stories have to end the same way.

The old man ran down the roster of the crew who were in his movie, six good men, dependable men, big-hearted men, who gave him their all.

Name by name.

"Dead. Dead. Dead, dead, dead."

Phil Fatolitis, with a faded tattoo on his forearm that says Melba, was the only one left.

October 9, 2006

15

ST. PETERSBURG

Folding the Map

Doris Yahn folded the map without trouble. That is, she folded it neatly, edges square, everything crisp and nice when she was done. Folding a map is an art. Lots of people can't do it. They try, but the map ends up a big fat mess that won't fit in the glove compartment. Doris Yahn had been folding maps for thirty-eight years. She was a trip planner for the American Automobile Association at its St. Petersburg office. She could fold a map and she could read one upside down. The day I watched her work in 2005 she was reading one upside down for a client who wanted to go to the Great Smoky Mountains in North Carolina.

As the client watched the map right side up, she efficiently drew a yellow line from St. Petersburg to Tampa, from Tampa to Atlanta, from Atlanta to Franklin, North Carolina. Then she assembled a special map booklet showing the route in more detail. "Have a good trip," she said.

"Thank you, Doris," the client answered.

Mrs. Yahn said she would be eighty-eight on her next birthday. Her white hair was as neat and proper as one of her maps, and she wore big glasses, dangly earrings, and a flowered blue dress. She spoke in a low, elegant voice she never raises even when she is taken aback by a request like the one she told me about. "Ma'am," said the preacher. "I want to bring the Lord to every prison in the United States."

Mrs. Yahn sighed that day and got out a bunch of maps. She began with the Florida map, drawing a yellow line from St. Petersburg to Tampa to Gainesville to Starke to Raiford. She also threw in a warning about the speed trap in Waldo. "You know, there are a lot of prisons in the U.S.," she warned the preacher. He knew.

She folded many maps that day.

One morning in 2005 a client wanted the fastest route to Chicago. Easy as pie. Another client wished to visit Paw Paw, Michigan. No problem. A client wanted help planning a six-month trip, from St. Petersburg to California, from California to British Columbia, from British Columbia to New Brunswick and back to St. Petersburg. That took a little more work, map reading, and folding.

Doris Yahn's workdays were always busy, but never busier than summer. In the summer, Americans enjoyed seeing their own country from behind the wheel. "It doesn't matter that gas is expensive," she said. "People want to travel. I've planned trips as far as Alaska."

Anchorage is 4,750 miles from St. Petersburg by road, Mrs. Yahn declared.

Clients who belong to AAA and need help plotting a course often end up talking to someone such as Mrs. Yahn. However, they seldom end up with a consultant quite as experienced. Mrs. Yahn unfolded her first AAA map in 1967, when cars still had vulgar tail fins and gas cost 33 cents a gallon.

During her tenure, interstates had been built and country roads had vanished. Motor vehicles shrunk from large to small, and grew from small to large again. During her career, safety belts and air bags came of age. Some luxury cars now included DVD players and Global Positioning Systems. GPS had failed to put her out of business.

In the year 2000, when she was eighty-three, she received her first computer lesson at the office. Now she drove her desktop PC like one of those NASCAR superstars. "We can plan a trip for someone on computer," she said.

But she remained an old-fashioned gal who preferred folding maps to maneuvering a mouse. "The problem with some of the maps we do on computer is too much detail," she whispered. "They start giving you directions from the moment you leave your driveway."

The day before she had handed a customer page after page of computer printout directions. She also handed him an old-fashioned book-let of maps, what AAA calls a TripTik. "Where's the wastebasket?" the customer said with a sneer. He was Mrs. Yahn's kind of guy. He discarded the computer map and kept the TripTik.

Woodrow Wilson was president in 1917, the year Doris was born in Akron, Ohio. A new Model T Ford cost $360, and there were more dirt roads in America then paved ones. But even then people needed direction. AAA was almost two decades old.

Growing up, Doris worked for her dad, a pharmacist. She graduated from high school and finished two years of college. In 1949, she married an engineer, and they had two children before his death eight years later from lung cancer. In St. Petersburg, she worked two years in a bank, a job she enjoyed until she learned that a new hire, a man, was making $10 a week more for doing an identical job.

"I asked why, and I was told he was married and had a wife to support," she said in that quiet voice. "I said 'What about me? I'm supporting two daughters by myself.' But it didn't matter to them."

She failed to get a raise, but two weeks later she started a new job with AAA. On her first day, a trainer spread a map in front of her upside down. The trainer asked, "Where is Marianna?" It took her a few minutes to find the little Panhandle town. In the twenty-first century it was nearly impossible to stump her on just about anything having to do with American geography. At home, she liked to watch *Jeopardy* and often beat contestants to the right answers about American cities.

Of course, she didn't consider herself a genius. Sometimes a client who arrived at her desk asked a question for which she was totally unprepared. "Can I drive from Los Angeles to Hawaii?" a client once asked.

"They haven't built the bridge yet," she answered.

Another customer wanted to travel the length of the Appalachian Trail. She explained that the trail began at Springer Mountain, Georgia, and meandered 2,160 miles to Mount Katahdin, Maine. "You do know it's a hiking trail, right?" she asked.

"Ma'am, you're wrong," the client answered. She marked the trail in yellow but did not argue.

Mrs. Yahn never remarried after her husband's death. Her daughter is now a schoolteacher, and her son is a baker. Her son lived with her. Sometimes she microwaved a meal, but she also enjoyed cooking when she had company. She roasted a good pork and had a reputation for preparing a fine meatloaf. She also enjoyed doing crossword puzzles and watching television programs about travel.

She shared with me her yen for traveling. Over the years she had traveled all over the United States. Her last great trip was to Yellowstone and Grand Teton national parks, though she saw them from the seat of a tour bus. The highlight of the adventure was a raft trip down the Snake River, where the guide allowed her to do the rowing. She was sixty-eight at the time.

She still drove herself to work every day in a 1998 Chevrolet Malibu. Before the Malibu she had owned a perfectly good car, a 1988 Oldsmobile that was demolished in an accident when a man in a hurry ran a red light on Central Avenue in St. Petersburg.

She never drove fast, and she advised her clients to observe speed limits. One time a young couple dropped by for assistance in planning a trip to Los Angeles. They were certain they could make the drive in a day. "Do you know it's 2,500 miles to Los Angeles?" she asked.

"We're going to take turns behind the wheel," the optimistic young man explained. Mrs. Yahn advised taking at least five days.

She also warned clients to avoid notorious speed traps. Every day she received bulletins about new speed traps and roads under construction. She consulted the bulletins before planning trips for her clients. Yet even an expert couldn't plan for everything.

One frugal client asked if she knew where he might rent a winter coat. Alas, that information had not been included in the morning's bulletin. "I am not criticizing our members because they are all very nice," she told me quietly. "But sometimes they don't think about what they are asking."

June 20, 2005

16

GIBSONTON

Making Biscuits

Everything was larger than life at Giant's Camp, an otherwise modest eatery on the Tamiami Trail near Tampa. There was the size 22 sneaker allegedly worn by the late Al Tomaini. And there were those biscuits, twice the size of hockey pucks but tasting more of the divine.

I went to the restaurant for the biscuits. Margaret Ingram, chief cook, had been performing biscuit wizardry for four decades. "They're made from scratch," the tiny white-haired woman declared as she marched around the hot kitchen in a cotton dress and gravy-stained apron. In Gibsonton, long a hamlet for the "who's who" of America's carnival sideshow royalty, Miss Margaret, as she was known, was a bona fide star.

Over the decades she had cooked for thousands of weary travelers and residents who could tell you about her fried chicken, her dumplings, her black-eyed peas. But her biscuits, flaky, moist, and perfect for dunking in a breakfast egg, were the draw for old-timers. "I'll eat anything she gives me," said eighty-year-old Willard Smith, a customer for a half century, as he perched at his favorite table by the window. "But I'm especially partial to her biscuits and gravy."

The dour carnival sideshow attraction known as the Lobster Boy, born with pincers instead of hands, was no stranger to Miss Margaret's cooking. Percilla the Monkey Girl and her husband, Emmitt the Alligator Man, also were regulars at the breakfast counter. The same went for Melvin Burkhardt, the Human Blockhead, who pounded nails up his nose without damaging his taste buds. Miss Margaret, seventy-six when I visited, never got the chance to cook for the Giant, but her imagination ran wild at the prospect. One platter of her biscuits never would have satisfied him.

"I hear he had a big appetite," Miss Margaret said during a lull in the kitchen. The Giant weighed 356 pounds without looking paunchy. The top of his skull scraped the sky at 8 feet 4½ inches. In 1940, he moved to Gibsonton, already a refuge for carnival folks, with his wife, who worked in the business, too. Born without legs, Jeanie was 2 feet 6. On the sideshow circuit she and Al billed themselves as "the world's strangest married couple."

In the old Florida before theme parks, their restaurant qualified as a tourist attraction to rival the greatest show if not on Earth at least in southern Hillsborough County. Customers who supped on fried mullet in tomato gravy did some major gawking for dessert. "I don't mind," the Giant liked to tell friends. "I'm peek-proof."

Al Tomaini was born in New Jersey in 1912 and suffered from a glandular problem that made him a giant. He met Jeanie at a fair in the Midwest, and they eloped to Niagara Falls and performed throughout the country. In 1940 they migrated to Gibsonton for reasons that included snook, redfish, and mullet.

Al liked fishing. He opened a business that catered to anglers on the Alafia River. "Bait, boat, and biscuits" could have been his slogan. Al had no idea what to call his place until his friend Frank Lentini, the famous Three-Legged Man, urged him to keep things simple. "Giant's Camp" was the sign Tomaini hung above his doorway.

The restaurant featured a tall ceiling to accommodate the proprietor, who often wore a huge cowboy hat and matching cowboy boots while riding herd at the cash register. Everything about him was enormous, even the monstrous ring decorating a finger. As customers paid for their meals, they often asked to try out the ring, so big it could have slid down a broomstick. Inevitably the most enamored patrons begged to purchase the ring.

"Oh, I could never part with this ring," the Giant always protested.

He usually allowed himself to be coaxed. As the customer bolted through the door, clutching the souvenir in triumph, the Giant calmly opened a box beneath the cash register. That's where he kept the stash of rings he sold daily to impressionable tourists.

Yes, he was a carny, but he counted himself a solid citizen, too. As the fire chief, he arrived at blazes in a custom-made vehicle renovated to allow for his tree-trunk legs. Sometimes his best friend, chief of police Casper Balsam, dropped by Giant's Camp to discuss business.

They never saw eye to eye on anything.

Casper was only 3 feet tall.

The Giant was only fifty when he died in 1962, which meant Miss Margaret never made his acquaintance. But sometimes she believed she knew him based on conversations with his friends and loved ones. Jeanie, his widow, was a frequent visitor to the restaurant until her death, at age eighty-three, in 1999. Photos of the Giant and Jeanie still covered the walls in 2006. One of his celebrated rings was mounted next to the front door. And about that humongous sneaker on the counter: Tom Thumb would have been proud to call it home.

Miss Margaret started working at Giant's in the early 1970s. She knew her way around a kitchen, having learned to cook from watching her mother-in-law, Ethel Ingram, in Alabama. Like many older rural women, Ethel took pride in the culinary arts. "She and her husband were sharecroppers," Miss Margaret told me. "What they grew is what they ate. If they couldn't eat it right then, they canned it. She made a good biscuit, too."

Miss Margaret baked her biscuits six mornings a week starting at 6 sharp. "I don't think I have a secret, except I do a lot of kneading," she said. Self-rising flour, shortening, milk, and salt were mixed together and shaped by hand on a buttered pan. Miss Margaret baked everything in a 350-degree gas oven for about ten minutes or however long it took. "To tell the truth, I never use recipes," she said. "Everything is in my head by now. I just taste things as I go along."

The thermometer next to the kitchen door said 92 degrees, but surely it must have been registering 10 degrees too cool. Miss Margaret didn't perspire; she was accustomed to hot kitchens. Finished with the biscuits, she began working on lunch. A turkey roasted in the oven, and soon potatoes, corn, and green beans were percolating in enormous pots.

In the dining room, waitresses hovered over customers like helicopters. A few words about the waitresses: Jeanie Tomaini, the Giant's wife, once joked that bad service and good food were the restaurant's trademark. During my visit, the service was prompt and occasionally polite. Although my hair long ago lost its dark sheen, I was addressed as "baby," "sweetie," or "darling."

But they were steel magnolias, those waitresses. Back in the twentieth century, a grumpy newspaper columnist had described a middle-aged waitress as looking worn around the edges. Harrumph! The newspaper from the wrong side of Tampa Bay was banned from the restaurant, then and forever. In the twenty-first century, feelings still seemed tender.

"It was rude for that writer lady to say that," Miss Margaret said, and nobody in the kitchen argued, not even the blushing pencil pusher for the Brand X Mullet Wrapper.

As I chatted with Miss Margaret in the doorway of the kitchen, a passing waitress, Margie, felt the need to gently stab my rear end with a fork.

"No," Margie announced to everyone within earshot. "He ain't done yet."

September 16, 2006

17

YBOR CITY

Coffee Talk with el Cafetero

Back in 2002 I seemed to read something different about coffee every day. On some days the story in the paper said drinking coffee was good for me. The next day the paper said coffee was going to burn a hole in my stomach. I drove over to Tampa to consult with the coffee maestro himself, Danilo Fernandez Sr. "Coffee is good for you," he told me gently. "In moderation."

Of course, moderation was a relative term if you grew up, as he had, in Ybor City, the Latin American community where coffee long had been part of the culture. As a young man, Danilo Fernandez had gulped at least a dozen cups daily. Now he was sixty-five and had reduced his consumption to a mere seven cups. I admired his discipline: He owned Naviera Coffee Mills, the last coffee factory in Ybor, and could have taken his coffee intravenously if he desired.

His grandfather had founded the factory in 1921 and named the business after the ship that transported him across the Atlantic from Spain. Naviera, which sprawled across half a block, supplied coffee to consumers, restaurants, and cafeterias throughout America. It also featured a walk-in coffee shop, El Molino, at 2012 E Seventh Ave., where Ybor City residents came for a fix of cafe cubana, the famous Cuban coffee, or cafe con leche, coffee with boiled milk.

Inside the factory, coffee beans sloshed round and round in huge vats. Roasting ovens glowed red, and machines spat and hissed. Out on the street, the heavenly fragrance of coffee wafted through the air. "If you grow up in Ybor, what you remember is all the wonderful smells," declared Fernandez, an intense, dark-eyed man with a thick white mustache. "When I was a boy, every block had a different smell. Okay? You understand? You'd smell the cod coming out the door at the fish markets. You'd smell the bread from the bakeries. And of course, the coffee was everywhere."

In the twenty-first century, modern Ybor was known more for its nightclubs, taverns, and tattoo parlors. Even the smell of roasting coffee was under the control of city bureaucrats eager to enforce air-pollution regulations. Although Fernandez had installed expensive odor-stifling machinery, there was no mistaking that serious coffee making was going on behind the sun-baked walls.

I know historians who say cigars put Ybor on the map. They wouldn't be wrong. But they wouldn't be telling the whole story either. "Coffee was just as important," Danilo Fernandez Sr. said as we sat in his office sipping coffee. Strong coffee had fueled the making of cigars.

Vicente Martinez Ybor, Fernandez explained, had moved his cigar factory from Key West to Tampa in 1886. Within decades thousands of workers in one hundred factories were making cigars by hand. Each factory boasted its own el cafetero: the coffee man. For a small fee, collected at week's end, el cafetero supplied each worker with what turned out to be an endless cup of bracing coffee. El cafetero would wheel his cart several times daily to the coffee factory of choice for a fresh batch.

Danilo Fernandez's grandfather, Carlos Menendez, got his start as el cafetero, delivering by bicycle. When he opened his factory, he was a small fish in a bigger pond; a dozen factories were already serving the coffee needs of the community. At the factories, infinite coffee was a treasured perk. No sane cigar factory owner would have considered ending the privilege; to do so would have risked wailing, the gnashing of teeth, or an expensive labor strike.

"Can you imagine workers being allowed to drink coffee all day on a Ford assembly line?" University of South Florida history professor Gary Mormino, author of *The Immigrant World of Ybor City*, once asked me. Ybor life revolved around a java fix.

Streetcar conductors turned coffee drinking into a science. Leaping off his car, a conductor typically rushed into the closest shop, ordered coffee, and poured it immediately into a saucer to cool it. Then he could bolt it down without burning his tongue and make it back to the car in time to collect new fares.

Restaurant waiters were required to read minds and remember faces. Who wanted their coffee solo, which meant black? Was it Fernando? Did Jorges like his coffee cortadito, a small cup of coffee with a drop or two of milk?

"The variants depended on the personal whim and pathology of the drinker," wrote Ferdie Pacheco in his book *Ybor City Chronicles.* "Strong men liked their coffee very dark (oscuro); politicians, lawyers, and burglars liked it half and half (mitad y mitad) and men with the weight of the world on their shoulders, with weak or failing digestive systems, liked it mostly milk with just a drop of coffee (clarito)."

Pacheco, who grew up in Ybor, later became a physician, Muhammad Ali's ringside doctor, and a well-known painter of his boyhood scenes. But he never forgot his days of waiting tables at the Columbia. "Size of cup was never stated but indicated by finger signals undecipherable to anyone but the waiters of the Columbia Café," he wrote.

In old Ybor, coffee was a serious business. Perhaps a man might let you make a joke about his wife, or wink at his daughter, but you took your life into your hands if you insulted his coffee.

On January 9, 1903, Ramon Garcia strolled into Rafael Mena's restaurant for a cup. Unhappy with the quality of the brew, Garcia argued with the proprietor. Bristling, Mena retired to the rear of the restaurant and returned as Garcia was paying his bill. "Mena drew a knife and slashed Garcia on the side of his head and face," reported the *Tampa Tribune.* "An ugly wound was inflicted, extending from the top of his head to a point near the chin."

The rude coffee drinker survived the encounter. There is no record of whether he took his future patronage to another restaurant.

Danilo Fernandez Sr. started drinking coffee when he literally was a babe in arms. But as a young man he resisted the business of his grandfather and his father. He sold shoes, he plucked chickens, he worked at a department store. Anything but coffee! At the University of Tampa, he studied business. One day he was needed to pinch-hit for an ill laborer at the coffee factory. A half century later he was still there.

Other coffee factories had come and gone, but his persevered. He credited hard work more than luck. He traveled across the country to sell his coffee and himself; his company imported coffee beans from all over the world, roasted and ground them. It packaged them and shipped them out the back door on the same day. Danilo Fernandez sold a blend of light roast, American coffee, and five blends of a darker roast often used in the famous Cuban coffee. "Cuban coffee is not a special kind of coffee, really," he told me. "It is a way of roasting coffee beans."

Many old-time Ybor residents, he explained, were poor—a pound of coffee had to go a long way. Beans were roasted longer than normal, almost to a burning point, to make them taste stronger. A thirsty cigarmaker could make an eye-opening cup with less coffee. He'd boil the water in a saucepan, add coffee, boil it for a few more minutes, and finally pour the mix through a cone-shaped strainer lined with cotton flannel.

In the twenty-first century, espresso machines did the same work. Danilo Fernandez Sr. didn't like espresso machines. He built his strainers out of wood and sold them at the factory's gift shop. Nobody but old-timers knew what they were. "Talking to the old people is part of the pleasure of the business for me," he said.

When he retired, he told me, his son Dan was going to take over. But not for a while. Three times a week Danilo Fernandez reported to the factory, did paperwork in his office, and drank coffee. Often he visited the factory gift shop to talk to customers about the old days.

He talked about the glorious history of Ybor, about all the factories and the shops and the sound of strumming guitars played by men sitting on their front porches. He remembered the wonderful smell of ripe guavas on backyard trees and the aroma of roasting pork wafting out of open windows.

Things changed in Ybor after World War II. "A lot of people who had seen the world came back and didn't want to make cigars like their fathers and grandfathers," Fernandez said. "They got educations, they did other work, they left Ybor."

The old Ybor began disappearing. Later the interstate cut Ybor in half, blocking neighbor from neighbor. Businesses failed; the crime rate rose. But now Fernandez liked to think Ybor was coming back, maybe not coming back the way old-timers wanted, but coming back, at least at night, when young people roamed the streets with alcoholic beverages in hand. Many had never visited Ybor during daylight; during the day, Ybor still belonged to the coffee-drinking old people.

"You know, the Ybor I knew was a thriving place," Fernandez told me. "Everybody knew everybody. If you were a kid, you didn't mess around. Okay? Somebody would say, 'I'm going to tell your father' and that was the end of bad behavior. And people, they really knew how to work. You know? Okay? When I was young, I never asked about money. I never asked for a raise! I might tell my boss, 'Sir, I just had another job offer. If I take it, here's how much I'm going to make.' If the boss valued you, he'd give you the raise. If not, you'd take the new job for more money.

"Now the young people, all they care about is how much money they are going to make. That's their first question. How much money? And they don't even know how to work. They think there's a Santa Claus. They think they're entitled to anything they want without sacrifice."

Danilo Fernandez Sr. poured himself a calming cup of strong black coffee. I asked him about the missing tip of a finger on his left hand. "Oh. It got caught in a machine years ago. Machine tore it off. They found the finger, but I didn't have time for surgery to put it back into place. I said, 'Just sew me up. I have to go to work tomorrow.' Okay? You know what I'm talking about? That was how it was in the old days."

February 18, 2002

18

FORT GREEN

Citrus Ladders

Robert Abbott's cell phone never stopped ringing the day I spent with him. "Go ahead," was how he greeted callers. The citrus business was like that in the summer of 2004, with so much fruit on the ground after still another hurricane.

Except for the cell phone, the forty-two-year-old Abbott, dressed in jeans, T-shirt, and a camouflage ball cap, was an old-fashioned man. In fact, he was something of a dinosaur. When he wasn't growing oranges and tangerines, he was building the ladders that a decreasing number of pickers throughout Florida were using to harvest citrus. Once, every orange in the state was harvested by a man atop a wooden ladder. Now the old-timey ladders were going the way of the manual typewriter.

"Aluminum," Abbott drawled in my direction. "More and more growers seem to want aluminum ladders." A few rich growers were even trying to eliminate aluminum ladders, human pickers, and insurance liability by using expensive machines that shook citrus from trees.

But folks with the last name of Abbott in central Florida's Hardee County, outside of Bradenton, didn't change their ways willy-nilly. His family had been building the rough-hewn cypress-and-oak citrus ladders for almost a century. As long as there was a demand, even a small one, he planned to keep on doing so.

His 5,000-square-foot open-air shed on State Road 62 smelled of cypress sawdust and sweat. Every once in a while he stopped talking as an electric saw roared to life nearby. A helper wielded a nail gun like an Uzi. A guy driving a front loader stacked ladders into neat piles.

Abbott was still building eighty ladders a day and nearly five thousand a year—about 20 miles worth of ladders if you lined them up. They ranged in size from 16 to 24 feet, though years ago he built a few 38-footers. They were propped up against ancient skyscraping trees that for the most part had been displaced by development or killed in freezes.

"A lot of ladders have gone through these hands," Abbott ruminated. "You know what I'm saying?"

He told me he was building fewer every year. Business had been down 35 percent since 2000 for reasons that included modernity and the desire of many growers to cut costs. Wooden ladder builders once were common throughout Florida's citrus belt, but now Abbott could name only one other. Abbott supplied 80 percent of the tiny market.

A citrus ladder was nothing like what a suburbanite might find at Home Depot. A wooden citrus ladder was extraordinarily wide at the bottom and very narrow at the top. The wide base provided stability in a grove's soft sand while the narrow top, leaned against the foliage, gave a picker room to get at the fruit. To the inexperienced eye, rungs seemed unnaturally far apart. But 17.5 inches, generations of Abbotts had discovered, was just right, allowing an athletic picker to climb quickly with an empty canvas bag and descend quickly when the bag was full. Pickers, after all, typically were paid by the pound.

An aluminum ladder was light, lasted forever, but usually cost $200 or more. A wooden citrus ladder was heavier, cruder, and cheaper. Abbott charged about $70 for his. They lasted a season or three in the grove, as Florida's climate and rough handling take their toll. Finished picking citrus from the tallest trees, workers sometimes sawed a ladder in half before attacking shorter trees. Occasionally a wooden ladder was added to a campfire on a winter night.

"It's a tough business," Abbott liked to tell folks.

He was born in Fort Green, a speck on the road just west of Wauchula, like his daddy, Jerald, and his grandfather, Edgar, before him. They were orange men, too. His kin had always grown them, but got into the ladder business about the time America went to war against Germany the first time.

Nobody got rich building ladders, though nobody went hungry either. Abbotts and their kin ate what they grew and what they shot.

Abbott still liked to venture into the woods with his gun and look for deer.

Hardee was, and continued to be, among the state's poorest counties. In the twenty-first century, almost 30 percent of children lived in poverty. Agriculture and phosphate mining were Hardee's most important industries, though a new prison just down the road offered other employment opportunities.

The 2004 hurricanes that traveled through Hardee made the poverty even worse. Trailers and rickety homes throughout the county were still in disrepair on the day I visited. Blue tarps covered tortured roofs.

"Hurricane Charley was the worst of them," Abbott said in an orange-blossom drawl. The storm was pointed at Tampa Bay when an unexpected turn at Punta Gorda brought it north along U.S. 17 toward him and his groves and his ladder shed. "Big dog," he remembered telling a friend before the telephone went dead, "this is one bad son of a gun."

His house survived, but thousands of Hamlin and Valencia oranges and Murcott tangerines ended up on the ground within the 300 acres of the family groves. Many of his finest trees—he was proud of his well-tended groves—were snapped in half or uprooted. "Yet I was one of the lucky ones."

Some neighbors lost 35 percent of their crop. Unlike him, they had no other work to fall back on. At least he had ladders. "In this business, with the profit margin so low, you need to diversify," he told me. "Otherwise something bad happens and you're gone. I really don't know what's going to happen to the citrus business in Florida."

Abbott worked in his shed, beneath the oak trees, starting at daybreak. If he wasn't in the shed, he was out in the swamps with a chain saw felling trees or driving a truck full of logs to a mill in Dade City or driving the truck, now full of lumber, back to the shed.

In the shed, lumber was shaved by a primitive, homemade machine his kin built sixty years ago. Another old machine cut and sawed. Years ago, rungs were whittled by hand. Now they were whittled by another ancient machine.

Workers chatted in Spanish and listened to *conjunto* and *norteno* music on portable radios. A citrus truck, roaring down the highway toward the juice plant in Bradenton, was the kind of music Abbott enjoyed. He sold most of his crop to the juice industry.

Fans paddled the still air. Boots kicked through sawdust and dirt. Phone rang. A grower in Winter Haven needed ladders. Phone rang. Wrong number. Abbott hated wrong numbers. They got his hopes up for nothing. He folded up his cell phone. "We're trying to be modern," he said. "But we're die-hard citrus people. And everything is changing."

At one time in Florida, citrus was almost always a family business passed down through generations. Abbott and his brothers hoped their children would keep up the tradition, but they were not optimistic. In the twenty-first century, juice was traded on the stock market and growers carried laptop computers in their pickups to keep up. "Used to be a grower knew every inch of his property," Abbott said. "Now that would be impossible for a lot of growers. There are some 50,000-acre groves in Florida now! Cadillac farming, I call it."

Abbott was not a Cadillac farmer. He was a Chevy pickup kind of orange man. His ladders, stubbornly wooden, belonged to the Model T generation.

November 29, 2004

19

LAKE WALES

Playing the Carillon

One time a convention of cantankerous crows collected on the bell tower. "Caw. Caw. Caw," they cried. Then, growing bolder—acting as if they owned the place—they set about making the kind of racket that gives crows a bad name.

"CAW! CAW! CAW!" It was 3 o'clock in the afternoon. If everything was to go according to schedule at Historic Bok Sanctuary in central Florida, William De Turk couldn't throw a hissy fit about bellicose birds. He was going to have to play the carillon anyway. Sitting at a big oak bench, hundreds of feet above the gardens but only a few feet below the crows, he struck the carillon keys with fists and feet. The corresponding bells began tolling. Mozart's "Ronda Alla Turca," performed on the carillon, shamed even crows into silence.

Everybody and everything got quiet when De Turk sat at the carillon. Anyway, that is how it was supposed to work. He was only the third carillonneur at the old tourist attraction since 1929. His predecessors, Anton Brees and Milford Myhre, had known how to quiet the crows, too.

"Quiet is requested during the recitals." So said the program handed to me on the day I arrived to meet the great De Turk. Visitors weren't supposed to talk during his performances. They were encouraged to turn off their cell phones. There was no worldly reason to eat crunchy potato chips in the garden. "We love silence," the carillonneur told me.

When the first note was tolled on the carillon, the Great Depression was under way and the former president, Calvin Coolidge, was sitting quietly in the audience. The bells—63 tons of bronze—remain in tune

At Historic Bok Sanctuary, William De Turk plays the carillon.
Photo by Jeff Klinkenberg.

to this day. The smallest, lighter than a bowling ball, weighs 13 pounds.
The heaviest is 12 tons.

When De Turk talked about heavy metal, he didn't mean the old
rock and roll band Black Sabbath. He knew the work of the Beatles,
but was more comfortable with classical music. Regular visitors might
have been startled to hear "O Danny Boy" on St. Patrick's Day, though
he called it "Londonderry Air," the formal title. I found him a somewhat
a formal man. He allowed a few close friends the informality of calling
him "Bill," but even people who knew him well addressed him as "Mr.

De Turk." Of course, courtesy titles such as "Mr." and "Mrs." seemed to go with the dignified territory of the sanctuary. Gardeners didn't wear bowlers and three-piece suits, but they ought to have.

Historic Bok Sanctuary was Florida's unofficial garden of serenity. There was no place in the state like it. A lush 250 acres of oaks and magnolias, camellias and azaleas, consecrated the top of 298-foot-high Iron Mountain. Benches, shelters, and shady spots provided vistas from which to admire not only the flora but the fauna—the butterflies, the birds, the squirrels, the fairies.

Actually, nobody had ever reported a fairy, but if they existed, I would have expected to find them here. Edward Bok, an American magazine editor, Pulitzer Prize–winning author, and wealthy philanthropist, began visiting Florida early in the twentieth century. In 1925, he hired Frederick Olmsted Jr., a landscape architect whose father had designed New York's Central Park, to create the garden. Bok hired a famous architect, Milton Medary, to build a tower to house a carillon. Bok was born in the Netherlands, the carillon capital of the planet, and thought Florida needed one. The tower is probably Florida's most beautiful, constructed with steel, red brick, Georgia marble, and Florida coquina. Bok hired Lee Lawrie to sculpt the statues of herons at the top and Samuel Yellin to design the wrought-iron gates and the heavy brass door decorated by a depiction of *The Creation*.

In England, John Taylor Bellfounders Ltd. forged the bells and built a traditional carillon. Carillons go back to the time of Shakespeare; about four hundred grace towers and cathedrals in Europe today. In North America, the Guild of Carillonneurs has a membership of five hundred. Unfortunately, there are only 190 available instruments, including four in Florida, so not everyone gets time at the keyboard.

De Turk knew the location of every carillon in the world. He had maps throughout his office, and pins in the maps that showed the cities that have carillons. He had played many of them. He beamed when fellow carillonneurs telephoned and asked about "Bok Heaven." In carillon circles, Mr. De Turk was widely considered the luckiest musician alive.

The ideal carillonneur would be a man about as tall and as strong as the basketball player Shaq O'Neal. The highest note on the Bok Tower keyboard, an F, is more than 7 feet away from the wooden slat that plays the lowest note, an E flat. It helps to have a wide wingspan. De Turk, who was sixty and delicately built, stood about 5 feet 7 inches tall. For him, playing the carillon was an athletic endeavor, something like playing goalie in hockey. To reach the keys, he scooted across the bench, hands and feet flashing. At the end of a performance, he could be drenched in perspiration.

He had worked at his music since piano lessons in first grade. "Unlike other children, I never had to be told to practice," he told me. "More frequently I was told to stop practicing." A music major, he graduated with honors from Ohio's Heidelberg College and got a master's studying organ at the University of Michigan. There was a carillon on campus; he took a lesson and was smitten. After a year of study at Historic Bok Sanctuary, he spent the next seventeen as carillonneur at Grosse Pointe Memorial Church in Michigan.

He became Myhre's understudy at the sanctuary in 1993; when Myhre retired in 2004, after thirty-seven years as the main man, De Turk became the featured carillonneur. De Turk had an assistant, Lee Cobb, who learned to play carillon at the University of Florida. They spelled each other at the keyboard and then tried to rest. It took power to depress the low notes on the carillon. "In Europe, some carillonneurs brutalize their instruments," De Turk said, banging the keys to demonstrate. "But we don't do that here."

Boompatta boompatta! Boompatta boompatta!

In the city, there seemed to be no escape from those bazooka bass speakers hidden in so many automobile trunks. Houses trembled. The ground quaked.

BOOMPATTA! BOOMPATTA!

At Historic Bok Sanctuary, no one had ever heard the Ramones yelping about their lack of cerebellums in "Cretin Hop." Nobody would ever nod along as R. Kelly rapped—BOOMPATTA! BOOMPATTA!—about fornicating in the kitchen next to the buttered rolls.

It was time to shush. De Turk had taken his seat at the carillon. Remember how Liberace used to roll his knuckles across the length of the keyboard so dramatically? De Turk did that on the sixty heavy wooden keys of the carillon without breaking any bones. "Arpeggiation," he explained. He usually didn't warm up, but he wanted me to see the possibilities.

With the sides of his hands or fists, he struck the keys. Attached to the keys were wires that disappeared through the ceiling and yanked the clappers in the bells. Bach's "Jesu, Joy of Man's Desiring" got a good workout, and there were no crows to ruin things.

"I crave silence," De Turk said. "There is not enough silence in the world. Everything is too frenetic. Mr. Bok was very wise to design a place like this. You know what my idea of a good time is? Sitting on my sofa with a glass of French wine in total silence." De Turk didn't own a cell phone. He hadn't bought an iPod. At home he had a grand piano and two polite golden retrievers, Cy and Sasha, who barked only if provoked.

When he needed to practice, he snuck back into the sanctuary after closing and played the carillon at night. If he needed to work something out during the day between performances, he played a practice carillon next to his office. The practice carillon was a duplicate of the performance carillon except for the bells. The bells in the practice instrument were small. It took little strength to make them ring.

Sometimes a visitor to the sanctuary requested a song. At least I did. De Turk is particular about playing only carillon-friendly music, so I was sure he would refuse my request. But I must have caught him on a good day. It was spring, after all; the orange blossoms perfumed the air around us.

"Yes, yes, I can do that," he said. He leaned across the keyboard of his practice instrument and played. A moment later the bells were tinkling. For the record, even "Chopsticks" sounded breathtaking on the carillon.

April 13, 2006

20

TAMPA

Pop Overton

When I asked for Hugh Overton at Cruise Terminal Two at the Port of Tampa I received only blank stares. But when I asked "anybody seen Pop?" I was speaking the native language.

"Why didn't you ask for Pop in the first place?" asked a luggage handler. Even the laughing gulls on the pilings squawked in derision.

No cruise ship departed or arrived without having to deal with Pop. When a ship docked, he was waiting. When it departed, he solemnly waved good-bye. He was the foreman of a crew that unloaded and loaded baggage and goods from every cruise ship at Terminal Two. To say he was an institution was to say a mullet was a fish that jumps. You got no argument.

He was sixty-seven and one of the oldest longshoremen, or stevedores, at the port. Actually, he believed he was the oldest and most experienced. He was nearing the anniversary of his fiftieth year on the waterfront.

"It's the only job I have ever had," he told me. "The port has been good to me."

He had performed just about every blood, sweat, and tears job there was. He had caught heavy lines thrown from ships and made them secure. Watching for the occasional tarantula, he had unloaded bananas. His back muscles protested, but he still had to tote millions of pounds of cement bags. He suffered from *mal de mer*, but often had to work on ships offshore, moving cargo when not wretching. "This is work that separates men from the boys," he harrumphed.

There was probably little doubt he was going to work as a longshore-man. In 1955, when he was seventeen, he traded high school for the waterfront. His daddy, Theo Overton, had done the same in 1933. Theo was among the first African-American men to work his way up to dock supervisor.

"I looked exactly like him. That's how I got called Pop. He worked me hard, my daddy did. I was kind of mad at him for giving me all the hard jobs," Pop said now. "But it was a good thing. If you are going to ever lead men, you have to know what hard work is."

At every dock in the United States, at every busy waterfront in Flor-ida—in Jacksonville, Melbourne, Port Everglades, Miami, Tampa—there were people such as Pop, longshoremen who handled lines, oper-ated forklifts, worked the cranes. Tampa's 250 longshoremen also drove new PT Cruiser motor vehicles, built in Mexico, off ships and onto the docks. They unloaded melons. They handled cruise-ship luggage.

Cruise ships such as the *Sensation*, which was part of the Carnival fleet and stretched 860 feet, was in port on the day I interviewed Pop. At 4:30 a.m., when Pop arrived at work, he looked at a sheet of paper and found out that the *Sensation* would dock in ninety minutes with 2,634 passengers. Now he did some quick math. Each passenger most likely would carry a bag or two. The eccentric ones might even carry three or four filled with coconuts or lava rock or, who knows, their bowling ball collections.

The ship would arrive at 6 a.m. The job would be to haul luggage off as quickly and as smoothly as possible and see passengers to their cars. Next, Pop's crew—thirty-six men that morning—would restock the ship with supplies. Finally, they would load a new crop of passengers and their baggage.

"We know what work is around here," Pop said proudly. "Oh, sweet Jesus, yes."

He had been born in Ybor City during the Depression. He remem-bered Ybor as a place that treated folks with black skin decently. Every-body was poor, but he remembered having fun, swimming in the creek, playing ball, talking to girls. But there were places that black people avoided.

"It was the South, and you had to be careful about staying away from where you weren't wanted," he said without a trace of complaint. He remembered those "White Only" water fountains and bus drivers who gave him the eye if he sat anywhere but on a rear seat.

It was different on the waterfront, on the docks, at the port. Black men found work. It was manual labor, but it was good, honest toil. "What I remember is working in the hold of those ships. Nothing was air-conditioned then. Oh, Lord Jesus, it was hot down there! No women worked there, so we men would strip down to our shorts. We'd be stowing canned goods. There'd be pallets of grapefruit. The thing we men dreaded most was ships coming in with cement.

"You didn't celebrate when the cement ships came in. A bag of cement weighed 94 pounds. We had a fourteen-man crew. In a day, each of us would move about five hundred bags. Sometimes it took a whole week to finish. Those bags, you'd hold 'em against your stomach when you lifted. By the end of the week you'd be missing skin and be all bruised up.

"Now we have a rule. If something weighs more than 50 pounds these days, two men have to lift it. Back then, it wasn't nothing for a man to lift a 94-pound bag by himself. People got hurt—people lost their arms and their hands and even their lives doing this work—but you didn't hear as much complaining as now. Now there is always Workman's Comp cases coming. More people are hurt doing less work. Different breed of men back in the day."

After a long day of unloading cement ships or watching for spiders and snakes hidden in the banana stalks, longshoremen slept well. They were always hungry. Dripping sweat, they'd head for the Gator Bar and order pork-chop sandwiches and chili and french fries and pay with a dollar bill and get change back.

Pop was still a formidably large man. He reminded me of a photograph of the folksinger Huddie Ledbetter, better known as Leadbelly, the guy who sang "Goodnight, Irene" and "Midnight Special." Like Leadbelly, Pop looked almost as wide as tall. I wondered if I could throw a sack of cement at his belly but didn't have the nerve. He told me he weighed 226 pounds, down from 240. He looked rock solid.

He lived alone. Used to be he and his wife, Jacquelyn, lived in a fine house on Rivergrove Drive in Tampa. She was principal at Dunbar Elementary and known for her warmth. She and Pop were married sixteen years and had three children. She was diagnosed with breast cancer in 1987.

"She was only fifty-one. I was working the *Regency C*, a passenger ship, when I got the call to come home. When I got home, I saw the fire truck and an ambulance. I went inside just in time to see her being zipped up in the body bag. She was only fifty-one. I can still see it like it just happened."

He couldn't bear to stay in their old house. So he moved to a little apartment in St. Petersburg. He told me enjoyed watching movies, especially movies that starred Steven Seagal, who usually portrayed a man's kind of man. Pop's favorite movie was *Under Siege*, in which Seagal played a navy cook who breaks up a terrorist plot to hijack a ship and its nuclear weapons. The sequel, *Under Siege 2*, was not as good, probably because the action took place on a train.

When he wasn't watching movies, he liked playing dominoes. He drove over to Nebraska and Seventh Avenue in Tampa and played with other older black men. The other men drank coffee and smoked cigars but not Pop. Pop told me he thought he was the only man ever born in Ybor City who never smoked cigars or drank coffee.

He said his health was good. He kept his blood pressure in check with medicine, diet, and exercise. He walked 3 miles a day even if it was raining. Last time he had checked his blood pressure, it was 130 over 80. He hoped he had good years ahead of him.

As a supervisor, he no longer had to work with his back and with his hands. Still, every once in a while, he was curious enough about his strength to swing some luggage on the waterfront. "Well, I'm not as strong as I used to be," he said sheepishly. "Used to be I was quite a man."

He told me he had been thinking about retiring as soon as he turned sixty-eight. But he wasn't sure; a man had to be cautious about retirement. There were good retirements and bad ones. He remembered when his hard-working daddy had retired. He fished and hunted whenever he could. Then he got lazy.

"He got himself this little bell. He'd sit outside and ring the bell and my mother would come running and wait on him hand and foot. She'd bring him iced tea or a sandwich, whatever he wanted. I said, 'Mama, you don't have to do all that. Daddy can wait on himself.' But she loved him and she did wait on him and, you know, he got to where he couldn't walk by himself. He passed in 1994 when he was eighty-five.

"I think a man has to stay busy. Even if he's retired, a man's got to work. My daddy was fine until he stopped working."

August 14, 2004

21

OKEECHOBEE

Hog Catchers

Greg Whidden was a rubbernecking driver whose head spent as much time outside the truck as inside the truck on the day we traveled together in 2006. He poked his head out the truck window whenever he was trying to catch wild hogs. "Whooooop!" he shrieked, watching his dogs. "Whoooop! Whoooop!" Trotting next to the truck in the predawn fog, the dogs bolted into the woods.

"Thooo-ugg!" Whidden yelled, sounding like Louis Armstrong with a sore throat. Perhaps somebody else would have gone with the traditional "Sooey" while calling a pig. For whatever reason, Whidden had been hollering "Thooo-ugg!" at pigs for the three decades he had been catching them by hand.

He was forty-four that year, all sinew and brown skin with the Mount Rushmore of Adam's apples. He was 6 feet 2 or so but weighed about 160 pounds in his dungarees, work shirt, ball cap, cowboy boots, and three-day beard. His jaws munched reflexively on a huge plug of Red Man. "Thooo-ugg!" he grunted again, spitting a juice projectile at an unfortunate oak.

"I'm telling my dogs to get me a hog," he yelled over the hellish squeal of his truck's frazzled shock absorbers. As the day broke at Kissimmee Prairie State Preserve, halfway between the central Florida cities of Okeechobee and Sebring, Whidden looked happy. At 54,000 acres, the preserve was a showcase of delicate wire grass, banana-colored wildflowers, gator-infested sloughs, and mysterious hammocks that served as a veritable box of animal crackers for endangered species. And it was crawling with hogs.

Hogs were anything but endangered. In Florida, they were something like the computer virus of the mammal world, completely destructive, known for a voracious appetite for fragile native plants, birds, snakes, and small animals. A couple of hungry hogs, rooting for vittles during the wee hours, could turn a lush field into a moonscape by sunrise. The state hired folks such as Whidden to get rid of them.

"Hear my dogs?" he yelled, steering his truck between craters dug by hogs with tusks like Turkish scimitars. He had trained his dogs never to bark unless they were hot on the trail of a hog. They were howling now.

"They're back in the hammock!" he said, gesturing out the window.

The truncated ring finger on the pointing hand appeared to have been gnawed by a wild animal.

"Hogs don't surrender easy," he said by way of explanation. "They're kind of like O.J. They'll do anything to stay out of the pen."

The brakes on Whidden's grape jam–colored Dodge Ram 1500 V8 Magnum four-wheel-drive pickup worked perfectly well. He simply didn't depend on them. When his dogs set off howling, Whidden leapt from the rolling truck, bounded to the trailer behind it, and released his quarter horse, Trigger. Moments later, astride Trigger, he vanished into the woods like a ghost. Whidden had earned his nickname, Spook.

Born and reared in the cattle country near Lake Okeechobee, he learned to hunt and fish and ride horses at an early age. He had steady work catching hogs because Hernando de Soto brought them to Florida in 1539. In the twenty-first century, hogs were found in thirty-one states. Hunters shot about 100,000 hogs a year in Florida. Hog removal specialists eliminated an additional 3,300 wild hogs from state property. The hogs gained ground anyway.

Spook caught hogs the hard way: by hand. He had nothing against guns but found it more satisfying to grab one while it was otherwise engaged by his dogs. Even so, the outcome was in doubt, since the hog often turned out to be a good deal larger than Spook, boasted bigger teeth, and feared for its life.

Spook sold his hogs at livestock markets. He received $30 to $50 for female hogs; sows were the easiest to catch and the best for eating. Boars were craftier, grew larger, and were harder to catch. Their meat verged on unpalatable. Spook sold them for $150 and up to hunting clubs that agreed never to release the boars into the wild.

Wild hogs don't look cuddly like Porky Pig. They usually are covered by brown or black bristles, avoid contact with people, and become dangerous when cornered.

Spook owned what had to be the marines of dogdom. They were mutts, they were curs, they were Heinz 57–variety canines. Many people who watched them in action wished their children could be as disciplined.

Spook began raising dogs for the purpose of catching swine in 1985. His father-in-law, Mabry Murphy, who often accompanied Spook on the expeditions, had raised hog-catching dogs for nearly a half century. "A good hog dog has to have heart," Mabry told me. A moment later, Spook came on the radio to say the boar hog he really wanted was still on the loose.

"A good dog has endurance," Mabry went on. "It has courage. Any dog will chase a hog, but the trick is cornering the hog, and then knowing when to pull away. You don't want a dog that's going to run off on you. You're looking for a businesslike dog that knows what he's there for."

Mabry and his son-in-law occasionally sold a dog for as much as $1,500. On workdays, their dogs, which weighed anywhere from 40 to 80 pounds, received two gallons of the best food they could eat. They had monthly appointments with the vet.

"We care about our dogs, but we don't treat them like pets," Mabry said. On those rare occasions when a dog delayed jumping into the truck bed on command, Mabry reflexively grabbed it by scruff of the neck and pitched it into the vehicle. Time was money.

Mabry's father had been a hog man too. So were his granddaddy and great-granddaddy. His nineteenth-century kin drove hogs, by horseback, from Lake Okeechobee to the shipping port in Tampa. Outside the city limits, Mabry's relatives poured molasses on the sand; when the hogs consumed the molasses, they also swallowed sand that made them heavier on the scales at the market.

A 500-pound wild hog was an enormous, formidable animal. Spook and Mabry dismissed stories they heard from braggart hunters or read in *Boar Hunter* magazine about half-ton hogs as beefy as VW Beetles.

Spook once had nabbed a 473-pounder. "I got him off a dairy," he said. "He was domestic, so he don't count." His largest wild hog was 416 pounds. "A wild hog don't sit around waiting to be fed. A wild hog, he's always on the move, always looking for something to eat. That keeps the weight off him."

A wild hog's favorite food was probably the acorn. Hogs also devoured palmetto berries. They consumed newborn deer. They ate reptiles, including protected indigos, and even rattlesnakes. They considered frogs and toads a delicacy. At Cape Canaveral National Seashore, they ate endangered sea turtle eggs and even turtle hatchlings. At Kissimmee Prairie, they ate quail. Biologists wondered if hogs were devouring the eggs and chicks of the ground-dwelling Florida grasshopper sparrow, another endangered species.

"Whenever Spook and Mabry catch a hog is a happy day for me," Charles Brown, the preserve manager, told me. In 2005, Spook and Mabry had harvested 249 hogs at the preserve. They captured 136 in 2004. Their banner year was 2001, when 463 hogs were removed from the fragile environment. They weren't running out of hogs to catch and they thought they never would.

Shooting on sight is probably the most efficient way to eliminate a hog. That may be possible on a private ranch, but it seldom happens in state or national parks. Gunfire, squealing hogs, and blood on the ground would disturb visitors with city sensibilities. In parks near urban areas, hogs are quietly trapped in politically correct baited cages. The method is somewhat effective but expensive and time-consuming because somebody has to check every trap in the park every day. However it is harvested, the story ends the same way for the hog, in a sausage, roast, or ham.

In south Florida, Spook Whidden's talents were in high demand. He caught hogs not only at state parks but on Audubon sanctuaries and at dozens of private ranches. Hired by Monroe County, he caught 69 hogs in a single week on Little Pine Key. Once the hogs had exhausted the food supply, they'd swim to the nearest island and begin again.

Alligators loved to eat Spook's dogs. He constantly fretted anytime his dogs had to swim across a pond. When a gator snatched one of his dogs—a twice-a-year occurrence—it would inevitably consume the dog's expensive radio collar. Between dog flesh and electronics, Spook would be out two grand.

"Everything has dried up 'cept for a couple holes, and they're filled with gators," he informed his father-in-law over the radio. Shifting into four-wheel-drive, Mabry Murphy drove toward the voice down the middle of a creek. Alligators scrambled out of his way. A moment later, a dog emerged from the woods and swam down the middle of the same creek. The oblivious dog made it to the bank without becoming a meal.

The lucky dog turned out to be Charley, born the year a notorious hurricane by the same name clobbered the state. Two years old, Charley loved chasing hogs. In 2005, Charley had a nice boar cornered and was waiting for Spook to arrive on horseback; the hog disemboweled Charley before Spook arrived.

"His guts was hanging out," Spook said. Spook tucked the guts back into Charley's abdomen and used a surgical stapler to close the wound. Years ago, he sutured his dogs, but the stapler is quicker. Less fortunate was the dog known as Buster, who chased an enormous boar into the palmettos a few years back. Spook lost radio contact, so it took a while to find Buster. Buster was alive, just barely, his windpipe punctured, but he refused to release the angry hog. Spook lost Buster but got the pig.

Spook never got enough sleep and had red eyes like Count Dracula. Hog catching was only one way he made a living. His day job was supervising construction crews for the City of Okeechobee's utility department. On weekends, he was a cowboy, the senior bronc buster at the rodeo. "I'm the oldest guy by a good twenty years," he said. He had broken both legs, an ankle, an arm, and every finger.

He looked weary without acting weary as he rode his horse next to the truck. Listening for his dogs, he'd suddenly trot off into the woods, returning minutes later dragging a pig behind the horse. He'd give his father-in-law a brief account, jump on Trigger, and vanish again. Within minutes, we'd hear discordant squealing.

Two bewildered hogs lay in the cage behind the trailer. Sows, they weighed 60 pounds or so, perfect, in Spook's opinion, for grinding into sausage. But there was another hog out in the woods that Spook wanted, a big boar that had eluded his dogs so far today. Spook was of the opinion that a boar hog is the smartest critter in the animal kingdom.

"Real wary," he said. A boar avoided other hogs except when looking for a mate or when being pursued by dogs. "A boar will run right straight through a herd of sows and confuse the dogs. They won't know who to chase." Boars never ran in a straight line. Boars zigzagged, changed directions completely, ending up behind the dogs.

Spook thought the most challenging boar to catch typically weighed about 150 pounds. Such a boar was fearsome but energetic and agile. "A dog-killin' machine," he said.

A dog howled.

"Thooo-ugg!" Spook shouted. Go catch that hog. The dogs raced through the palmettos with Spook just behind them on his horse. An hour passed. Two hours. Spook kept in touch over radio. Almost got him. Nope. Lost him. Sometimes the dogs barked along the road. Then their barks faded away.

"Thooo-ugg!"

The hog jumped the road once. Twice. Hog scrambled through a pond, sprinted across a prairie, snuck back into the hammock, tried his luck in Duck Slough. Three dogs caught up. Defiant or exhausted, the boar stayed put.

Show time.

The dogs didn't rush the hog until Spook leapt off his horse. Then they charged, dodged, retreated, charged again, baring teeth and snapping. The hog growled back, hissed, squealed, slashed air with lethal yellow tusks.

All the while, Spook drew closer, an inch at a time, to those tusks. Not yet. Not yet. Spook had been battered and torn by many a hog in his career. The 5-inch scar on his thigh was proof.

The idea was to grab the hog by the leg and pull it off its feet. Easier said than done, but that's exactly what he did. Wham! The boar was on its back, jaws popping with rage.

Grabbing a hog, Spook once told me, is like catching a rattlesnake. "If you're gonna catch him, your heart better be in it. If you turn loose his head and just hold him by the tail, things ain't gonna be pretty."

Spook knelt on the boar's shoulder below the neck. He carried cord between his teeth. He reached, somehow, past the boar's frantic tusks and looped the cord around the front hooves. He tied what must have been the fastest double half hitch in history, pulled the knot tight, and used the momentum to reach back and tie the rear legs. The hog-tied hog squealed.

Now Spook looped a rope around the tail. He dragged the boar from the woods to the trailer. Trigger, the horse, sweated profusely. The dogs panted. Spook looked ready to go again.

The boar was black with tiny eyes and an uninviting personality. Spook knelt on the 160-pound boar once more. As it popped its jaws, Spook untied his knots. I stood on the bumper of his truck just in case; Spook told his father-in-law to get ready.

Mabry opened the trailer door.

The trick is not hesitating, not giving the boar a nanosecond of hope. Grabbing one back leg and one front leg, Spook swung the hog into the trailer lickety-split and pronounced the day a success.

No bones broken. No gutted dogs. No fingertip deficit like that one terrible time.

Spook shrugged and looked sheepish as he told his famous story about the revenge of the boar.

"The dogs had him bayed up on the edge of palmettos. I got out to catch him. He turned, he was in there, and he turned, and when he turned he seen me, and I was way too close at the time, and he run at me, and I put my hands out to grab him by the ears to keep him off of me, but he was faster'n me. Bone was stuck out there, and the fingernail was lifted up, bitted at an angle. Didn't hurt till I got back to the house."

For the love of heaven, what happened to the doomed fingertip?

"I hunted for the piece. God give me that finger, and I wanted to leave there with what God give me."

Spook had to leave the fingertip out there next to the palmettos. The boar got away too.

September 16, 2006

22

PALMETTO

Snead Island Boat Works

Jimmie Alderman was an old-fashioned fellow. He had a computer but preferred a pencil and paper. He owned a new car, but often drove his prized 1931 Ford. His favorite boat lacked an engine. It was a sailboat he constructed using plans from 1911.

Jimmie was eighty-one when we talked. He told me how much he hated to part with old things. The yellow photograph behind his desk showed an ancient shack that had been built in 1907. Sentimental, he refused to scrap the shack. In 2005, the shack provided storage for old boating gear he knew he would never throw away, but possibly donate to a maritime museum.

Snead Island Boat Works, Jimmie's business near Bradenton, belonged in a museum, too. Nearly a century old, it loomed over the Manatee River like a haunted house.

"There aren't too many of us left," he said. He was talking about old-fashioned boatyards. An old-fashioned boatyard was a place boats were repaired. Sometimes a boatyard sold boats, and sometimes a boatyard stored boats, but for the most part a genuine boatyard was like an old-fashioned garage where elbow-grease labor was performed.

At Jimmie's boatyard, men with fiberglass under their nails scraped hulls, straightened propeller shafts, and refitted masts. They wore steel-toed boots, smoked unfiltered cigarettes, and expressed themselves with grunts. The stray dogs and cats that showed up periodically never went hungry.

When I was a kid, every coastal county in Florida had two, three, five, or ten boatyards like Snead Island Boat Works. But in the twenty-first century, they were an endangered species. Florida had become too modern, and too expensive, for old-fashioned boatyards to exist on the highest-priced real estate remaining, the waterfront.

A mariner who did business with Snead Island Boat Works had to go into the office. There, a clerk recorded the transaction into an old-fashioned ledger. Jimmie Alderman had computers at his place, but he didn't trust them.

"Nothing wrong with a ledger," he said. "A ledger never stops working in a thunderstorm."

Among the first mariners to use the Manatee River shoreline were Tocobaga Indians. Then came the Spaniards. In 1843, Edward Snead claimed the 740-acre island near the mouth of the river as his own. In 1907, Ed Pillsbury established the boatyard. In 1935, the Pillsburys sold it to Edward Bishop, who sold it to Jim Alderman, who handed it off to his son Jimmie. Jimmie still came to the boatyard every day, though his son Gary, fifty-four, was manager.

Captain Jim Alderman—that's what everybody called Jimmie's daddy—died in 1990 at the age of ninety-two. The old man loved wood boats. He loved wood, period. Before he ran the boatyard he was in the lumber business. He had a lumberyard in Tarpon Springs, in Pinellas County, where Alderman Road still bore his name.

The sawmill burned down in 1925; Alderman moved south to the Manatee River for a job on a boat and at the boatyard. Captain Jim's boy, Jimmie, remembered helping build a boat at age five. Jimmie still had the boat and many of his other old boats. Scattered about Snead Island Boat Works, they looked seaworthy.

Jimmie told me he officially began working at his daddy's boatyard while in high school. "At a boatyard, you started at the bottom," he said. He showed me his scars, souvenirs from scraping razor-sharp barnacles. Boats were always built from wood in those days. They needed constant scraping and painting and repair. "It's different now," Jimmie said. "Work isn't as hard because of modern equipment."

The 4-acre yard smelled of fiberglass and creosote, though a south wind carried the fragrance of the river. Outside Jimmie's window, mullet jumped. Occasionally he looked out the window and watched a fishing guide casting for snook.

Jimmie had grown up eating mullet and snook and grits. Nobody who lived on water had gone hungry during the Depression. "I built my first sailboat out of a rowboat when I was fourteen," he said. "I sailed up and down the river though sometimes I went into the bay and camped on one of those islands. I'd bring sardines, crackers, and a jug of water and was in heaven."

In June, he'd wade for scallops. "You don't see them now, but back then there were thousands. I'd bring a bucket back to the boatyard and clean them. Have you ever cleaned scallops? Well, then you know it takes a lot of time. The sun would go down and you'd be eaten alive by mosquitoes and sand flies while you cleaned those scallops."

Jimmie served in the army during World War II. He was transported to Europe on the *Queen Mary*. In the North Atlantic, the ship pitched like an enraged bull. He had sea legs and never threw up. He liked standing on the ship's fantail and looking back at the wake. "I always thought they needed to flat haul the *Queen Mary* out of the water and adjust her props," the old boat man said now. "She really vibrated." He took a bullet in Germany, and sometimes the hip still hurt, but he hated complaining.

He liked to walk from his office to the huge tin shed next door. Inside the shed were old boats. The *Little Islander*, a wood beauty, lay next to the *Skip Jack*. The *Skip Jack* belonged to him. He built it out of cypress and juniper in 2004. He modeled the *Skip Jack* after the commercial fishing vessels that once plied the Manatee River. He liked to sail it out on the river on breezy days.

On most mornings he and Maribel, his wife of sixty-two years, drove to the boatyard in their 1931 Model A. He always was partial to 1931 Model A's. He bought his first in 1941 for $50 and took Maribel out on a date. He said he wished he could still find a 10-cent milkshake. "Well, everything changes," he said.

Jimmie Alderman told me he worried about the future of old-timey boatyards in Florida. "Maybe they'll go inland," he said hopefully. "When we got started, waterfront was affordable, but now the only affordable land in Florida is in the middle of the state. Maybe people will have to trailer their boats to those places."

At least once a month developers came sniffing around the boatyard and tossed impressive numbers Jimmie's way. Jimmie listened but always answered the same way.

"Not interested."

His son Gary, who managed the place in 2005, told me he had the same philosophy. Gary had two daughters, one a senior at Clemson and the other an insurance saleswoman. Jimmie dreamed that his granddaughters might take over the boatyard one day. But they made no promises.

At 5:30 p.m. sharp, the boatyard closed, and Jimmie and Maribel said their good-byes. Often they drove into town for groceries before going home. They drove out of the old yard past the mango trees and the poinciana trees and headed east toward town. Sitting in their 1931 Ford, at an intersection graced by a Walgreens, a CVS Pharmacy, and a Checkers, they waited for the light to change.

June 28, 2005

23

EAST POINT

Highway Patrolman

I am one of those nitwits who wait until the needle points to empty before looking for a service station. Driving one afternoon in the Florida Panhandle, I found myself wishing I had brought hiking boots for what promised to be a long walk when I ran out of gas.

I felt less anxious once I escaped the lonely woods known as "Tate's Hell" near the Apalachicola River and drove onto U.S. 98. At least if I ran out of gas on the busy coast highway, I might be able to thumb a ride. Then, rising in the distance like an oasis, was a Chevron.

I did my credit-card stuff and pumped gas into my parched truck. As my anxiety ebbed and the gas flowed, my eyes were drawn to the sticker I see on gas pumps everywhere I go.

"Warning," the sticker read, "If You Don't Pay for Your Gas You Could Lose Your Driver's License!" Next to the warning was a photograph of a Florida Highway Patrol trooper. Not just any trooper, but about the fiercest-looking trooper in the history of troopers. On the sticker he wore a Smokey Bear hat low on his forehead like one of those nail-eating Parris Island marine drill instructors. Under the hat was a shaved head.

He had serious eyes, no-nonsense eyes that bored into yours, eyes that made you want to drop down and give him twenty pushups. He had the neck of a bull and the shoulders of a linebacker and hands that could pop your skull like a cantaloupe if you gave him cause. Even if I were poor, even if I were desperate, even if I were a habitual criminal, I would not steal gas if I thought he might come after me.

Highway patrolman Anthony Stone. Photo by Jeff Klinkenberg.

As I stood pumping gas and musing about the trooper from hell, a Highway Patrol vehicle happened to drive up and park on the opposite side of the pump. The interesting coincidence prompted me to steal a glance at the driver.

I looked a second time. Then a third.

Finally, with the hair rising on my neck, I walked over and cleared my throat. "Excuse me," I said, trying not to squeak. "This might sound like an odd question, but aren't you . . . ?"

"Yes, sir," he said. "I'm him."

He introduced himself as Trooper Anthony Stone. Crushing my hand in a serious handshake, he said that yes, sir—certainly, sir—he would be happy to talk a few minutes. He told me he was thirty-four years old. He told me he was born in Clearwater and raised in Crystal River. He joined the marines after high school, and the Highway Patrol after the marines. Stationed in Quincy, near Tallahassee, his job was patrolling U.S. 98, where people, frankly, didn't steal much gas.

"Old-fashioned values up here, sir," he said. "It isn't much of a problem."

In most of twenty-first-century Florida, especially urban Florida, stealing gas was a problem, especially as the price of gas went up. "Pump-and-run" is what Trooper Stone called the phenomenon where a thief pumps gas and then flees before paying.

In 1999, it was considered epidemic. That's when Florida Petroleum and Convenience Store Association communications director Rue Luttrell called Highway Patrol Deputy Director Ken Howes and asked for the loan of a trooper who might model for a public information campaign. Luttrell wanted a "serious-looking person" for her "don't steal gas" campaign. Howes didn't have to think long.

In North Florida, Trooper Stone was a well-known spit-and-polish straight arrow. Soon his photograph was pasted on gas pumps from Key West to Pensacola—more than forty thousand pumps on any given day.

I asked Trooper Stone about fame. "I don't think about it, sir. But people do recognize me, yes sir. Not long ago, I was doing some off-duty work in Tallahassee and somebody asked if I were that guy. Every once in a while people ask for autographs. I would rather give them an autograph than sign my name on a traffic citation."

I asked why he thought he had been picked to be the gas sheriff. "I don't know for sure, sir," he said. "I do know I am serious about my work in the Highway Patrol. I love my job. It's more than giving speeding tickets for me. I enforce drug laws and just help people. I am also an ex-marine. When you become a marine right after high school like I did, you're like a puppy. They have trained you for life."

I told him he looked like a marine. "Thank you, sir. I still press my uniform every day. I still shine my shoes every day. I wash my car every day. It's a habit."

As we talked, I worked up my nerve. I wanted to tell him what graffiti artists in urban Florida did to his gas-pump photograph. They wrote "I'm gay" over his picture, gave him devil horns and vampire teeth. I was especially nervous about telling him the "I'm gay" part. Instead I mentioned the frequent Hitler mustaches.

"Yes, sir. I'm aware that people do that. But you know, they don't do that up here. We have small-town values up here. Plus, people know me. I'm around. When people know you, they treat you like a human being."

In the city, most of us went through life feeling anonymous. We didn't know our neighbors, much less the guy who sold us groceries or the woman behind the counter at Exxon. In the city, we stopped for gas at huge service-station supermarkets, where the aisles were jammed with bags of chips. The typical gas thief favored the pump nearest the road, filled his tank, and left the hose on the pavement. Then he jumped into his car and made his escape. Most Florida stations made customers pay in advance or use credit cards. The honor system no longer worked.

Up in the Panhandle, in Trooper Stone's territory, where kids still chased tadpoles in ditches, life seemed innocent. As we chatted, he waved at people who stopped for gas, greeting many by name. A tough-looking guy on a motorcycle roared up, apologized for the interruption, and showed Trooper Stone his license.

"Thank you for stopping me that time, Trooper," he said. "I paid my fine and got a new license. I wanted you to know I'm squared away now."

"Way to go, sir," said Trooper Stone. "I'm happy to hear that."

I asked Trooper Stone if he ever chased gas thieves.

"Yes, sir, it does happen, though not very often. Like I said, everybody knows each other around here. If you steal from this station, you're stealing from a person you likely know. It's not like in the city."

He told me about one chase. "Two couples were in the car. It was a man and his wife and that man's parents. But when I stopped them they had a credit-card receipt for the gas. One of the women had also kept a travel journal where she had written down how much gas they'd purchased and what kind of mileage they'd been getting. They had their gas purchase as well documented as I have ever seen. My advice to everyone is to hang onto that gas receipt. Sometimes a clerk will make a mistake."

I thanked Trooper Stone for his time. He thanked me in return and crushed my hand again.

As I started driving off, he suddenly reappeared at my window. For a terrible moment, I was afraid I had forgotten to pay for my gas.

"Sir, I just wanted to get one thing straight. I don't want it to sound like I think everybody who lives in the city is dishonest. Of course they're not. But up here in the country, you know, we still do believe in family values."

April 6, 2004

DANGEROUS FLORIDA

24

WEEKI WACHEE

Cave Diving

Those of us who have never explored a Florida underwater cave wonder why anybody in their right mind would even be interested. Sitting at the breakfast table, eating Shredded Wheat, we imagine the descent into the cavern, the thrill of exploring an alien world, and then the moment when the diver realizes that something has gone terribly amiss.

We imagine the panic and the backtracking, the black shadows dancing across the walls in the fading light of the lantern, perhaps the fleeting thought of loved ones who will miss their husband or son or daddy until the end of time. From there everything goes downhill.

What we call real Florida is a lovely, benign place most of the time. It is the osprey whistling from a tall pine, the fellow selling collards on a street corner, a wade fisherman reeling in a spotted sea trout, a chorus of pig frogs yodeling their backyard Grand Ole Opry on a wet summer night. The postcard real Florida is the reason so many of us enjoy living here.

But parts of real Florida come with risk. A day at the beach can end in the jaws of a shark. Alligators lurk among the lily pads. A lightning bolt spoils a shelling trip. In an underwater cave, a broken light bulb, the wrong mix of gas in an air tank, the smallest error in judgment become catastrophe. Yet most of us are willing to take the risk—and generally it is a small risk—to fully experience Florida and to live our lives as completely as possible.

With its spectacular mixture of the wild and the tame, Florida is unlike any other state. Our population is 17 million and growing. We have major cities, major universities, major art museums, championship sports teams. A restaurant in South Miami Beach, Joe's, serves the best stone crab claws in the world. It is hard to imagine anything better than sitting on the sand behind the Don CeSar and toasting a St. Pete Beach sunset with a glass of fresh-squeezed orange juice in late January.

But look before jumping off a dock or sea wall in our civilized state. In the wilderness of a Florida lake or sea, animals with unspeakable appetites cruise the shallows. We might be mugged in Manhattan, but we won't be devoured by wild beasts.

Much of wilderness Florida, of course, has vanished, tamed into housing subdivisions and shopping centers and theme parks. Yet it is still possible to get lost here. A boat trip can end in tragedy; it happens all the time. But there are places in Florida, in the Everglades and Big Cypress, in Gulf Hammock and Chassahowitzka, in Apalachicola and Aucilla, where a hike in the woods can end badly for the explorer who is sloppy with a map and compass.

Most of us have never experienced Florida's greatest wilderness. Underground Florida is too inaccessible and demanding and claustrophobic for ordinary people. We have dry caves that are smaller versions of the spectacular caves found in Kentucky and in the American Southwest, caves that feature awesome rocks and formations and countless opportunities to fall a long way to death.

But few places on the planet have underwater caves to rival ours. Most are accessed through crystal-water springs in central and north Florida. Some are miles long and hundreds of feet deep. Some are narrow and twisty, others cavernous. Divers require specialized equipment, training, and nerve. Like test pilots, astronauts, and ancient mariners, cave divers are a special breed willing to die for their passion.

Since 1960, more than 430 cave divers have lost their lives in Florida, Mexico, and the Caribbean, according to the National Speleological Society. Most were foolish, underequipped rookies, but some were obsessively careful people who knew exactly what they were doing until the end.

By most accounts, John Robinson Jr., thirty-six, of St. Petersburg, and Craig Simon, forty-four, of Spring Hill, were careful, well-trained, experienced cave divers who used state-of-the-art equipment. By most accounts, they were up to the challenge of exploring Eagle's Nest, an underwater cave in Hernando County.

For cave divers around the world, Eagle's Nest is a mecca, the Grand Canyon of underwater caves. It begins in an ordinary pond, about 200 feet wide, in the woods. At the bottom of the pond is a kind of chimney that descends hundreds of feet into a cavern large enough to contain most of a professional basketball arena. Beyond what divers call "the Main Ballroom" are longer tunnels and crannies that descend even deeper. How far do they go? Nobody knows.

And nobody can know what happened in the last few hours and minutes and seconds in the lives of those two adventuresome men on June 12, 2004. We can only imagine.

We can imagine the two friends driving past the Home Depots and McDonald's and Olive Gardens of U.S. 19 and turning west at Weeki Wachee on State Road 50. They drive pickup trucks off the pavement into the woods. For 5 miles or so, they bounce along a winding dirt road that turns into truck-swallowing sand and mud. But their trucks are equipped to handle deep sand and mud. It is simple to get lost here, to take the wrong fork in the road—in fact, there are many wrong forks—but they don't. They drive through sand pines and palmetto thickets and oak hammocks and cypress swamps and finally park.

They unload their dive equipment and their underwater scooters. They are miles from pavement and anyone else. When they aren't talking, they can hear wilderness Florida in a way city people can only dream of. They hear the cries of red-shouldered hawks and the chirps of the cardinals and the chattering of squirrels. Perhaps they even hear a turkey. The woods are full of them.

They pull on their insulated suits, adjust their tanks and masks and lights, and lumber into the water. Cold, the water is 72 degrees, but cave divers don't mind. The bird sounds vanish the instant the divers' heads go under. Now the sound track is their own breathing and the gurgle of bubbles and perhaps the hum of the scooters if they are operating.

Below them is the dark hole of the cavern shaft, the abyss. The Main Ballroom awaits.

As they descended into that clear water last weekend, what were they thinking? What were they feeling? They must have felt like they were immortal.

June 22, 2004

25

GAINESVILLE

Mojo

Don Goodman, who still loved alligators, once was right-handed. Now he did everything with his left. He buttoned his shirt and zipped his pants, steered his car, and even opened a can of peaches one-handed. He learned to shave and tied his shoes with the wrong hand. The director of Kanapaha Botanical Gardens near Gainesville, he tended plants one-handed without much of a struggle. When he led a tour at his lush 62-acre park, one arm was good enough for pointing out the splendid palms and water lilies the size of magic carpets. Pausing at a pond, he gestured with his remaining limb. "That's where Mojo used to bask on the bank," he told me. Mojo was the alligator that had crawled over from a nearby lake about a year before my visit. "When a gator is about 6 feet long, it's a lizard. When an alligator grows larger, when it really bulks up, it's a dragon. Mojo was about 12 feet long. He was a dragon." Mojo wasted no time eating Kanapaha's other alligators. Always hungry, he went on to prey upon aquatic turtles. When he seized a heavy turtle in those massive jaws, the crunch echoed throughout the park. "You know how alligators will roar at other alligators? Mojo was so dominant that when it thundered, he'd roar back at the thunder."

As Goodman and I strolled along the pond, he automatically looked for Mojo. "In a strange way," he said, "I miss him. He was magnificent." Mojo had a crooked back. At first, park employees nicknamed him Quasimodo after the *Hunchback of Notre Dame*. That was shortened to Modo and finally to Mojo. If an alligator can be a celebrity, Mojo was. For a while, he was the most photographed alligator in Florida. He'd lie motionless on the bank for hours, oblivious to the hundreds of amateur photographers who crept near. He lay so still many were sure he was a fake. But he wasn't. He was just biding his time. Usually after dark he'd slither into the pond and look for something to eat.

Although you wouldn't have known it from reading the papers, large alligators ordinarily pose little danger to humans. Millions of Floridians swim in lakes, rivers, and springs every summer without harm, yet in a typical year only a dozen or so bathers are bitten. Almost all survive to swim another day; a fatality happens about every two years. Almost without exception it is a large, hungry alligator to blame. Usually the victim has gone swimming in murky water, far from shore, often at dusk or after dark. The alligator submerges, cruises along the bottom, and surfaces under the swimmer, jaws agape. The alligator drowns the swimmer before tearing him or her into bite-sized pieces.

Goodman knew all of this. Since boyhood he had been interested in reptiles. He was born in 1944 in Missouri, a poor state for finding alligators, but a wonderful place for snakes. He collected rat snakes and king snakes and even kept copperheads and rattlers. His parents balked at letting him have an alligator, but otherwise encouraged his passion. Eventually he got his doctorate at the University of Florida, studying under the famous herpetologist Archie Carr. He also met his wife, Jordan, at UF. She was a herp woman. Their idea of a perfect date was to go out and catch barking tree frogs by hand. They'd place the little frogs on the steering wheel and head for the nearest Steak 'n Shake. As the waitress leaned in to take their order, they'd poke the rear ends of the frogs, which sang out their sad songs in unison.

Neither of them stuck with herpetology. Jordan went on to become a nurse, and Don followed his new passion for growing things into establishing the botanical garden, which he opened in 1978. Yet part of him never stopped loving reptiles. When Mojo showed up, he was thrilled. At last he had a pet alligator. Initially, Jordan enjoyed watching Mojo too. But she lost her enthusiasm. "He's just too big to have around," she told her husband. "He could be dangerous. Get rid of him."

Don put off a decision. "I have to admire my wife's discipline," he told me. "She has exercised Herculean self control by not telling me 'I told you so.'"

Goodman had curly red hair, a moustache, and a wiry build. He was not only the founder of Kanapaha Botanical Gardens, but its most enthusiastic worker. He liked manual labor. It kept him fit. Unlike a lot of bosses, who get stuck in the office doing paperwork, he enjoyed dirty hands. September 23, 2002, was no exception. He had been watching with dismay as algae grew along the bottom of the main pond. As it broke loose and floated to the surface, it became an eyesore in the otherwise stunning park. "I'm a swamper," Goodman always told people. He decided to clear the pond of algae himself. The pond was a good half acre wide or so. It was going to be an all-day job.

It was hot, so he got an early start, though he didn't wade into the water right away. First he looked for Mojo. When Mojo was basking on the bank, Goodman never worried. Mojo was basking on the bank, asleep, hundreds of feet away from the section of pond Goodman intended to clean. He waded into the water with confidence. For two hours he cleared algae while wading in thigh-deep water. It was hard work and Goodman got hungry. At noon he broke for lunch.

He returned at 1:30. He waded into the pond once more. For some reason it never occurred to him to look for Mojo. Live and learn. While Goodman was eating lunch, Mojo had been rambling. He had crept into a new section of pond. In the turbid water, he lay hidden on the bottom.

Oblivious, Goodman slowly worked his way toward those terrible jaws. "It's amazing how a few seconds can change your life," he told me. "That's all it took. One second you're in the water doing what you love. The next second I'm stumbling out of the pond with half my arm gone."

I took Goodman to lunch at a Gainesville restaurant. I felt guilty asking him to talk about the catastrophe. But Goodman, a scientist who valued fact, said he didn't mind. "I never saw him," he said of Mojo. "He must have seen the shadow of my arm and just reacted. Suddenly, there he was, in front of me in a big swirl of water. He grabbed my right arm just below the elbow so fast I wasn't immediately aware we were attached."

Picking at his luncheon chicken with his left arm, he said, "Usually, when an alligator latches on to a person, it's a mistake. Once you raise heck, bang him on the nose, he lets go. You end up with a few bite marks and a story to tell. Those are the rules of engagement; it's unfortunate that alligators sometimes behave irresponsibly. Mojo was so large he didn't care."

Goodman swallowed some iced tea and continued. "He pulled me to my knees. I didn't feel pain at all. I was all adrenaline. I got back on my feet and yelled, 'Help! Alligator!' The second time he jerked me with great force completely underwater and I swallowed a mouthful. I thought I might die. I somehow struggled to my feet once again. Mojo started spinning. That's what a big alligator does. It spins, drowns the prey, tears it apart. He was spinning but I wasn't. That's when I knew. I looked at my arm. It was attached to Mojo by a little rope of flesh. I still had complete clarity of mind. I realized that it was either part of me or all of me. I was going to have to give him my arm. I backed away and broke that rope of tissue and waded out of the pond."

A park employee, planting a butterfly garden, sped over in a golf cart to help. As she drove, Goodman worked on a tourniquet. At the office, as she called 911, he drove the cart into the parking lot and waited for paramedics. "Can I do something to make you more comfortable?" the paramedic asked. By now Goodman was feeling a burning, searing pain.

"Well," he said, "there's a bottle of Tylenol on my desk."

While the ambulance raced for the hospital, Shands at the University of Florida, state trappers arrived and killed Mojo. They slit his stomach and removed Goodman's arm. It was too mangled to be reattached. Goodman was released after three days. Three weeks later he returned to work, but felt tired. When I visited six months later, he was back to cleaning ponds, though much more careful about alligators. Well-wishers who wanted to shake hands grabbed his left.

He wore a prosthesis on the right. It was a high-tech model that looked real. When he flexed his bicep, the hand opened. When he contracted the tricep, the hand closed. He was capable of drinking water from a glass, though not a Styrofoam cup. The hand lacked sensitivity and he crushed cups. His arm still hurt. He had tried hypnosis and acupuncture, but the pain persisted. He invited me to accompany him to his weekly visit to Dr. William Baker, a University of Florida neurologist. "Phantom pain is difficult," Baker told him. "We don't know much about it, frankly. Your brain still thinks your arm is there. The pain probably will go away in time, but we don't know for sure."

Goodman smiled wanly. "It's the ultimate insult," he said. "I lose my arm, and the arm that isn't there still hurts." Baker prescribed medicine that would help him endure the worst moments, when he felt a crushing pain—almost like something large and strong had gotten a hold of his arm. "In my mind," Goodman said. "I guess Mojo still has me."

The Goodmans lived minutes from the park. They had an outdoor swimming pool in their backyard. On a good night, the pool collected aquatic vertebrates that interested them. One morning they harvested a peninsula newt from the pool and dropped it in their indoor aquarium for further study. Within minutes the newt got too close to a hungry African clawed frog. The frog bit off the front left leg of the newt.

Over the next week Goodman watched the wounded newt regenerate a new limb. "I'm envious," he said. "It kind of gives me hope."

May 5, 2003

26

ST. PETERSBURG

The 1935 Hurricane

A day after Hurricane Katrina destroyed New Orleans in 2005, I drove over to talk to Floyd Russell at his house on Snell Isle in St. Petersburg. As we chatted in his den, horrific images of New Orleans and Mississippi kept rolling across the television screen. After a while Floyd got up and changed the channel. Soon he was fidgeting. He switched back to hurricane coverage that showed more destruction, homeless people, more dead bodies on his TV.

He hit the mute button and said, "I get tired of it. After a while I am hungry for news other than the hurricane. With the sound off at least I can read the headlines about other news crawling across the bottom of the screen."

It wasn't that he was indifferent to the suffering. The opposite was true. For him, watching was especially excruciating. His feelings had everything to do with what happened to him when he was an eight-year-old boy living with his family on south Florida's Matecumbe Key, in the little community of Islamorada.

Life in the Florida Keys in 1935 could have been a page torn from *Tom Sawyer*. He and his cousins—fifty-three Russells lived on Matecumbe alone—played in the lime groves and collected fiddler crabs on the beach. They waved to the train as it chugged across the island on its way to Key West 80 miles distant. Nobody had electricity on Matecumbe in 1935, and the stars almost cast shadows.

On Labor Day, a storm blew in from the Atlantic. When it was over, thirty-eight of his relatives were gone. They were victims of what is still considered the most powerful hurricane to ever strike the United States.

Floyd was seventy-eight when we met. For most of his life he had somehow lived with the memories of those 200 mph winds and the 18-foot tidal surge. I didn't think he would talk to me about them. "I really don't like to live in the past," he said. On the other hand, he had always been the family historian and felt obligated to tell the story of how he lost his mother, two sisters and two brothers in a matter of hours.

During hurricane season, even if there were no storms on the horizon, Russell and his wife, Melissa, watched the Weather Channel as if they were hypnotized. "You better pay attention if you live in Florida," she told me.

In the twenty-first century, it was impossible for a hurricane to sneak up on the United States. Satellites noticed the storms as soon as they formed off the African coast, in the Caribbean, or in the gulf. Then meteorologists studied computers and wind models and predicted where the storm might go.

In 1935, forecasting was only a step or two above reading tea leaves. A ship out in the ocean might experience tropical winds and notify the U.S. mainland. If winds were especially strong, the news might make the radio or the paper the next day. On the Keys, no sane person depended on the media to save his skin. Everybody had a barometer. Floyd's dad, James Clifton Russell, had one. So did Uncle John next door. For generations, Russells had lived with storms, first in coastal South Carolina, then in the Bahamas, and finally on Matecumbe Key beginning in 1854.

When the barometer showed 29.92 inches of mercury, everything was normal, safe to climb into a boat and sail to the reef to catch snapper and haul lobster traps. When the barometer fell, seagoing folks took notice.

On that Labor Day, the barometer headed south. In Miami, it was noticed, too. The Florida East Coast Railway dispatched a train to evacuate the island. Under normal conditions, Matecumbe's population numbered several hundred, but it had swelled that summer. More than six hundred unemployed World War I veterans were on Matecumbe building a highway. Living in primitive camps, they were vulnerable to even weak tropical storms.

The evacuation train was delayed leaving Miami. It was delayed again when a broken cable above the tracks snagged the locomotive. Finally, around dusk, it reached the Keys. By then, Russell family barometers were at 27.90—and falling by the minute. The bruised sky looked like it had been inspired by Edvard Munch's painting *The Scream*. Water flew over the islands in winds stronger than what any human in North America had ever experienced.

Floyd Russell's favorite chair in his den was one of those cushy recliners on which he rested his feet while perusing his Bible or watching the news. A husky man with blue eyes and white hair, he was dressed in an orange jumpsuit like one of those NASCAR mechanics. A pronounced cowlick hid a prominent scar; whatever had struck him in 1935 had performed a favor. It had stolen at least some of his memories. But not all his memories, Lord no.

He told me that the Russell clan lived in wood houses, up on blocks, on the shore of the raging Atlantic Ocean. As winds grew, Floyd's dad and Uncle John chose to take their families to higher ground, a relative term in the Keys. It meant 6 feet above sea level. Matecumbe was barely a half mile wide. The two families marched inland a hundred yards to the packinghouse where key limes were sorted before shipping. As the winds shrieked and water rushed through the door, the creaking house came apart. Floyd's dad shouted, "Let's get out of here!" Better to take their chances in the storm.

Seven decades later, in his Snell Isle home, Floyd Russell leaned forward in his comfortable chair. "The thing I can't stop thinking about is the decision the adults in that room had to make at that very second. I mean, there were two men in there and two women—but nine kids. Who was going try to hold whom? I always think about that."

Barometers on the island were registering 26.35, the lowest ever recorded in the United States. It was a compact storm; the eye was barely 8 miles across. Yet eye-wall winds exceeded 200 mph with higher gusts and tornadoes.

Floyd's dad grabbed his arm and opened the door.

"People were instantly blown away or washed away—I'm not sure. Something hit my head, I don't know what. I don't know what happened except I guess the Lord wanted me to live."

By the time he came to, the water had receded. His dad grimly led him to a freight car flopped on its side at the railroad tracks. Ancient coconut palms had been uprooted or snapped in half. Bodies lay everywhere, in wreckage and under fallen trees. Some people were sandblasted to death, their skin gone. One talkative survivor had been impaled by a tree limb. He was offered morphine but asked for two beers instead. He drank his beers, the limb was pulled from his abdomen, and he died.

Floyd's dad left the train car to search for his family. He found his daughter Florene and his wife, Charlotte. He knelt over Charlotte and removed her wedding band. When Floyd married Melissa fifty-two years ago, he slipped the same ring on her finger.

I asked Floyd Russell about how a boy or man recovers, emotionally, from such a trauma, and he did his best to answer. He said he depended on prayer and his faith in God and focusing on the present. "You know, I think the Lord builds into children the ability to endure. Later on it hit me, but I just tried to stay busy. I tried not to dwell on the past."

After two days his dad put him on a boat and sent him to friends in Miami. He had to go by boat because the train tracks were gone or twisted like pipe cleaner, never to be rebuilt. A week later those friends sent him by boat to live with family friends in Key West.

Meanwhile, the rest of the world was slowly discovering the horror. Officially, 408 bodies were recovered, including 259 World War I veterans. Ernest Hemingway arrived from Key West to write an essay for a socialist magazine, *New Masses*. The title of his article was "Who Murdered the Vets?" Hemingway was furious about that delayed rescue train. He provided a terrific account of the hurricane's aftermath.

"The railroad embankment was gone and the men who had cowered behind it . . . were all gone with it," he wrote. "You could find them face down and face up in the mangroves. . . . Then further on you found them high in the trees where the water had swept them . . . beginning to be too big for their blue jeans and jackets that they could never fill when they were on the bum and hungry."

In the heat, bodies swelled and began to rot. A boat hauled 116 for burial in Miami. The remainder were placed on a pile of broken railroad ties and rubber tires and burned on Matecumbe.

Floyd Russell's dad never located the bodies of three of his children. For years afterward, skeletons were discovered on offshore islands. Two decades after the hurricane, a developer's bulldozer on Matecumbe uncovered three skeletons, sitting behind the wheels of three different automobiles. The automobiles all had 1935 license plates.

Floyd Russell spent the next few years in Key West, returning to Matecumbe on weekends and summer vacations. The lime groves were gone, but he helped his dad, the postmaster, sort and deliver mail. He enrolled in a military school in Georgia when he was thirteen. Drafted during World War II, he was selected by the army to study Japanese at Yale. The war ended, and he graduated with an architecture degree instead. After he married Melissa, he worked in New Jersey for her dad, not as an architect but as a publisher of medical books.

Only in 1960 did he and Melissa return to Matecumbe—just in time for a Category 4 storm known as Donna. They spent the hurricane huddled in the attic as the ocean washed into their living room and lapped at the ceiling.

They rebuilt again. They built a house on the island that became known as "Floyd's Fortress." It featured reinforced walls, a sturdy roof, and steel shutters that a coconut fired from a cannon might not have dented. In Floyd's fortress, bedrooms were downstairs, and the most valuable possessions, his beloved piano and organ, were on the second floor.

The Russells have a son, John Clifton, known as J.C., who was a mortgage broker in St. Petersburg. In 2000 they moved into the same Snell Isle neighborhood where their son lived. Their home on Brightwaters, across the street from the water, was one of those sprawling ranch-style houses where everything outside and inside seemed perfectly placed—even the prized candy dish resurrected from the sand that covered the island after the 1935 hurricane.

On the dining room table built by his late father from Florida Keys mahogany, Floyd spread old news clippings and photographs of his family taken in 1934 and a chart showing who in his family lived and who in his family died on that terrible night of September 2, 1935. He was the last survivor.

He ushered me into the backyard to show me something. "I believe in having hurricane shutters," he said on the patio. "I have pretty good ones. Look here. I have accordion shutters. They are easier for a man my age to open and close."

He demonstrated how you work the shutters. "Just grab them and slide," he said, grunting. "See? They run along a little track."

The shutter hung up, stuck. "Ah, look at this! Wasps built their nests right in the tracks. Mud dauber wasps. I got to get rid of these mud dauber wasps before we have a hurricane."

September 18, 2005

27

ST. PETERSBURG

Revenge of the Sandwich

If Johnny Cash had been a fish, he would have been a goliath grouper. Goliath grouper are very macho. They like their colors dark and have baritone voices. The biggest kid on the grouper block, goliaths grow up to 800 pounds. They lurk in the deep shadows of fishing piers, bridges, and reefs. When disturbed, or when they're just feeling their oats, they sing. The rumbling sound, which originates in their swim bladders, can be heard a long way off.

When Dan MacMahon was skin diving off Sarasota on a summer afternoon in 2003, he hoped to spear something for dinner. He had no plans to go after a goliath grouper, which were protected by state law. He wanted to spear a corpulent black grouper or hogfish or something equally delicious.

"I ended up spearing a nice cobia," said the Pasco County resident on the day we talked.

When he heard rumbling emanating from the reef, he didn't mistake it for "I Walk the Line." He was pretty sure a goliath grouper was warning him to keep his distance. Not for an instant did he think the goliath was singing a different tune, one that could have been called "Hand Over That Cobia Or I'm Going to Make a Sandwich Out of You."

Don MacMahon's hands and legs and toes and fingers were still in one piece the day we met. Oh, he showed me a few old scars from encounters with marine life or boat propellers. But he also showed off a brand-new scar and a story to go with it.

"Things happen out there," he said.

Dip your toe into the gulf and you entered a primal world where something might bite, pinch, sting, or even swallow you. Pugnacious blue crabs dreamed of well-turned ankles. Sea lice the size of pinheads burrowed under your bathing suit and soon you were begging for Benadryl.

In deeper water, you kept your eyes open for stingrays and jellyfish. They hurt, but at least they wouldn't eat you. Bull sharks, tiger sharks, and lemon sharks occasionally demonstrated an appetite for human flesh.

But only the most paranoid bather feared a grouper.

"They're pretty docile," Lew Bullock, who studied grouper for the Florida Marine Research Institute in St. Petersburg, once told me. "The only exception I can think of is this pet goliath grouper I had in a tank for a while. I caught him when he was 3 inches long. Called him Big Otis. Eventually he got to be about 3 pounds. One day I was feeding him by hand to impress a secretary. I guess I was paying more attention to the secretary than I was to Otis. Suddenly his mouth was around my arm. They don't have big teeth, they have lots of tiny teeth, but it hurt. Big Otis raked my arm pretty bad. It doesn't pay to try and impress a secretary."

Score one for Big Otis. But most of his ilk usually ended up on a bun with onion, tomato, cheddar cheese, and maybe a pickle on the side.

Grouper sandwiches are as Florida as Key lime pie. Next time you wolf down a grouper sandwich, thank Dan MacMahon, among the most experienced commercial spearfishers in west Florida. He was born in Atlanta in 1959 but raised in Port Richey close to the gulf. He started diving when he was eight and began spearfishing as a teen. For decades he managed a grocery store while dreaming of the weekend and the fish. In 1998 he quit the grocery business to spearfish for the market full time.

"I love what I do," he told me. "When I'm down at the bottom, I'm as comfortable as most people are in their living rooms. Oh, I've had a few bad moments, with sharks, but I'm still alive."

You name it and he had tangled with it. He had speared large mutton and mangrove snapper, amberjack, cobia, and the delicious hogfish.

Grouper were his specialty. He had brought to port black grouper, red grouper, and speckled hind grouper. When it was allowed years ago, he regularly speared goliath grouper.

Back then, they were known as jewfish. Nobody knows exactly how the name jewfish came to be. A few Bible scholars suspect that the leviathan of Jonah's Old Testament tale was in fact a hungry grouper of enormous proportions. Others believe the grouper derived its name from a Jewish law that prohibited the eating of shellfish or "unclean" fish. The *Oxford English Dictionary* credits the name to an outdoors writer, somebody named Dampier, in the sixteenth century. "The Jew Fish is a very good fish," he wrote, his quill pen on fire, "because it hath scales and fins and is therefore a clean fish, according to Levitical Law."

Perhaps if the fisheth in question had been sleek and beautiful, nobody would have brought up the possibility of anti-Semitism. But the giant grouper is rather homely, a toad with fins, with beady eyes and a maw of a mouth, brown and mottled to better blend in among the rocks and the barnacles. In 2001 the jewfish became the goliath grouper.

What do they eat? They eat whatever happens by. Scientists who have conducted stomach-content studies say they eat mostly lobster and crabs. But fish too. Dan MacMahon once was cleaning one when a small hammerhead shark tumbled from its gut.

Photographs of huge goliath grouper once were staples of Florida newspapers. Fishing tackle often included ropes, chains, and hooks the size of a small anchor. If the goliath were large enough, in excess of 400 pounds or more, often a tow truck was employed to haul the monster from the sea.

St. Petersburg's most famous goliath grouper story involved a Boo Radley–type character, the mysterious loner known only as Slim, who haunted the waterfront in the 1950s and the 1960s. Hands frequently dripping with fish slime, Slim prowled the downtown piers and seawalls armed with a spear. I couldn't find anyone who remembered Slim's last name, but I found lots of people who recalled him. Slim, who had one leg shorter than the other, towered almost 7 feet. He liked whiskey, poetry, and was quick with a knife. He often fished for goliath grouper at the downtown pier.

"Slim was sitting on a piling dangling his legs in the water," remembered Jimmy Kelley, a retired shrimper whose dad used to run a tackle store on the pier. "Suddenly, Slim screamed. The grouper had him by one leg."

"Sure, I remember that," said Dale Mastry, who owned a tackle store in St. Petersburg. "When he jumped up he was bleeding like a stuck pig."

Dan MacMahon didn't scare easily. When he went out on a fishing trip, he stayed for days at a time a hundred miles from land. Big seas didn't bother him. He made his peace with lightning decades ago.

He went out with a small crew. One man always stayed on deck while the others did the spearfishing. Dive. Approach a fish. Fire the spear. Put the fish on a stringer. Look for another fish. When the stringer is full, return to the surface. But be careful. A bleeding fish in the middle of the ocean is an invitation to mayhem.

Once or twice he'd had a bad moment with a hammerhead that tried to take fish from his spear. Another time a huge shark that could have been a great white made a pass at him and a friend. But that didn't keep him out of the water long.

I wanted to know about his most recent trip. He told me. He told me he had taken friends on a dive trip to south Florida. On the way back, MacMahon wanted to show them an offshore spring known as the Green Banana. It's about 50 miles west of Sarasota.

Ordinarily he wouldn't dive there. Too much competition from recreational divers. But it's an interesting place, a deep hole on the bottom about 165 feet down. "Goliath grouper were all over the place," Mac-Mahon said. He and his dive buddy heard them before they saw them. Boom! Boom! The huge fish were doing their best Johnny Cash imitations.

MacMahon had speared a cobia. An enormous goliath—MacMahon guessed 500 pounds—swam out from beneath a rocky ledge. Like a gorilla pounding on its chest, it boomed. As MacMahon grabbed the cobia, the grouper swam uncomfortably close.

"It came up from below me. It wanted that cobia. Pretty soon its huge head was between my fins. I pushed it away with my spear gun."

Annoyed, the goliath boomed again. "Suddenly, he grabbed me in the middle of my right leg. You know how a dog will shake a rag? That's what he did to me. He shook me like I was a rag."

The goliath spit out MacMahon. Then it came again. MacMahon re-loaded his spear gun. It is against the law to shoot goliath grouper, but MacMahon felt like the smallest link in the food chain. He shot the grouper. As it quivered and spiraled into the great hole on the bottom, MacMahon headed in the opposite direction.

He bled all over the boat. When he stopped bleeding, his friends took photographs of his leg, scraped from ankle to above the knee, the diameter of the goliath's maw.

Nobody said, "Revenge of the Grouper Sandwich." They didn't have to.

A few days after I spoke with MacMahon, I headed over Dockside Dave's Restaurant in Madeira Beach. It was close to noon, and I was thinking about a grouper sandwich. So were other people. Every stool at the counter was taken.

Out back, co-owner Kevin Matheny opened a bin. Inside the bin, among hundreds of pounds of ice, were the corpses of freshly caught black and red grouper. He filleted a nice black.

He walked into the restaurant with two fillets and handed them to Scott Lusco, thirty-five, the cook. "The secret is fresh fish, spices, and keeping the peanut oil at just the right temperature," Lusco said. Into the fryer went the grouper. Even in the noisy restaurant you could hear sizzling.

A few minutes later, he put the plates on the counter with a bunch of napkins. The grouper fillet was bigger than the buns. It was hard for a human mouth to get around the girth of those sandwiches, but jaws up and down the counter managed nicely.

September 2, 2003

28

SUMMERDALE, ALABAMA

Bull Sharks

Chuck Anderson needed his one good hand to pull the swim goggles over his head. When he wore the rubber fin on his stump, he felt as strong in the water as the old triathlon champion he once had been. Only one thing was different. When he swam in the Gulf of Mexico, he felt as vulnerable as the humblest mullet.

"Clear water, no problem," he said in 2006. "Dirty water, or when I can't see what's around me, I'm an unhappy guy."

Alligators may have had a better press agent, but the bull shark has always been the gulf region's most fearsome animal. Robust creatures, they sometimes exceed 9 feet and 500 pounds. With their massive heads, wide jaws, and voracious appetites, they easily live up to their name. "They have one of the highest levels of testosterone in the animal kingdom," said Dr. Robert Hueter, director of shark studies for Mote Marine Laboratory in Sarasota County. When a bather was killed or maimed in the South, especially in the gulf, the bull shark was inevitably the prime suspect.

Bull sharks fed on large prey close to shore during summer—just when folks are going to the beach. Bull sharks had no particular taste for the human metatarsal. But add millions of swimmers to a subtropical ocean and stir in hundreds of feeding sharks, and sooner or later somebody got unlucky.

Even so, sharks bothered about fifteen swimmers a year in Florida, prompting exasperated marine biologists to remind us that driving to the beach was more dangerous. "Say the word 'shark' and the first image most people conjure up is a *Jaws*-inspired white shark devouring unsuspecting bathers," said George Burgess, director of the International Shark Attack File on the University of Florida campus.

For the record, nobody had ever been mauled by a great white shark in Florida. Whites are a cold-water animal that rarely venture close to shore in southern oceans.

In the South, we have the bull shark. Which, as Chuck Anderson told me, was plenty of shark to go around.

A swimmer anywhere in the world has a 1 in 11.5 million chance of becoming a shark-attack victim, according to the International Shark Attack File. Nobody in a century had been attacked by a shark at an Alabama seashore until Chuck Anderson went for his triathlon training swim in 2000.

The most likely place in the world to have an unhappy encounter with a shark was Volusia County on Florida's east coast. Swimmers who visited the beaches of Daytona Beach or New Smyrna didn't automatically land on the menu, even though thousands of bathers cavorted in turbulent water loaded with baitfish and sharks with poor vision. During summer, schools of small blacktip and spinner sharks—usually 4 feet long or less—chase sardines and mullet through the surf. About a dozen times a year they ended up mistaking a hand or foot for a meal. The victim showed up at an emergency room with stitches and a story to tell. In the twentieth century, 182 swimmers were nipped by sharks in Volusia County but never a fatality.

Shark experts differentiated between what happened on Florida's east coast and on the gulf coast. "On the east coast, we have what I call 'shark bites,'" said Mote Marine's Bob Hueter. "In the gulf, we have fewer incidents, but they are often what I call 'attacks.' The animals are bigger and do more damage."

A 400-pound bull shark had killed sixty-nine-year-old Thadeus Kubinski after he dove off his dock near St. Petersburg in 2000. In 2001—"The Summer of the Shark," according to *Time* magazine—a bull shark removed the arm of eight-year-old Jessie Arbogast while he played in the gulf near Pensacola. Doctors reattached the arm, though the boy suffered brain damage from loss of blood.

If bull sharks were looking to gobble humans, nobody would be safe in the water. But they generally use their powerful jaws and serrated teeth to devour stingrays and sea turtles. They are especially fond of tarpon, the popular game fish known for strength, endurance, and jumping ability.

In the summer, schools of the silver beauties swim along the gulf beaches. Over at the Redington Long Pier, in coastal Pinellas, anglers hook tarpon and watch in dismay as bull sharks bite the fish in half. A bull shark occasionally chased a hooked 7-foot tarpon into the surf.

"Everybody on the pier yells 'Shark!'" explained angler Ken Bednarski. "All the swimmers run out of the water." At Boca Grande, in Charlotte County, bull sharks made life interesting for tarpon and tarpon fishers during summer. "Bull sharks have developed pack hunting techniques," said fishing guide Dave Markett.

Like the more dramatic-looking but less potent hammerheads, bull sharks lurked under boats and waited for an angler to engage a tarpon. A free-swimming tarpon usually could evade a bull shark, but a hooked one nearing exhaustion was easy pickings. Sometimes several bull sharks tore apart a 150-pound tarpon as anglers watched.

Scientists studied the phenomenon. In most of the world, shark populations were declining because of overfishing and habitat destruction. "But in Florida, fishermen say they have never seen so many bull sharks," said Mote's Hueter. "We're trying to find out if that's true, and if it's true, why."

"Serpents, bears, hyenas, tigers rapidly vanish as civilization advances, but the most populous and civilized city cannot scare a shark far from its wharves," Henry David Thoreau wrote in *Cape Cod*.

In 2005, toxic red tide killed millions of fish in west central Florida. The dead and dying stacked up against seawalls. For bull sharks it was better than a fast-food restaurant. In St. Petersburg, early-morning strollers saw them feasting along docks and seawalls.

Bull sharks are common in Florida bays. They even like canals that feed into the bays. In fact, they are the only known shark species that can live for long spells in freshwater. They swim 2,500 miles up the Amazon River. They attack bathers in Central America's Lake Nicaragua. A dead one was found in Florida's Lake Okeechobee one summer. Residents of the Land of Lincoln have spotted bull sharks in the Mississippi—1,800 miles from the gulf.

In the ocean, an immature shark becomes food for countless predators. In freshwater, a young bull shark that evades a sluggish alligator is probably going to reach adulthood.

A Mote Marine Lab scientist, Michelle Heupel studied bull sharks in the Caloosahatchee River, which fed into Lake Okeechobee. She netted them 18 miles from the gulf, fit them with radio transmitters, and studies their movement. "They're very sturdy sharks," she said. "They're built like linebackers. They're very aggressive, yet when I net one, it always seems calm. It's like it knows it's the king of the hill."

Chuck Anderson was born in 1955 and grew up in Alabama. He was a water boy, one of those southern kids who couldn't get enough of swimming, skiing, and fishing in Mobile Bay. His dad—everybody called him "Lefty" even though he had both of his arms—was a football coach. Chuck played quarterback in high school. He threw a tight spiral, never suffered from a lack of confidence, and thought he might have a career after high school.

It didn't happen. He got his bachelor's and master's degrees, taught social studies in high school, and ended up a football coach like his dad. Folks in south Alabama still called Chuck "Coach" even though he had directed the athletic department for Baldwin County's school system since 2001.

He spent working hours traveling from school to school in his Ford pickup, his cell phone at the ready. Sometimes a caller from a school asked him to jot down a phone number. "Too dangerous," he explained in a fried mullet accent, explaining that his only hand was gripping the phone and he was steering with his knees. His bike, running shoes, and swimming equipment were in the truck bed. He had weighed 275 pounds until he started exercising thirteen years ago. Now he was a solid 225.

He had competed in triathlons all over the South, including Florida, mostly in the Panhandle but also in Pinellas and Sarasota counties in west Florida. He lived fifteen minutes from the gulf, where he had done most of his eighty-seven triathlons and hundreds of training swims. Nothing bad had ever happened to him—except once.

He used a prosthetic only when riding his bicycle. He slipped the stump into a fiberglass sleeve on the handlebars. He pedaled 35 to 70 miles a week, ran another 20, and tried to swim a mile or two. The water in a pool is always clear.

He told me he tried not to be self-conscious about the missing arm. In south Alabama, and in the Florida Panhandle, he was known for his sense of humor and good cheer. Strangers shook his left hand. In their photos, Anderson beamed and waved the stump at the camera.

The Timex Triathlon watch on Chuck Anderson's right wrist beeped at 5:15 a.m. It was June 9, 2000, and he had a date at Gulf Shores with triathlon buddies. He wanted to stay in bed but finally thought "the heck with it" and got up. If he wimped out, he'd never hear the end of it.

He liked those training swims in the gulf. They were challenging. They were macho. In the gulf, there is no black line on the bottom to follow. In big waves, you swallow water. In turbid water, you fight your fear of drowning, of swimming into a raft of jellyfish, of the unspeakable appetites of big fish.

He parked at the Pink Pony pub, a landmark on the beach. He was early. So were two other athletes. They decided to do a short swim while waiting for the rest of the gang to arrive.

Richard Watley swam out first. Soon he was swimming along the beach 200 yards out. Anderson and Karen Forfar swam together about 150 yards offshore. Anderson was a strong swimmer, but Forfar was better. She forged ahead.

Anderson glanced at his Timex: 6:38 a.m. He and Karen would swim for another seven minutes before joining the main party of triathletes on the beach. Then they'd swim their regular 1.25 miles.

It was a windy morning. Bruise-colored clouds scudded across the sky. In the high waves Anderson tried not to swallow the gulf.

Something very large and very heavy smashed into his thigh. It hit so hard he was nearly blasted out of the water.

He yelled with all his might at whatever was below him to "STOP! STOP! STOP! NO, NO, NO!" as if his tormentor were a bad dog. Then he shouted for Karen to get out of the water.

His first impulse was to swim toward shore like an Olympian. Then he thought better of it. If something was approaching, he wanted to see it coming.

He floated on his back, pointed his head toward shore and kicked and paddled. Nothing. He ducked under the water for a fast look. Through his goggles he saw a dark shape emerging from the gloom.

He stuck out his right arm to fend it off.

He felt contact, but no pain despite the blood in the water. He stared at his hand in disbelief. Only the thumb remained. Beseeching God in one breath and shrieking profanities in the next, he managed to paddle toward shore. He took another peek in the water. Too late. The shark rushed up and bit him on the stomach before vanishing into the murk. Shore seemed a long way off.

The beast came up 20 yards away. It swam straight for him, dorsal slicing the water like something out of *Jaws*. The former quarterback tried a stiff arm. His arm ended up inside the shark's maw. The shark dragged him 15 feet to the bottom, shaking him the whole way. He wondered if he'd see his kids again.

The shark surfaced with him in its jaws. Then a miracle.

The shark, about 8 feet long, sped toward the beach. Anderson felt like he was water skiing. His heels dragged bottom. Man and beast stopped. Anderson lay on his back on a sandbar with the 300-pound bogeyman crushing his right side. He was afraid the shark was going to bite off his face. At least it would have to release his arm first.

The shark wouldn't let go. As it began wiggling free of the sandbar, Anderson staggered to his feet and tried to reclaim the limb. He jerked on the arm three times, adrenaline masking the pain, but the shark hung on.

He hauled on his arm with all his might, using his back like a landscaper trying to uproot a dead hibiscus. A surgeon later described what happened as "degloving." The skin and muscle below the elbow were raked off the bone by the teeth.

Anderson heard a loud pop. The shark had just bitten off his hand.

He tumbled backward as he fell free. He somehow got up and lumbered through the shallows to the beach. He glanced at the bare bone and decided he wouldn't look again. Karen Forfar, his swimming buddy, took a long look and screamed. "Next time I do a triathlon," Anderson gasped, "I'll be in the physically challenged division."

He told her he was going to bleed to death if he didn't get a tourniquet. The sixty-two-year-old woman began peeling off her one-piece bathing suit, but a construction worker came by and offered his shirt instead. Out in the gulf, Richard Watley, the last triathlete in the water, was on his way in, oblivious. As he approached the sandbar, the bull shark bit him on the knee and buttocks. Bleeding, Watley jogged out of the water and reclined on a bench near his buddy.

The ambulance arrived. Watley's injuries weren't serious. Examining Anderson, paramedics radioed for a helicopter. "He's lost a lot of blood," a paramedic said. Anderson heard everything. He never fainted.

It was too overcast and windy for a helicopter to land. The patient arrived at South Baldwin Hospital in the ambulance. In the operating room, Dr. John Rodriguez-Feo completed the amputation, staunched the bleeding, and reattached muscle. Happy to be alive, Anderson in upcoming weeks enjoyed serenading nurses with that Jimmy Buffett song.

"Fins."

"I don't blame the shark," he told friends. "It was just being a shark. In fact, I feel sorry for it. That shark is going to have to wake up every morning at 5:15 when my Timex starts beeping."

He focused on learning how to live without his arm. His wife, Betsy, helped him button his pants. She tied his shoes. At least nobody expected him to wear a tie to work.

He relied on his teeth to do a lot of the work.

"If I lose my teeth I'm in trouble," he told Betsy.

He told his wife he wasn't going to quit triathlons. She wasn't surprised. After all, he had gone for a 3-mile walk his first day out of the hospital.

Physical therapist Jennifer Davis agreed that having a goal might help her patient. "The clients who are afraid to climb back onto the horse never seem to fully recover," she said. "It's the passionate people who do well. Chuck had this passion about doing another triathlon."

At first, Davis encouraged him to move what remained of his arm. When he could do it without grimacing, she attached weights to the stump. Muscle appeared. Initially he couldn't swim a lap in the pool without exhaustion. Soon he could swim sixty. Davis modified a swim paddle to fit the stump. Now he swam fast, like Tarzan.

He wouldn't embarrass himself in front of the other athletes.

On April 21, 2001, ten months after his injury, he showed up at the Mullet-Man Triathlon in Florabama, held at the border of the two states. His friends were overjoyed to see him. The national media was in attendance. He tried to put aside his fear when the starter's gun sounded.

He ran 4 miles in twenty-eight minutes and pedaled 16 miles in forty-eight. He covered a quarter mile in the gulf in less than six minutes. He finished first in the over-200-pound division of the triathlon.

Hundreds of people slapped his back, saluted his courage, pumped his left hand.

He hated every second of a swim that had once brought him pleasure.

He and Betsy divorced in 2002. "What happened to me was much harder on my family than on me," Anderson told friends. Betsy, who had never smoked, died of lung cancer two years later.

Their children tried to cope with their mother's death and what had happened to their dad. Their son, Sam, confronted one fear by hanging posters of bull sharks in his room. Laura, their daughter, eventually had the courage to dip her toes into the gulf.

"My theory is that something like this could never happen twice to people from the same family," she told friends.

Her dad kept competing in triathlons. In 2004, while swimming in a race in Mobile Bay, he felt like something awful was about to happen.

WHAM!

Something large and ominously heavy crashed into his head. He stopped dead in the water and screamed for help. It wasn't a bull shark.

It was a log.

He finished the race, but hated the panic and the fact a lifeguard had

Chuck Anderson. Photo by Laura Anderson.

helped calm him down. He decided he was sick of triathlons. "I've done enough of them," he told friends.

In 2005, he changed his mind. He'd confront his fears. He trained hard for the annual Sandestin Triathlon held in the Florida Panhandle in August. He felt his strength and confidence return.

A month before the race, Jaimie Daigle, fourteen, was paddling a boogie board in the gulf near Destin when a bull shark grabbed her. She bled to death.

Two days later, Craig Hutto, sixteen, was wade fishing for spotted sea trout in the gulf near Apalachicola. A bull shark mutilated his leg, which had to be amputated at the hospital. Anderson decided not to do the triathlon.

I asked if we could drive over to Gulf Shores, where the bad thing had happened to him. Pelicans bobbed in the rough gulf beyond the breakers, and bathers crowded the shallows behind the Pink Pony on E Beach Boulevard. Jimmy Buffett was on the jukebox, and it sounded like "Fins" at first, but turned out to be that sturdy beach-bar anthem "Margaritaville."

The guy who called himself Lefty looked out at the water. Then we walked down the sidewalk as he looked for the bench.

The blood-stained bench where he had rested his mutilated body summers ago was gone. For years the bench had served as a macabre tourist attraction. Hurricane Ivan finally washed it away.

Now there was no sign of what had happened to him on the Gulf of Mexico beach, no sign of the bull shark that had gotten hungry.

June 25, 2006

LIVING AND DYING

29

ARCADIA

Al and Karen Smoke

In an iPod world, Karen and Al Smoke were as old-fashioned as their windup Victrola. Every morning, before Al made the bed, he cranked up the Victrola Player Tone, as it was known, and listened to one of his scratchy 78-rpm long-playing discs. He made the bed while serenaded by Irving Kaufman warbling "I'm All Bound 'Round with the Mason-Dixon Line," which had been recorded during the silent-film era.

After supper, as the chuck-will's-widows began their nightly symphony out in the woods, Karen weaved a rug in the living room and talked to Al, who listened because he knew it was good for him. When they got married two decades ago, the first thing she did was ferry him to the urologist. "He had six kids by his first wife," she told me the day I visited in 2006. "Enough damage. I had him fixed."

Al was seventy-six, and Karen was fifty-five. They lived in a little house on the Peace River, more than a mile from the nearest paved road. Their idea of happiness wasn't owning a lot of new stuff. It was about living as comfortably and simply as possible.

They survived life in Florida without a telephone. They did without air-conditioning. They got their power from solar panels, so they never wrote a check to the electric company. Thoreau would have understood.

"Our life is frittered away by detail," he wrote in *Walden*. "An honest man has hardly need to count more than his ten fingers."

When the Peace River flooded, the Smokes got around by canoe.

"Simplicity, simplicity, simplicity," Thoreau wrote.

In 1854.

I tried to imagine Thoreau in the twenty-first century, fidgeting behind the wheel of his Prius while creeping through Tampa on I-275 at rush hour. Talk about the mass of men—and women—living lives of quiet desperation. Honk, honk, honk! Modern desperation is seldom quiet.

As our lives become more complicated, most of us yearn for simplicity. We think of buying a little place in the country, a weekend place at first, somewhere we can retire. We'll give away our useless possessions. We'll grow tomatoes, tackle *Ulysses*, turn off the phone. Especially turn off the phone. Turn off the television, too. Breathe deeply, watch the birds, talk to our spouse. Maybe play Parcheesi.

That's the dream anyhow. But the fact is, most of us probably would lose our sanity without modernity, without air-conditioning, without *American Idol* on the big-screen plasma, without the canary yellow SUV to tote the kids to soccer practice. Speaking of kids, yours just came into the house to show off the new tattoo and ask for a hot pink cell phone for her birthday.

A kindly neighbor once offered Thoreau a doormat.

"It is best to avoid the beginnings of evil," he said.

The Smokes met in rural New Jersey, where Karen ran a printing press and Al repaired machinery at the same company. They got married and moved to Miami when their company did. Miami has many charms, but the Smokes found the exotic city too busy and crowded. Al had grown up on a dairy farm, and Karen had been one of those girls who never played with dolls. "I liked frogs and snakes."

They began saving money for retirement and a move elsewhere. One day, Al witnessed a triple shooting. He told Karen, "Let's get out of here." They had discovered the Peace River on a camping trip. They bought a couple of acres near a bend in the river outside Arcadia in 1985.

They pitched a tent and began their labor.

Here is something I learned about the Smokes when I visited. They could do practically anything with their hands. When Al was in the navy, he was considered the sailor with the highest mechanical aptitude aboard the aircraft carrier. Karen was an able plumber, seamstress, quilter, mechanic. She wasn't afraid of electrical work. A chain saw was an extension of her arms.

Karen and Al Smoke. Photo by Jeff Klinkenberg.

There were no roads into their property, so they carried supplies in by canoe. They opened a road between pines with chain saws. Al rented a bulldozer and cleared land for the house. They built it on stilts. It has two levels. The only room with walls is the bathroom. Otherwise, there are no partitions to block breezes. The house has about 1,200 square feet of space, a 22-foot ceiling, and twenty-six windows. Sunlight never falls upon the windows because of the eaves, verandas, and screened porch.

They cook with propane. They have a wood-burning stove in the living room.

They have their own well and pump. They have a composting toilet. They were among Florida's solar-energy pioneers. Al bought twenty-two used solar panels and a dozen used batteries. They crank out 13.2 volts for their house.

At night, Al enjoyed strumming a battered Martin guitar—acoustic, of course—by the glow of an electric lamp. Karen read her beloved books. She got most of them from the library in Arcadia, though she owns several copies of her favorite book, *Cross Creek*. She identified with author Marjorie Kinnan Rawlings, an independent, tough-talkin', solidly built gal who gave up city life to live in the Florida backwoods with few luxuries.

Mail was virtually the only way the Smokes communicated with the outside world.

They owned a television, a 13-inch, 12-volt Sansui purchased at a truck stop. It had a color picture. "Look at this," Al said demonstrating the primitive antenna. "I can tune in about six stations." In the evening he watched the weather report and *Antiques Roadshow*. On weekends, the Smokes listened to *Prairie Home Companion* on radio while Karen worked on a quilt.

"When they made a movie about *Prairie Home Companion* a few months back, we thought about driving to Sarasota and seeing it," Al said. They never got around to it. Last movie they saw, in an actual theater, was *Close Encounters of the Third Kind* when they lived in Miami. In 1977.

People were always wondering what the Smokes missed about city life.

When asked, they'd become quiet, look at each other, work hard at giving a good answer. The real answer turned out to be: nothing. When something important happened, they found out about it eventually.

They didn't hear about September 11, 2001, until September 13.

They didn't hear about the space shuttle disaster until the next day, when Karen's dad drove out to tell them.

During another visit, her dad suffered a massive heart attack. The Smokes had no way of dialing 911, so they put the frail old man in their 1983 VW bus and sped toward Arcadia. He died on the way.

They still missed him, but they consoled themselves with the thought that he had died in their company and never had to be connected to tubes or wires at the hospital.

The Smokes didn't run out and buy a phone. "We know some people who have gone mainstream," Karen said. "They've bought a cell phone."

They skinny-dipped in an old cattle trough to cool off, though I only had their word for it. They bathed in an outdoor shower.

They grew collards, kale, broccoli, green beans, and okra. They gave up on tomatoes, squash, and melons because of the mildew. They grew grapes, bananas, grapefruit, oranges, and tangerines. They grew persimmons. Al liked to eat peanut-butter-and-persimmon sandwiches.

Sometimes they entertained guests for lunch. Karen expected them to clean their plates. "If I take the trouble to prepare the food, that's what I expect." She'll ask, "Don't you like my food?" I was careful to reach for seconds.

They seldom ate meat. Karen said, "We can't afford it." They lived below the poverty line. Al received a $900 Social Security stipend every month. They had a little money in the bank. He devoted thirty-five years to his company before retiring, but it declared bankruptcy and he had lost his pension.

In the 1990s, the Smokes started a business to tide them over. They called it the Non-Electric Toy Co. They made playthings for children out of wood. Al did most of the work by hand, though a generator powered a few tools. The minute he fired up the generator, Karen tossed clothes in the washing machine. They used God's own air to dry their tattered clothing.

Al played marbles as a kid. Why couldn't modern children? One toy, Marble Race, boasted a series of ramps that transported marbles from start to finish line. Another Rube Goldberg device featured a series of levers and doohickeys and thingamajigs. It moved marbles down a ramp to a box at the bottom. Their most expensive toy, which I couldn't find at Wal-Mart, was priced at $29.

They sold virtually all their toys by mail. They'd drive to Arcadia in their 1949 Hudson and scavenge cardboard boxes from the supermarket. They packed their toys in those boxes and shipped them away. Every once in a while, they sold their wares at craft shows, just enough to attract some mail orders. Al told me that a small business had requested one hundred marble machines. Al had to explain that he lacked an assembly line. He and Karen made toys one at a time. After two weeks they'd finished twenty-three toys.

In their most profitable year, the Smokes made $5,000.

Hurricane Charley barreled through central Florida in 2004. The Smokes watched the storm coming up the river toward them on their television.

They didn't have to watch television to know it had arrived. The house shook, but no windows broke.

Through the windows they saw huge oaks going down, saw branches flying. It took them a long time to clean up. Three other tropical storms followed in the next few weeks. Their house became an ark. Alligators snoozed below their deck. Armadillos looked at their porch with envy.

For a while, a trip to town involved paddling a canoe more than a mile through the woods to where they had parked their car on the pavement. "Of course, we never lost electricity," Al said, playing with his mustache. "The solar panels gave us what we needed. And we cook by gas. Getting by day to day was no problem."

The Smokes liked to think they lived in paradise. But in the twenty-first century, living simply was getting complicated. The Smokes had invested more sweat than money when they built their house. They estimated it to be worth at least $35,000.

In 2006, they were spending a third of their income on home insurance. The Smokes discussed the possibility of one of them getting a job in Arcadia, about 10 miles away. Karen said she might enjoy working in the library. Then she changed her mind and said, "I would rather stay in the woods."

They watch red-shouldered hawks and otters. Every once in a while their chickens started squawking, and they checked the coop for bobcats, foxes, and rat snakes. Rat snakes liked to eat chicken eggs.

Pig frogs grunted like wild hogs. At night, barred owls went "Hoo-hoo a-hoo. Hoo-hoo a-hoo aw."

As the years went by, modern Florida more and more was intruding on their simplicity.

On weekends, campers often canoed to the bank on the other side of their river. The Smokes heard them, the shouts, the music—what did you call it? Rap, maybe, industrial music. Anyway, there was lots of deep bass pounding across the river, pounding through the woods to their house.

"Drunken orgies," Al said of the campers. "I've seen people having sex on the riverbank."

Karen had yet to be so lucky.

"But I saw these guys standing on the riverbank, seeing who could pee the farthest," she said.

Those guys with weak bladders should have counted their blessings. Karen must have been in a good mood the day she watched them.

She didn't burst out of the woods brandishing her chain saw.

September 21, 2006

30

BRADENTON

Going Barefoot

The smartest guy I met during the summer of 2004 was Jim Desorbo. Hot and miserable weather had put the rest of us in bad temper, but not him. He was calm and cool, dressed casually for the season, careful to avoid a ridiculous coat and tie, and, whenever possible, shoes.

"No better place in the world than Florida to go barefoot," he told me on that steamy Saturday. "I love the feeling of the ground under my feet, and I love the sense of freedom. Freedom is what this country is all about."

A forty-five-year-old pharmacist, he usually wore tasseled loafers to his place of business in Sarasota. Then off they came. He reckoned that 80 percent of his waking hours were spent with feet deliciously free of leather. "I'm not a weirdo," he explained. "In fact, I consider myself pretty normal from the ankles up."

I wondered about his encounters with the shoe police. "They happen," he admitted. The shoe police included the high-heeled shopper in Publix who noticed his bare tootsies and announced her disgust, and the welcomer at a Wal-Mart who suggested he would be more welcome wearing something other than skin on his size elevens. Another shoe sheriff, it turned out, was his wife, Michelle, who required that her husband wear shoes to church and other formal gatherings, at least when he accompanied her.

He complied, though he sometimes employed stealth footwear: a pair of ragged boat shoes that boasted everything but a sole. "When I wear them, it's a rush. I feel like I'm getting away with something," he said.

Freedom's just another word for nothing left to shoe.

"A lot of people have closed minds," Jim Desorbo lamented. When Floridians thought of bare feet, the image that came to mind was that of flower children, Janis Joplin hippie girls, long-haired Abbie Hoffman hippie guys with dirty feet. Pot smokers! Free-love advocates! Liberals!

"I'm not a radical," Desorbo said. "I'm not an exhibitionist. I don't have a foot fetish. I'm just a guy who enjoys going barefoot in Florida."

He had grown up near Albany, in a New York valley named after an ancient Mohawk tribe whose members kept their moccasins handy all year. When Desorbo was a boy, barefoot season lasted a couple months if he was lucky.

Of course, it was different in post–World War II Florida, where kids often spent three seasons with feet gloriously bare. With their calluses thick and yellow, shoeless children routinely crossed smoldering parking lots without flinching. Adventuresome youngsters scampered up coconut trees like monkeys, bare feet clinging to rough bark. Even more depressing than returning to school in September was returning to the habit of wearing shoes for even part of the day.

In the twenty-first century, Florida kids were meticulously shod, wearing shoes everywhere but to bed and perhaps the swimming pool. Nervous parents fretted about hot pavement, glass, sprinkler heads, and what the neighbors might say.

It was enough to make Desorbo's feet start sweating. Migrating to Florida in 1984, he began making up for lost barefoot time in 1999. At first he did without shoes inside his house. Soon he was ambling sans shoes around his Manatee County subdivision. The outside world, with its scorpions, fire ants, and rusty nails, beckoned.

"The first time I walked across a parking lot during summer, I blistered the bottom of my feet," Desorbo said. "Then I learned the trick. Walk on the paint; it's cooler there. Roll your feet outward and walk on the edges. Of course, I have pretty thick calluses now. It's not that big of a problem."

For folks who considered bare feet their Nikes, public relations was the larger problem. Initially, Desorbo and his naked feet were self-conscious. A rude stare threw him for a loop. Then he discovered the Society for Barefoot Living. The Society for Barefoot Living was established by a computer software writer named Paul Lucas in California in 1994. "I wanted to see if there were more people like me," Lucas wrote to me in an e-mail. There were.

The society claimed more than one thousand members. The Florida chapter, with thirty-six devotees, was among the largest in the United States. The main club benefit was information through its Web site. For example, club members learn that there is no law, in any state, specifically forbidding driving a motor vehicle with bare feet. In the glove compartment of his SUV, Desorbo carried a letter from the Florida Highway Safety and Motor Vehicle Department stating the facts, just in case. In his wallet he carried another letter, from Florida's Department of Business and Professional Regulation, explaining the law as it pertains to bare feet and businesses. Basically, there is no state law, though stores and restaurants can set their own rules.

"If I go into a restaurant and somebody says I can't because there's a law, they're wrong," Desorbo said. "But if that's the restaurant's policy, I'm polite and never make a scene."

He hadn't missed a meal. He kept a pair of restaurant-friendly flip-flops in his car for emergencies. If the restaurant was hoity-toity, he wore his soleless shoes and tried not to giggle.

Barefoot men have barefoot heroes. They include the philosopher Socrates, who walked around ancient Athens asking embarrassing questions until he was made to swallow poison. John Chapman, aka Johnny Appleseed, traipsed across Ohio wearing a sack but no shoes. Abraham Lincoln relaxed in the White House by taking off his shoes and letting his tortured feet draw breath. In 1960, Abebe Bikila ran a marathon over Rome's cobblestone streets in bare feet and won the Olympics.

When Desorbo exercised, he wore shoes because his gym required it. When he rode his bike, however, the pedals were caressed by bare skin. During a hiking trip to the Georgia mountains, bare feet did nicely, thank you. "There were some sharp rocks under the leaves, so I had to go slower," he said. "But basically it was no sweat."

Bare feet do sweat, by the way, but they seldom stink. Smelly feet are caused by hot, enclosing shoes. For the same reason, Desorbo never worries about athlete's foot.

A public bathroom? Look for a handicapped stall.

"They are cleaner. I figure most handicapped men or people sit more than stand when urinating."

A filthy gas station urinal? Not the end of the world to a barefooted man. Urine, Desorbo learned from the Society for Barefoot Living Web site, was not a toxic waste product: It is 95 percent water, 2.5 percent urea, and 2.5 percent minerals, salt, and enzymes. When a barefooted person stepped in dog droppings, he knew immediately and didn't drag it into the house.

"I haven't stepped on glass," Desorbo said. "My feet are so tough that sandspurs don't even bother me anymore. Worst thing that happened was I tore a nail off bumping a shopping cart wheel in Publix."

He waited until the parking lot to launch a scream. Didn't want to hear somebody remark, "What did you expect, stupid?"

He wore shoes when he bowled and wore skates when he visited the ice rink, but he refused to wear socks with the athletic footware. He showed me his spectacularly barren sock drawer. He didn't own a single pair.

He bragged about the ease of flying. Last time he took a plane, he ambled around Tampa International Airport without shoes, and nobody complained. At the security gate, nobody had to instruct him to take off his shoes for inspection.

"But when I was walking on the plane, the flight attendant told me I needed shoes. I had my flip-flops ready. Took them off when I sat down. It was no big deal."

July 27, 2004

31

ST. PETERSBURG

Tommy

The person who manned the takeout line where I bought lunch in St. Petersburg was a guy everybody knew as Tommy. Tommy was a muscular, baby-faced man in his early twenties with jet black hair and pale green eyes. Much of his body was covered by tattoos, including ones he did himself when he made a living as a tattoo artist. When I got to know him in 2003, he was taking college art classes at night. He had talent.

At the cafeteria where he worked the noontime shift, he enjoyed joshing with customers. Usually his customers joshed back, though sometimes they looked at the tattoos on those big arms and didn't know what to make of him.

I was famished after a long bike ride and stopped at Tommy's station for lunch. I ordered pasta. What he put in my takeout carton was so modest I raised my eyebrows in protest.

"Don't worry," he said. "You get a side dish with that."

"Well, I hope so," I said.

He gave me a look and laughed.

"Hey, man!" he said. "Happy Hanukkah."

I'm not Jewish, but I recognized an anti-Semitic "Jews are cheap" remark when I heard one.

"What do you mean by that?" I bristled.

"Hey, man," he said, throwing up his hands. "I'm not going there."

But we did end up going there.

Back at the office, and later at home, I fumed. The more I thought about it, the more my "harrumph" seemed inadequate.

We have all heard racist and anti-Semitic jokes. And like many of us, I have found it easier to walk away than to make a big stink. Of course, if you know right from wrong, walking away is cowardly.

This time I felt the need to do something. Then I talked myself out of it. I was scared to confront Tommy and put off visiting him for days. Then one morning it just happened. I went into the cafeteria for coffee and there he was when I stepped through the doors. Tommy wiped his hands on his apron and walked over to see what I wanted. Gulping, staring at his tattoos, I told him why I'd come. He didn't flinch.

"Yeah, I remember it," he said in a low voice. "I'm really sorry. The second I said those words, I knew I'd said something stupid and that I was wrong. I try to be funny; sometimes I try to make light of things, but I don't think enough before talking. That wasn't funny. I'm really sorry."

His response caught me off guard; I guess I thought he'd deny any responsibility. After all, that's what everybody seems to do these days. Tommy apologized again, and we got to talking.

He told me he was twenty-four, a high school dropout who left home at sixteen but later got his degree after taking the General Educational Development test. Now he was attending college and working to support himself.

I was fascinated by those tattoos. I asked about the "Tommy Boy" tattoo on his wrist. "I did that one myself. A pretty girl held my hand while I did it so it didn't hurt much. I should have gotten her phone number."

But he forgot.

"You know something," he said, noticing my interest, "people who have tattoos aren't treated the same as other people. The other day these ladies came up for food in my line. One of them was holding this book. I asked what she was reading. It was the Bible. I asked what chapter. She looked a little suspicious at me but told me 'Galatians.' I said, "Oh, yeah! That was one of Paul's letters.' The lady said, 'YOU KNOW the Bible?' Sure I know the Bible. I guess if you have tattoos, you can't know anything about the Bible. Right? I guess I know a little about prejudice."

But Tommy, and people like me, probably needed to know more. I asked Tommy if he wanted to go for a walk.

We walked over to the Florida Holocaust Museum at 55 Fifth Street S in St. Petersburg. It's across the street from where I work, but I'd never visited. I asked Tommy if he wanted to go inside. Perhaps he was more open-minded than he might have seemed at first.

"I'd love to," he said.

When you enter the museum, you know right away that everything is different. Because the world is full of crazies, you can't visit without an encounter with security guards. The guards stared at Tommy's black clothing and his tattoos. But I was the one carrying a pocket knife. I left it at the security desk.

The museum was filled with schoolchildren. The museum was quiet except for the low, calm voice of a tour guide, an older man named Sandy who asked the kids, "Do I look like a Jew?" The kids didn't know how to answer. Sandy pointed to a photograph of a Gestapo guard using calipers to measure a human nose. "If your nose was a certain size then, that meant you had to be a Jew," Sandy said. For the record, Sandy, who is Jewish, had a small nose.

I felt like crying. When you go into this museum, you feel like crying. I looked at Tommy's baby face, at his eyes both large and wet, for a reaction. "How strong did these people have to be?" he whispered. "How strong did they have to be just to get up and keep on going?"

We examined another photograph. In the picture, hundreds of Jewish prisoners were lined up next to a deep trench. Ideally, they would fall cleanly into the trench after they were shot. That way the bulldozers could get to work and the guards wouldn't bloody their hands during the burial.

"Oh, God!" Tommy whispered.

Tommy was born in Miami but never knew his mother and dad. He told me about his adoptive parents. He liked them well enough, he said, but they were insensitive to his desire to be an artist. "Of course, they'd have their own story, but we don't get along. I felt I had to get out. They didn't think art was a good career."

I asked Tommy about his former line of work. "Not enough art in it," he whispered. "Usually, somebody would come in and pick a tattoo pattern—we had these patterns on the wall—and that's what you had to do. No creativity. Well, maybe sometimes. One time this guy came in, a skinhead, and wanted me to do these white supremacist things. I said 'No way, man.' But he kept telling me that's what he wanted. I said, 'You go outside with those things, somebody is going to kick your ass.' But I ended up doing the tattoos. God! That was stupid, too. Now I wish I hadn't."

The centerpiece of the Holocaust Museum is a dilapidated boxcar. Officially, it is known as Auschwitz Boxcar #113 0695–5. Brought here from Europe, the boxcar had room enough for 40 people. But guards routinely loaded it with 140 men, women, and children. Some suffocated right away. Others died along the route with the smell of urine, vomit, and fecal matter in their nostrils.

"Try to imagine what it was like," Tommy whispered to me. "They're in that boxcar. They're terrified. They're sick. They're saying to themselves 'It can't get any worse. It can't get any worse.' But, of course, it did. The real horror began when the boxcar arrived at the death camp."

Tommy suddenly looked excited. "I'm an artist," he said. "I have to get this out. I see this as a charcoal drawing. I want to come back and draw this."

The following week, Tommy became a regular at the Holocaust Museum. He sat in front of the boxcar with his pad and his charcoal and sketched. He'd show me his work every day, and it looked perfect to me, but not to him. He saw only the flaws—no, he told me, he didn't have it, not quite yet, but soon, he promised me, soon, just give me another day, and he'd go back for another round.

Every day, after a few hours of serving buttered grits or pasta or fried chicken at the restaurant, he'd walk over to the museum for another try. Sitting in front of the boxcar, listening to hip-hop on his headphones, he worked on his Holocaust drawing.

Finally he finished his sketch and gave it to me. He signed it, which is how I learned his full name, Thomas G. Mandzik.

"I'm worried that people who read about me might think I'm Hitler's child because of something dumb I said without thinking," he said. "I would hate for that to happen."

I would hate for that to happen, too. First impressions—well, you know. They aren't what they're cracked up to be.

"You know what?" he told me the other day as he served me lunch. "I think they should take people who are truly anti-Semitic to the Holocaust Museum and make them look at that boxcar. I mean it. Make them sit down and look at it for an hour. The really hateful people, they should put inside. Make them stand inside that boxcar and feel what it was like."

April 27, 2003

32

ELLENTON

Freedom Riders

Winonah Myers, a gray-haired contrarian of sixty-four, woke before dawn. Then she drove her yellow Ford pickup through Bradenton to the Sunshine Skyway Bridge and collected tolls. The best part of her job was watching the sun come up over Tampa Bay. The worst part was feeling perpetually sleepy and having to work in the cramped dimensions of a tollbooth.

She had bad memories of tight spaces. When she was nineteen, she spent much of a year in the most notorious lockup in the South, Mississippi State Prison, better known as Parchman Farm. The gas chamber was a few cells away from her death row cubicle. At night she whispered through the ventilation system to an inmate who later was executed. "I was a little baby when I was in prison," she told me in 2006. "I was scared to death."

On June 9, 1961, Myers and four other young civil rights activists, some black and some white, walked into a train station in Jackson, ignored the "colored" waiting room, and took their seats in the "white" waiting room. They were quickly arrested for breaching the peace.

Myers and her friends were known as Freedom Riders. A U.S. Supreme Court decision had prohibited segregation at interstate public transportation facilities—at airports, train, and bus stations—but the law was ignored in the Deep South. People of color were supposed to know their place, no matter what federal judges said.

Freedom Riders, including white people like Myers, challenged the tradition by drawing worldwide attention to the reality of southern living. They got themselves arrested. Then they clogged the jails. Eventually the government was embarrassed into enforcing the law.

Freedom Riders David and Winonah Myers. Photo by Bob Croslin.

Before the year was out, nearly four hundred Freedom Riders had been arrested. Many served brief jail sentences and happily got out. Not Myers, who stubbornly refused bail, refused even to file an appeal. Jailed on June 11, she stayed behind bars until Christmas Day.

Of all the Freedom Riders, white or black, she served the longest sentence.

You know what she liked best about winter on Tampa Bay? White pelicans. Visitors from the North, they migrate to Tampa Bay in late fall and remain until spring. Some mornings the gargantuan birds, larger than their common brown cousins, flew over her toll booth on their way to the feeding grounds. She could also see white pelicans from her mobile home on the Manatee River. Myers and her husband, David, often lounged at their dining room table and admired them through a big picture window.

Growing up in Ohio, Winonah appreciated nature, too. After prison, she worshipped it. "The sky," she told me. "The fresh air. The birds."

The story of the Freedom Riders for years served as a footnote to the civil rights movement. New generations learned about Rosa Parks, lunch-counter boycotts, and Dr. Martin Luther King Jr., but the achievements of the Freedom Riders often slipped through the cracks. But a new book by University of South Florida historian Raymond Arsenault had changed their status. As *Freedom Riders: 1961 and the Struggle for Racial Justice* received national attention, so did the men and women who were participants. Winonah was in the book. So was her husband, David, sixty-five in 2006. He had been a Freedom Rider, too.

About half the Freedom Riders were white and half African-American. Many were college students, preachers, and attorneys. David Myers was twenty-one, a poor Indiana farm boy and among the few white students enrolled at Central State University in Ohio. Winonah had grown up in poverty in Cleveland. She ended up at Central State because it was inexpensive.

"It was an exciting time to be alive," she told me when I visited their mobile home near Bradenton. "There was all this idealism. There was the Peace Corps. There was VISTA. There was the space program. There was John F. Kennedy and Martin Luther King. Life was full of possibilities."

David Myers was a handsome upperclassman, excited about making the world a better place, excited about the civil rights movement, excited about dating Winonah—Winonah Beamer then—who shared his idealism. From the moment they met, he knew they would end up together. At their dining room table, with their cat, Moe, on her lap so many years later, she said, "Oh, please. You never said anything to me."

"Well, I meant to," he said.

History happened first.

David Myers was a talker in 1961. He was a dreamer. Almost a half century later, the wide-eyed boy had heart disease and diabetes, but he still rode his Honda motorcycle every day. He still liked to canoe. And he enjoyed good conversation. He talked too fast and seldom stayed seated more than a minute at a time. Among mainstream civil rights activists, Freedom Riders were initially seen as radicals, or fools. It was considered suicidal for black men and white women, or white men and black women, to travel together into the heart of Klan country as if they were friends or even intimates.

John F. Kennedy had been elected president in a close race, thanks in part to black voters casting ballots for the first time. Kennedy felt beholden to them, but he was also loath to antagonize conservative white southern voters. Meanwhile, the Soviets were active in Berlin and Cuba. The last thing the Kennedy administration wanted was another racial crisis in the South. But that's what it got.

On May 4, Freedom Riders boarded a bus in Washington, destination Deep South. In South Carolina, the Klansmen waited with clenched fists. While visiting his family home on Mother's Day, David read in the paper about a Freedom Ride in Alabama where activists were beaten with pipes as they fled a burning bus. David told his mom he wanted to be a Freedom Rider. "This has to be done."

"But not by my boy," she said.

Over in Ohio, Winonah was having a similar conversation with her mother. They became Freedom Riders about a week apart. David first.

On May 28, Myers and seven other Freedom Riders boarded a Trailways bus in Montgomery, Alabama. It was escorted by federal troops and law enforcement officials into Mississippi. David remembers thinking he might be killed, but nobody approached the bus. Still, the moment they walked into the bus station in Jackson, they were arrested for breaching the peace.

They pleaded no contest and were pronounced guilty. Myers served thirty-two days, mostly in city and county jails. He remembers the experience as fairly pleasant. He shared a cell with sixteen other white men—even in jail the races were segregated. The food was unappetizing, but conversations were grand.

Jail keepers allowed the national press in for a visit. David was flattered to grant an interview to the famous columnist Westbrook Pegler.

Naive, David didn't know that Pegler had come south to discredit the Freedom Riders. Pegler lamented that "bands of insipid futilities of the type called bleeding hearts" were giving Jackson, Mississippi, a bad name. Working himself into a tizzy, Pegler complained about Myers and his "wispy whiskers and the start of beatnik sideburns" and his Quaker background. "His soul suffered at the thought that someone (God, of necessity) had created a difference between him and his black brethren." Pegler was so angry he wrote about Freedom Riders a week later. "They wouldn't fight anybody for anything, but they didn't think it wrong of them to affront a local social system and kick up riots and civil war with painful, even fatal results."

Eventually David and other inmates transferred to Parchman, a prison where inmates often picked cotton by day. Life was especially trying for black inmates, historically punished with lashings from the whip known as "Black Annie." The famous bluesmen Leadbelly, Bukka White, and Son House had been inmates during the 1930s; Leadbelly's famous "Midnight Special" is about life there.

After an uneventful week, David was returned to the county jail and a few days later was released.

Winonah's ordeal was only beginning.

Winonah, when I visited her and David, was usually quiet at first. Quiet—and taciturn. She'd listen for a while, maybe as she ate, as David and I spoke. She'd cock her head as she took in the bushwa, then interjected a sharp remark, accompanied, perhaps, by a swear word. Eventually the sentences poured out.

On June 9, 1961, she and four Freedom Riders boarded an Illinois Central train in Nashville and got off in Jackson. As she remembered it, hardly anyone took notice in the station except city police captain J. L. Ray. When she mimics him even now, he comes off sounding like the white sheriff of *In the Heat of the Night*. "You in a heap a trouble, now. Git up and move on."

Nobody in the train station budged.

"I said git up and move on."

Nobody budged.

"You cain't set here. Ah'm arresting you for breach of peace."

Winonah told me she tried to practice "forgive and forget," but her tone suggested otherwise.

The sheriff escorted everybody to Hinds County Jail. Twenty inmates were housed in a cell intended for eight. Ten days later the women were trucked to Parchman.

"Female guards strip-searched us. There wasn't a place they missed if you know what I mean. I was scared to death. They took us to the maximum security unit—at the other end of the hallway was death row and the gas chamber. Two of us shared a cell 6 feet by 9 feet, but that included a toilet and a sink and two beds. We never got out of the cell to exercise. We got to shower twice a week. This was summer with no air-conditioning. You got two minutes to shower before the water went off automatically.

"A lot of the other inmates, I mean the Freedom Riders, were kind of, pardon my French, bitches. They wanted to control every minute and every hour of every day. Our leaders wanted us to exercise in our cells, all together, do ballet pliés, jumping jacks, you name it. Somebody in another cell would shout out French lessons. Somebody else lectured on Greek and Roman mythology. Then we'd have to sing. My cellmate would say, 'Winonah isn't singing.'

"One girl had an asthma attack. The other girls began chanting in unison 'E-MER-GEN-CEE!' I could see the guards laughing, so I just grabbed the bars and rattled my cage, made such a racket they had to come out. They took the sick girl away and some of the other girls were mad at me. They said the way I had rattled the cage was uncivilized. I didn't care what they thought. And after that they left me alone. I didn't mind solitude.

"We had only the Bible to read. I tore out the stiff cardboard frontispiece and used it to block the light on the ceiling. They left the light on all night. Shine right in your eyes all night. I had to train myself to wake up at 2 and at 5 when they did the inspections and take the frontispiece off the light, else I'd get in trouble.

"Breakfast was always corn bread that had these chunks of corncob still in it, grits with gravy and fatback. Lunch and dinner were always beans, potato, something mushy. We drank chicory coffee. Your digestive system always cycled between constipation and diarrhea.

"We were allowed to write a letter to blood relatives once a week, but they always censored your mail going out and coming in. We got a piece of toilet paper 5 feet long every day. One time I wrote a letter to David on the toilet paper and gave it to an inmate who was being released from prison. She hid it in a sanitary napkin and smuggled it out. That's how David found out how I was doing."

Most inmates, feeling like they had sacrificed enough, left prison within a month, bailed out by the civil rights group the Congress of Racial Equality. Winonah remembers being in no hurry to leave. "To stay even longer was going to be even more dramatic. I did the crime so I was going to serve the time, so to speak. Let the nation see what they were doing to us. I stayed. That was it."

Eventually she was the only Freedom Rider in the prison. With no cellmate, she had room to run in place to keep up her strength. She lost track of time—couldn't have told you if it was Friday or Thursday or Sunday. Sometimes she talked to the guys on death row through vents. High school kids, studying civics, toured the prison. Everybody wanted to set eyes on a real Freedom Rider.

"She don't look very dangerous to me," Winonah heard a student whisper. Winonah snorted to herself: "You'd be surprised!"

Sometimes the prison matron visited her cell for a talk. The matron urged Winonah to think about the error of her ways and to repent. The matron liked to play gut-bucket country music in her office loud enough for Winonah to hear. One day she must have switched stations by accident because Winonah suddenly heard Johnny Mathis singing "Chances Are." Winonah burst into tears. She used to listen to that song at home.

They let her out on Christmas Day in 1961. David came to fetch her. From prison they took a bus to the black part of Jackson and visited friends on Lynch Street. Winonah enjoyed her first bath in more than six months. Then they grabbed a bus back north, eager to escape Mississippi.

She and David married on April 7, 1962. David never finished college, but had a long career as a newspaper photographer in the Midwest until his retirement four years ago. Winonah finished her education and taught mentally challenged adolescents and adults for years. She and David had three daughters and three grandchildren.

David told me he never stopped thinking about his days as a Freedom Rider. A few years ago he was watching television and the documentary *Eyes on the Prize* came on. He couldn't stop crying.

Later he talked to a psychologist. The psychologist said, "You feel guilty that you didn't do more. And only now are you acknowledging how frightened you were. You also feel that what you did has been sadly unappreciated."

"You hit the nail on the head," David said.

Winonah told me she never felt guilty or sad. She told me she never cared whether or not anyone appreciated her.

"When I was mad in the cell, I was mad in the cell. When I was sad in the cell, I was sad in the cell. When I got out of prison, I was glad."

David kept his souvenirs in a box in the living room, mostly newspaper clippings about the Freedom Riders. He prized those Westbrook Pegler columns that attacked him as a bleeding-hearted wimp. He told me he wished he had kept Winonah's toilet-paper letter. He didn't remember what she wrote. She didn't either.

He had a part-time job working for the Department of Agriculture inspecting fruit for parasitic flies. Winonah told me she enjoyed her humble job at the tollbooth. It only paid $6.25 an hour but she felt lucky to have it.

When she had filled out the application, she had answered honestly about her prison record. The interviewer told her, sorry, we can't hire you. Winonah, remaining calm, explained the circumstances of her time in prison. She explained how the Kennedy administration eventually enforced the desegregation laws in the South. She explained the U.S. Supreme Court decision that overturned the convictions of every Freedom Rider who had filed an appeal.

Of course, Winonah's conviction still stood because she had served her complete sentence without appeal. But she got the job.

On a winter morning in 2006, the sun rose like a glorious pumpkin over Tampa Bay. Pelicans glided over the mangroves, and belted kingfishers raised a ruckus from the power lines. As the morning ripened, Winonah Myers was too busy to watch birds.

All those anonymous people going to work. All those anonymous people going to play. On a normal shift, 1,500 cars drove past her toll-booth for destinations unknown.

Winonah, the taciturn woman, nevertheless felt herself wishing they would stop for a chat. She would tell them: "Prison wasn't all that bad. In fact, it's a good place for thinking about who you are and what you did. It really gives you time to ponder life. In a strange way, I liked it. I learned something about myself. I could survive. I recommend going to prison."

Of course, Winonah never actually shared that thought with anyone passing in the slow lane.

"Thank you" is all she said, collecting their dollar. "Have a nice day."

March 4, 2006

33

TAMPA

The Bone Man

Taft Richardson Jr. was a bent-over man with a bald head and a generous white beard tipped with dreadlocks who walked Busch Boulevard like an Old Testament prophet. He was a natural-born preacher, Lord Almighty, and I listened to him testify as I thumbed through his worn Bible. He didn't stalk the streets to preach, though if someone needed spiritual help, he was happy to give it. He was merely looking for dead animals along the highway he could drop into his sack and take home.

He believed in the resurrection of the bony. Perhaps the dead cat in the middle of the road stinking to high heaven wasn't really a cat. Maybe it was something else. Maybe it was an angel of God. Or maybe just clouds, man, just clouds.

The tail! The dead cat had a beautiful tail. Back home he used the bones in his sculpture of a lizard. He also used bones from a cow, horse, dog, pig, turkey, armadillo, and turtle in the sculpture. But the very end of the lizard tail was the tail from the roadkill cat.

He called that sculpture *Watch and Pray*. "The eyes follow you, man," he told me in 2006. "And that piece of bone on the head, that fish bone that looks something like a headdress, it represents prayer."

Florida had no shortage of artists. They painted pictures of sunsets and pelicans. They blowtorched mangrove roots out of copper. They whittled grouper out of wood and molded panthers out of clay.

Of all the artists in Florida I had ever met, Taft Richardson Jr. was the most unusual. "Bones, man," he said. "It's like I can keep the animal alive if I make something out of his bones, a-huh. The bones aren't dead to me, a-huh. Sometimes I can pick up a bone and the vibe is so strong I got to put it down, man. Something about bones is sacred to me."

Taft Richardson lived in a neighborhood in Tampa called Spring Hill. His place at 1005 E Skagway Ave. was the only house on the block. His nearest neighbors were a brick factory and a repair shop for car-wash machines. The railroad tracks were about 100 feet away but seemed closer.

When he sat in his yard during the day, Richardson had to almost shout to make himself heard. POCKETTA-POCKETTA! roared the brickyard machine. CHOOCHOOCHOO! rumbled a passing train.

"You know what, man," Richardson said in his preacher's patois. "If you listen to it, if you pay attention to it, you hear it as noise. But I get in this state, a-huh, and the noise becomes music, a-huh. I'm building something, man, and I got this music. It's beautiful."

He was sixty-two the summer he told me his story. He had grown up in the neighborhood. He left Tampa for a while, tried to make a living with his art in Washington, did construction work, but moved back when his mother was ill. He rented the house, turned it into the Garden of Eden. He didn't call it the Garden of Eden—that would have felt immodest—but everybody else did.

His yard represented the only green in the industrial neighborhood. He grew pecans, avocados, mangoes, oranges, grapefruit. He had shade, man, shade and mosquitoes. The mosquitoes seldom bothered him, but sometimes they aggravated other people so he kept a can of Off! at the ready. Off! didn't kill mosquitoes; it discouraged them. He didn't believe in killing. "I used to eat meat, but dealing with all the bones I stopped eating meat," he said.

The bone art started at his kitchen table in 1968. He remembered eating beef ribs. He remembered gnawing the meat off the bones and stacking the bones on the side of the plate. Soon he had a stack of bones.

"GIRAFFE!"

That's what he remembered yelling. The bones had spoken. Make us into a giraffe.

"The Bone Man," Taft Richardson Jr., and his Bible. Photo by Jeff Klinkenberg.

"I didn't do it, God did it," he said. "God gave me my calling."

He was about twenty at the time. He had two strong parents and friends who cared about him. Yet he felt adrift. He felt the streets calling him, as they called to other men who grew up in poverty and sometimes ended up in jail.

He liked to tell people he was saved by the bones.

His daddy was named Taft Richardson too. Taft's daddy was an auto mechanic and a boat builder. Taft's daddy could make anything with his hands and passed on those skills to his seven sons. His mother could do anything in the kitchen and in the garden. Neighborhood folks said she could heal the sick with plants. As a little boy, Taft Jr. was ill with asthma until his mother fed him herbs, goat's milk, and prayer. Even the matriarchs in the community were awed. They called her "Miss Mary," a term of respect.

Taft stuffed his pockets with bones. He stuffed his shirt with fruit. He was always playing with the bones. It was almost like he was waiting for a message. "I thought he was weird," said his older brother, Harold, sixty-nine, when I talked to him. "Then one day, years later, I came home for a visit. Taft was in the backyard with his bones. I went out there to see what he was doing with them.

"Oh, my God! I never saw anything like it!"

The crucifix, which he called *The Answer*, stood 4 feet high. He had constructed it from cat bone and pig feet and cow leg. He had built the crown of thorns using teeth from garfish.

Glory Hallelujah! was a crane made from the bones of a rooster, raccoon, and dog. The crane's head leaned back with open beak and crowed at the dawn.

Occasionally he sold a sculpture for a few hundred dollars. More often his art was displayed in museums in Tampa and Orlando and in coffee-table books such as *Just above the Water: Florida Folk Art*, written by University of Central Florida professor Kristin Congdon and Florida Department of State folklorist Tina Bucuvalas.

"He is an amazing human being and an excellent artist," Bucuvalas said when we spoke. He is "one of a large group of African-American artists who base sometimes idiosyncratic painting and sculpture upon their strong Christian spiritual beliefs. Many of these people also consider themselves preachers and consider their art as a way to spread the word."

Richardson usually carried bones home and deposited them in his backyard and let the ants do the work. The advantage of his neighborhood was that he was the only full-time resident on the block. So he heard few complaints about odors.

Used to be he drove his truck along the interstate and collected great bones from roadkill deer and alligators and hogs. The gasoline got expensive, and he traded the truck for a bike. Now he walked, though his friend with a truck sometimes took him on a road trip.

A few weeks before my visit, Taft and his friend saw turkey vultures circling over the edge of the city. After the scavengers picked clean the bones, the artist hauled what was left of the horse all the way to his backyard.

"I'm going to make it a serpent," he announced. "That's what the bones told me."

A friend ate a freshwater turtle and presented it to the artist. "That was one angry turtle," he said. "I'm going to make that turtle into a cobra."

In the backyard he had lockers full of white bones. He had containers of glue made from crushed bone and paste. He had interesting rocks and plants and pieces of tin. The house he shared with his wife, Rosa, was somewhat of a museum as well, full of paintings and bone sculptures. "Hey, man," the artist said. "What do you think of John the Baptist's head?" Fish. Cat. Turkey.

John was among his favorite biblical figures. John was a prophet who spoke spiritual truth to power. John was an eccentric, too, wearing animal skins and eating locusts and honey. Richardson liked honey but he would never have eaten a locust. That would be killing.

Florida was different when he was a boy. The neighborhood was different. White people had their own schools and churches and stores and black people had theirs. Of course, separate didn't mean equal.

The artist told me he sometimes missed the old days. He recalled fondly the small community of close-knit families. Most households had a father and a mother. Kids got into mischief, but loving adults often saved them from themselves.

Richardson told me he worried about his neighborhood now. Many children didn't know their dads. Some never saw their moms. Many kids became adults too soon.

For years, Richardson and his brother and other grandparents in the neighborhood had been running an artist's camp at the Garden of Eden. Every day kids from other blocks in the neighborhood came to work on their art.

They drew pictures, they painted, they sang, they sculpted. Of course, they heard a lot about the Bible. Some children were older teens, some were too young for school. "If the child can walk, he can dance," Richardson said. "If he can color with a crayon, he can paint."

Sometimes the children and their teacher investigated the curbs for bone, glass, and cans, which they used in their art. A bedspring abandoned on the roadside might turn out to be a daddy longlegs spider, after all. "It's a struggle man, from the womb to the tomb," Taft Richardson Jr. said. "We have to take care of our children."

He funded his children's program through his art and collected donations from kindhearted people. He held a fish fry most Saturdays to raise money.

In the early evening, after the kids had gone home, after the brick factory had turned off the pocketta-pocketta machine, he enjoyed his yard. He could even hear the cicadas.

"I feel like I'm in the wilderness, man. I feel like John the Baptist. A-huh. A-huh. It's not the wilderness of John, it's an urban wilderness."

The high-crime urban streetlights shined yellow through the pecan branches into his yard. He walked into the house, grabbed his Bible, read the scripture about the time a disciple asked the teacher for a good prayer.

"Our father, which art in heaven," is what it said in the King James in his lap. The artist was sure King James actually meant to write "Our father, who arts, in heaven."

Anyway, that's how he preferred to read it.

August 13, 2006

34

ST. PETERSBURG

Plume Hunter

The old Frenchman must have adored the view at Dogleg Key. The old Frenchman, whom other plume hunters called Chevelier, loaded his shotgun and waited for the birds to return to the roost. He especially relished shooting roseate spoonbills. To him their gorgeous crimson feathers looked green as dollar bills.

Chevelier, the most notorious plume hunter who ever drew breath in North America, was the scourge of pretty birds from the Everglades to Tampa Bay in the nineteenth century. He lived for a spell close to where I lived in southern Pinellas County, along wading-bird-infested Boca Ciega Bay. Frenchman Creek in St. Petersburg was named after him.

Plume hunters sold feathers that stylish women in New York and in Paris wore on their hats. Chevelier and other hunters almost eliminated wading birds from Tampa and Boca Ciega bays. Spoonbills, whose colorful feathers were as valuable as gold, suffered most of all.

In Tampa Bay, they stopped nesting in 1912 and did not raise young again for almost seven decades. In Boca Ciega Bay, the waterway separating St. Petersburg from its beaches, breeding spoonbills were last reported in 1881. By the time the plume trade was outlawed, about a century ago, it was nearly too late.

But now, in the twenty-first century, life was looking better for spoonbills hoping to raise a family. Take that, Chevelier.

Ann Paul scanned the mangroves with her binoculars on a spring day in 2005. Paul, who worked for the National Audubon Society, kept track of fifty thousand pairs of waterbirds on eighty islands in west central

Florida. Dogleg Key, near John's Pass in Boca Ciega Bay, was among those islands.

"There's one," she said. The spoonbill preened like a grande dame at a New Year's Eve ball. She was white and pink and gold. Her feather-less head enjoyed a green tint and a few sexy freckles. But it was that improbable Alice in Wonderland bill that provoked our double takes. I imagined two wooden mixing spoons clacking together.

As we watched, another spoonbill hopped childishly from branch to branch toward mama bird. The new arrival, hatched weeks ago, was mostly white. The chick bobbed its head ridiculously for attention. Mama ignored the "I want food NOW!" tantrum.

In 2003, Ann Paul and her husband, Rich Paul, the manager of Audu-bon's Florida Coast Island Sanctuaries at the time, were doing their annual breeding bird survey of west central Florida islands. They were flabbergasted to see a handful of nesting spoonbills in Boca Ciega Bay. "When Rich and I saw we had nesting spoonbills in Boca Ciega Bay again it was a real cause for celebration," Ann Paul told me. "I'm talking about a champagne moment."

A good time to kill was at dusk. A man with a shotgun and a skiff, hid-ing in the shadows, could make real money when the birds returned to their mangrove island roosts. When birds were breeding, when they were incubating eggs, the industrious plumer could even slay birds at high noon.

Nobody went to jail. It was perfectly legal. In fact, almost everything in pioneer Florida was legal. If something moved, or even if it didn't move, likely it would be harvested and sold. Loggers felled trees that were ancient when the first Europeans had arrived in Florida. Miners scalped the land for phosphate, and commercial hunters sold deer meat and bearskin rugs to the highest bidders.

Fancy ladies in northern cities adored those colorful feathered hats. An ounce of feathers was worth $20 in New York, the world headquar-ters for the millinery trade. A pair of spoonbill wings, typically turned into fans, fetched $7 at a time when most Floridians lived in poverty.

The New York ornithologist W.E.D. Scott wrote an account of his depressing visit to Boca Ciega Bay in the spring of 1887.

"I had been here six years before, and it fairly teemed with bird life then," he wrote in an ornithological journal, the *Auk*. "Every tree and bush on this large area contained at least one nest, and many contained from two to six or eight nests. A perfect cloud of birds was always to be seen hovering over the island in the spring and early summer months. . . . It was truly a wonderful sight, and I have never seen so many thousands of large birds together at any single point."

The Frenchman and his assistants took up residence at Maximo Point, near today's Sunshine Skyway Bridge near the mouth of Tampa Bay. Typically they would shoot birds and then process the feathers back at the shack.

"Only a few cormorants were to be seen," wrote Scott in his journal, ". . . and though I spent several hours looking over the various parts of the island, I found no other large birds breeding."

Scott tried to find out what had happened. "I am told by persons living near, whom I have every reason to believe, that it took these men five breeding seasons to break up, by killing and frightening the birds away, this once incomparable breeding resort. Of course there were other plume hunters who aided in the slaughter, but the old Frenchman and his assistants are mainly responsible for the wanton destruction. . . .

"It is scarcely necessary to draw any conclusions or inferences. This great and growing evil speaks for itself."

Chevelier's first name was Jean, though sometimes he called himself Alfred. He also used the last name Lechevallier. "His name was shrouded in confusion, possibly the result of Cracker unfamiliarity with the French language," wrote Stuart B. McIver in his history of the plume trade, *Death in the Everglades*.

Born in Canada, Chevelier listed his trade as "taxidermist." He was considered a leading citizen in Florida. A bay in Everglades National Park bears his name. A defunct company in the Big Cypress that helped build the Tamiami Trail was named after Chevelier.

His name first showed up in Florida's public record on March 16, 1881, on the day he paid a huge sum, $1,800, for 120 acres at Maximo Point in St. Petersburg. But he knew it was a good investment.

One of Chevelier's neighbors was John A. Bethell, a founder of St.

Petersburg. An accomplished hunter, Bethell shot bears, panthers, and alligators on the peninsula for food. But he pronounced himself disgusted at Chevelier's venality.

"There were plume and song birds of every description that the Creator had placed here to beautify and adorn Man's Paradise," he wrote in *History of Pinellas Peninsula* in 1912, "but the lawless marauders just about destroyed everything that came in reach of their powder and lead.

"The worst scourge that ever came to Point Pinellas was one Chevelier, a Frenchman from Montreal Canada, who located just west of Point Maximo for the purpose of killing birds for their plumes, feathers and skins."

Two Chevelier assistants bragged about harvesting eleven thousand plumes and thirty thousand bird eggs in a single season. Their best day, during nesting season, was one thousand plumes. They harvested the parent birds and left the chicks to perish in nests. Chevelier liked killing pelicans, and sometimes sold their pouches for wallets.

Having wiped out Tampa Bay's bird population, Chevelier moved to the greener pastures of the Everglades.

He died in 1895, his reputation intact, about two decades before laws were passed to put an end to plume hunting.

Ann Paul was a fiftyish woman with blond hair and skin burned by wind and sun. Her hands were scarred from encounters with a variety of birds, some rescued from entanglement in discarded fishing lines, and some captured for scientific purposes. She had been born in Gainesville, educated at Cornell, and spent much of her time in a boat patrolling the bay.

She told me her favorite time was when the spoonbills were mating in the spring. "We don't know that much about their biology," she said, "but mostly the adult birds are looking each other over. They are dressed in their best finery—their feathers have the best color of the year. Spoonbills do a lot of what we call 'skygazing.' They'll stare up at sky and open their bills wide. They are letting the rest of the world— spoonbills that might be flying overhead—know that they are spoonbills and available for mating."

At some point, amorous spoonbills take flight. They fly around an island in a high, tight spiral. People who have watched the phenomenon say it looks like the spoonbills are happy. Scientists loathe ascribing human emotions to birds so they simply say the reasons are a mystery.

Spoonbills at Boca Ciega Bay build basket-sized stick nests about 12 feet up in the mangroves. A female will lay one to three eggs. Both parents take turns incubating. The eggs hatch about a month later. Both parents take turns foraging for food. Sometimes a spoonbill will fly 30 miles to find feeding grounds that are just right. A spoonbill feeds by touch in water about a foot deep, sweeping its bills to and fro, snapping up crabs and minnows. Then it returns to the nest and regurgitates food into the chick's bill. Chicks are always hungry. They beg for food from dawn to dusk. Spoonbill parents look beautiful in the spring, but weary.

By 1920, Florida's spoonbill population was down to fewer than thirty pairs. In the twenty-first century, there were eight hundred nesting pairs. The largest nesting colony was found at Alafia Banks, in Hillsborough County, in Tampa Bay, where Ann Paul watched over three hundred nests.

The colony at Dogleg Key in Boca Ciega was more modest. She had counted nine nesting pairs, up from the six pairs she had seen in 2004. "This is a good place for them," she said, studying the island through her binoculars. "They have chosen to raise their young in the right neighborhood. There are no opossums, raccoons, or house cats to get at their nests. And no thugs to bother them."

Chevelier would have adored the view. But probably for the wrong reason.

June 5, 2005

35

GAINESVILLE

David Stevenson

Even on a gloomy morning, Forest Meadows Memorial Park was beautiful. Tucked between Newnans Lake and Hawthorne Road, the old cemetery felt like country even in the city of Gainesville. A light drizzle dripped off the shiny leaves of the magnolia tree that towered over the plaque marking Jimmy Cash's grave.

"James H. Cash," said the tombstone. "Beloved Husband of Louise. 1943–1971."

There were no flowers on the grave, not even the plastic ones that sprouted from the earth everywhere else, but not because nobody cared. They did. Louise, who went by Louisa now, remarried after five years of numbing depression and moved to Tennessee, but she had fond memories of Jim. Her kids spread out across the country, all except David. He was forty-two when I met him in 2005, a property appraiser, and lived an hour away in Starke.

David—his last name was Stevenson—forced himself to visit the cemetery every now and again, accompanied not by flowers but his own grief and guilt about what had happened so many years ago in a little country lake, when he was just a little boy who was crazy about his new stepdad.

"How can a nine-year-old boy kill a big, strong man like Jimmy?" he asked me. "I know it wasn't my fault, but I'd really like to know."

Haunted by ghosts that were more than three decades old, David Stevenson impressed me as a man in search of a life preserver. Sometimes he was sure the life preserver was within reach, and his eyes crinkled up in a wan smile behind wire-rimmed glasses. At other times the old phantoms rose up, wanting to drag him under. As he told me his story, his eyes grew vacant and looked away. Sometimes he stopped talking altogether, lost in the memories of that haunted lake of his boyhood.

What had happened wasn't his fault. Everybody told him so then, and they told him now, and deep down he knew they were telling the truth. He was only a boy, for God's sake.

So why does he feel that way?

It was a pleasant Florida boyhood, he told people. "I've read *Huck Finn*," he said. "I was *Huck Finn*." When he was at his job, appraising property, he could drive past a river or a forest or a lake or a swamp and see the little boy he once had been, fishing for bream, building forts, shooting a .22 at pop bottles, studying the sky for flying saucers, launching grapefruits like cannonballs at boulders that should have been pirate ships.

David's father, Louisa's first husband, was engineer Warren Stevenson, a midwesterner who moved to Florida when even cities seemed like towns. They married in 1962, and David and his sister came along a short time later. David liked his father, who taught him to value outdoor Florida. At the same time, his dad was as quiet and conservative as his mother was volatile and liberal. Their marriage failed; even now Louisa blamed her own immaturity. David was old enough to miss having a dad.

Jimmy Cash, a twenty-seven-year-old Tennessean fresh from the Coast Guard, came along about a year after the divorce, in 1970. He and Louisa met at a party at the University of Florida, where Jimmy was taking advantage of the GI Bill to get a degree in building construction. It was a whirlwind courtship. Louisa—twenty-nine years into a happy third marriage—still enjoyed talking about memories of her second husband, Jimmy.

"He was full of life is what I remember most. He had a great personality. He had big plans about how his life was going to go. After he died, a few weeks later, I was going through his closet to get rid of his clothes. He didn't have a lot of clothes, or shoes, but what he had he kept in perfect order. That was so Jim, and so unlike me. He had it together."

David's memories of his stepdad were also achingly sweet.

"He fished with me. Took me to the carnival in Gainesville and loved all the scary rides, even the Bullet, the one that turned you upside down. Didn't mind playing Monopoly. Because he'd been in the Coast Guard, I guess he knew all these complicated knots. He taught me all these cool knots. He taught me how to fight, you know, how to box. He was kind of butch, macho."

David had an old picture of Jimmy taken shortly before Jimmy died in the lake. In the photo, Jimmy stares coolly into the camera like he's the movie star James Dean, holding a stringer of catfish. You can see a twinkle of rebellion in Jimmy's eyes, and the hint of a tattoo on his left forearm. Jimmy got the tattoo on a wild evening in the Philippines during his Coast Guard days. He swore he was ashamed of that eagle tattoo, but to David it was kind of cool his new stepdad had one.

"I was very, very lonely after my divorce," Louisa told me once. "I prayed and prayed after my divorce that I would meet someone who would love me and love my kids. After I met Jim, I promised God that if Jim asked me to marry him I'd go back to church."

They married in the fall of 1970. "I always felt guilty I didn't go back to church," she said. "It was like I had used God as a puppet to ask him for a favor, and when God granted me the favor, I just put that God puppet back on the shelf like he was a toy."

The marriage, however brief, was memorable. Louisa remembered laughter and love.

"I don't want to make him out like he was a saint," she said. "Of course, he was human. He had his own dark side. I remember, this one night, when he got real serious and heavy and told me this terrible story. It was so terrible I didn't interrupt him or ask him questions. I just let him tell it."

Jimmy told Louisa he'd once killed a man. Didn't feel a trace of remorse. He was aboard a Coast Guard ship in the South Pacific. At sea on a dark night, Jimmy waited in hiding for another mariner to pass along the slippery deck.

"Jimmy said he pushed that man overboard. He said the man had it coming. He said the man just disappeared off the face of the Earth that night. Jimmy said people thought it was an accident, though they always wondered if he might have had something to do with it, but Jimmy said nobody ever made the accusation."

Louisa was sixty-two when she told me that story. Many years had passed. It was still hard for her to believe that Jimmy could have hurt anyone.

"Jimmy was not a violent man. Not even close. He never beat me, or beat the children, so I didn't know, and I still don't know, what to make of that old story except I think it had to be true. I know Jimmy was married once, before we met, when he was very young and living in the Philippines. I know his first wife left him for another man. I always wonder if maybe that man was the man he pushed off the ship. But I don't know.

"It's ironic, isn't it? Jim may have been responsible for drowning another man. It's kind of like karma."

During the marriage, the Cash family lived in Melrose, a rural community east of Gainesville known for pecans and outstanding fishing. They rented a tin-roofed Cracker house on State Road 21 on Lake Melrose, a good place to catch speckled perch and swim.

On May 7, 1971, David and his little sister were swimming when Jimmy came out of the house in his bathing trunks. Spring was going full tilt. The lemony scent of magnolia blossoms would have been in the air; pileated woodpeckers must have been excavating caverns in old pine trees. In the late afternoon, the water in the lake would have been cool. Most men would dip their toes in, make a joke about the cold, and creep in, if at all. Not Jimmy. Jimmy was Jimmy to the last moment of his life. He took a flying leap off the dock.

He apparently didn't know, or apparently had forgotten, about the tree stumps in wait just under the water's surface.

You can't see the dock from State Road 21, by the way, but you can see the lake behind the house. For years, David refused to even drive past the house and tried not to think about what happened there. About a year before he called me up he changed his mind.

So: On a winter's day, in 2005, he sat in his Dodge Ram in Melrose and worked up his nerve to talk about what for most of his life he had avoided talking about. Beyond the house was a hill, and beyond the hill was the lake. He let the engine run but turned off the CD player and that album by Kansas, the '70s band that had a mournful hit, "Dust in the Wind."

"Jimmy went in headfirst and came up holding his head, kind of shaking it, but face down in the water. It was just like Jimmy to play around like that, to goof off with me, so I played along with him. I got him in a bear hug and held him under. He was like a rag doll, but I kept thinking he's going to jump out of the water grinning.

"Well, he didn't do that. I pushed him farther down toward the bottom and stood on his back. I stood on his back. Stood on his back. Now in the back of my mind, I'm thinking he's goofing, but my little sister, she said, 'David, something is wrong,' so we let him up. He was all purple."

They dragged him from the lake, David told me in a southern drawl so soft and quiet that I had to lean over to hear.

"I ran to the house and called my mom. She took one look outside and freaked."

Louisa was a registered nurse. As she blew breath into Jimmy's lungs, David tried calling on the telephone for help. It took a long time for paramedics to arrive. David wasn't sure his instructions were clear enough. The paramedics didn't have a respirator with them.

"A neighbor took my sister Cindy and me to their house to wait. I remember we watched cartoons. Can't remember which cartoons, but we focused on them. Maybe we were in shock, maybe what had just happened hadn't sunk in. Nothing sunk in until a neighbor ran in and said, 'He's dead! Good God! He's dead!' A while later my grandparents arrived and took us to their house in Gainesville. I never spent another night in Melrose."

Louisa asked a priest to do a funeral service. The kids didn't go. At home, Louisa held David tight and told him it wasn't his fault, that he should put the thought out of his mind. Later, she regretted that advice. It might have been good for David to think about it and to talk about it.

"Mostly I was numb," Louisa said. "My parenting was poor. I was sick for a long, long time. I wasn't stable to begin with, so everything got worse."

In the fall, she had a baby. Jimmy's baby. Named her Missy.

Louisa moved from Gainesville to Naples. Jimmy had bought a good insurance policy, thank God, and Louisa didn't have to work. She said she was incapable of working, of thinking straight, of following through on much. She was too sapped by grief to do anything sensible. She remembered buying a house on a vacation to North Carolina, driving home to Florida, and deciding the new home was a mistake. David remembered moving twenty-one times before he was an adult.

"I would spend a lot of time up in her room at night talking about life," he said. "One night while Mom and I were talking, it was about a year after Jimmy died, I look out the window and see this giant man in a tree watching us. The man was actually leaves and limbs, but it was perfect looking, like a man. It was one of the most amazing things I have ever seen. I would look away and then look back—the man was still there. I mentioned him to my mom. She was shaken, too. She had seen him before, and she thought it was Jim saying he was in heaven and happy."

David, barely ten, smoked pot with his mom. "I read the Bible and smoked marijuana," Louisa told me. "For some reason, pot and the Bible seemed to go together. I was so lost."

Terrible years passed. Louisa married again, her kids got a new dad, and slowly she put her life back together. She gave up pot but hung on to Jesus.

David tried to do his best. A smart kid, he barely got by in school, unable to concentrate, lonely, racked by guilt. After school he delivered papers, bagged groceries, learned carpentry, had the first of many girlfriends. One broke his heart, but often he broke up with a girl before she could break up with him. When you're close to someone, he believed, you will hurt badly if they go first.

He earned a finance degree from the University of Central Florida, bought a house in Starke, lived alone, of course. Considered himself a poor candidate for marriage. David rented movies. Identified with *Being John Malkovich*, a strange film about stolen identity. Read *War and Peace* just to see if he could. Can tell you lots about Pierre Bezukhov and Anna Pavlovna and the Battle of Austerlitz. Numbed himself with alcohol or cannabis.

He saw doctors and gave up intoxicants. He experienced good days. But just when he thought he was over the hump, the bad ghost would come calling and suggest that Jimmy's death was no accident.

David once wrote me an e-mail about such a haunting:

"When you're standing on someone's back and they are drowning under you—nefarious thoughts did float through me at that moment. Sometimes I think maybe some force outside of me took over my body and I did it on purpose—or maybe I just have a totally damaged soul or am quite mistaken with too much imagination.

"I remember that moment—I am not sure it was all me at that moment—Jimmy was taking the place of my dad—maybe my territory was being threatened and I tried to harm him."

David Stevenson likes to garden. His house in Starke sat on 6 acres. He grew onions and tomatoes. Tomatoes were hard to grow anywhere in Florida, what with the nematodes and aphids and too much sun or too little, but he must have had a green thumb. Barring a hard freeze, he told me, he might have a beautiful crop come spring. Spring—a time for regrowth, for optimism.

He told me he was learning a new skill, optimism. He had taken up golf, a game that requires concentration and work, one shot at a time. He enjoyed shooting baskets. When the ball dropped through the hoop, it was a good feeling, a job well done. He is very shy but had forced himself to make new friends.

He got to know his neighbors.

They were Jerry and Sylvia Teston, easy folks to talk to, despite their own daunting problems. Years ago, Jerry got hurt in an auto accident, lost a lot of blood, and required a transfusion. Now he was dying of AIDS.

David had so much respect for Sylvia, an attractive woman with beautiful skin and a steady gaze. When she wasn't taking care of her husband and her aging mother, she was working as a waiter and finishing her college degree.

Jerry died, and David offered his regrets. A year passed. Sometimes he and Sylvia talked at the gravel road. If nothing else, David understood grief. He asked if there was anything he could do.

Sylvia threw David a life preserver. Well, could he fix her front door? A few jalousies needed fixing, too. He once had worked a summer as an apprentice carpenter and fixed everything in her house, even the toilet and towel racks. In return, she invited him to supper. Turned out she was a good cook who could do wonders with chicken and mashed potatoes.

And so it went for months. They never went out on an official date. Cautious and gloomy, David disliked the idea of a date. A date was a commitment of sorts, and he believed it was safer to keep things casual. His idea of a get-together was a meal at her house, quiet talk, a rented video, a polite good-night.

The ghost was still there, standing on his back, pushing him down.

One day early last spring, Sylvia, who was thirty-six, told David she had accepted a real date with another man, a nice guy from Macclenny. She didn't know where the date was going to lead. But she was interested in getting to know this man anyway. Unlike David, he wasn't afraid.

It was another life preserver, though neither David nor Sylvia knew it.

David hated the idea of Sylvia going out with another man. His first impulse—the old self-destructive one—was to say good-bye before he could get hurt. But he didn't. He is unsure why, except he had been thinking a lot about the past, about confronting the old ghosts, about daring to give up his guilt and get well. Perhaps Sylvia was part of that.

He telephoned and asked her to go on a walk.

"Will you marry me?" he blurted out.

It was the first optimistic thing he had done in many years. "I know it's April 1," Sylvia told him, "but you'd better not be kidding."

They were married by a justice of the peace on April 28, 2004. On their honeymoon, they traveled to St. Augustine and stayed at a B&B next to Ripley's Believe It or Not museum. They took a carriage ride that was part of a "Haunted St. Augustine Tour." David was relieved to see no ghosts.

At Sylvia's urging, David was attending church again, a Catholic church because David was raised Catholic and said he values tradition. Sylvia belonged to Grace Community Fellowship Church, where congregants spoke in tongues. But she also accompanied David to Mass at St. Edwards, too.

I took them to dinner. As we ate spaghetti, they talked about having a child before too long.

Sylvia really wanted a child.

David said, "Oh, I don't know. I'm forty-two. Maybe that's too old. I don't know if I could be a committed father."

"Well, you didn't think you could commit to getting married," Sylvia said. "But here you are."

David didn't attend Jimmy's funeral in 1971. Nobody wanted that little boy to see that poor man in his coffin. For a long time, David stayed away from the cemetery. When he turned twenty-one, he worked up his nerve. Wept at the grave and asked Jimmy to forgive him. Ten years later, he visited again. Wept.

Now, in the winter of 2005, we went together. He parked his truck on the cemetery road next to a canopy where another funeral service was about to begin. Workers arranged seats in neat rows in front of a freshly dug grave.

Ignoring the preparations, David walked past tombstones, reading as went along, until he got to Jimmy's grave. He hunkered down and brushed away a dead leaf and thumbed the sand out of the depression in the letter "A" in the name James H. Cash.

He didn't say "Hello, Jimmy" or "Jimmy, I'm so sorry" or tell Jimmy about Sylvia and then instantly feel like a weight had been lifted from his shoulders. That would be a nice ending, but it would be one of those TV movie endings, pat and unbelievable.

"You know," he told me, "I don't know how this story is going to end. I'd like to think it's going to have a happy ending, but I don't know. I think I'm on my way, but it's hard, you know . . ."

He climbed back into his truck, started the engine, and drove slowly out of the cemetery. As he headed out, a long procession of cars, lights on, turned in. Another day, another funeral.

March 13, 2005

36

VERO BEACH

Mosquito Man

What the late Roger Tory Peterson was to birds, the imperial Richard F. Darsie Jr., Ph.D., was to mosquitoes. If it flew, if it whined, if it bit—and even if it never bit—he could describe it at length. The white-haired Darsie liked to study mosquitoes through a microscope at the University of Florida's Medical Entomology Laboratory, on the state's east coast. He liked to study eggs, larvae, and pupae. Sometimes he went searching for a good puddle, scooped larvae into a vial, and raised the larvae to adulthood. That way he could identify a mosquito through its life stages.

Every quarter century or so, he updated his tome, *Identification and Geographical Distribution of the Mosquitoes of North America, North of Mexico*. U.S. booksellers were not sweeping *The Da Vinci Code* off their shelves to make room for a technical science book when I visited him in 2005, but it hardly bothered a dedicated mosquito man. Eight hundred readers had shelled out $75 for the newest edition, a 384-page volume cowritten with Washington, D.C., entomologist Ronald A. Ward.

"Who will buy this book? Are you kidding me?" Darsie asked, dismayed by my ignorance. "Every mosquito-control district in the U.S. should have this book, every agency that has any dealings with mosquitoes, and every university library that has an entomology department should have this book."

Though humanity fretted about terrorists, AIDS, and Ebola, as teeth were gnashed regarding the unspeakable appetites of sharks and alligators, the most dangerous threat to *Homo sapiens* most likely remained the humble mosquito.

In the developing world's tropics, mosquito-transmitted malaria was killing nearly 2.7 million people a year, according to the Centers for Disease Control and Prevention. Although malaria had been virtually eliminated from North America a half century ago, no mosquito expert was sleeping soundly. With bad luck, the disease might fly in on a mosquito's wings. Dengue, another sometimes fatal mosquito-borne disease, was active along the Texas border. Encephalitis, which can be fatal, flared up annually somewhere in the United States. West Nile virus was showing up from New York to Florida. That is why "Know thy enemy" was the credo of folks in the mosquito business, and why Darsie was their Yoda.

"Mosquitoes belong to the phylum Arthropoda, class Insecta, order Diptera" is how he began his book. "They are bilaterally symmetrical insects; adults are covered with an exoskeleton and bear jointed legs and two functional wings. A second pair of wings is represented by knobbed halteres. Mosquitoes may be distinguished from other dipterous insects by the presence of scales on the wing veins and by mouthparts in the form of an elongated proboscis, adapted for piercing and sucking. They are holometabolous; that is, they have four dissimilar stages in their life cycle: egg, larva, pupa and adult . . ."

Mosquito scientists tried to avoid writing like Hemingway. The famous author, however, would have appreciated the effort. He once came down with a raging case of malaria.

As Hemingway recovered from malaria in 1922, he was not interviewed by Richard F. Darsie. But it wouldn't have been out of the question. Darsie happens to be old enough. "I am sorry," he told me, "but I never discuss my age."

A colleague did. "It is hard to talk about Dr. Darsie without bringing up his age," declared Jonathan Day, a UF entomologist and national expert on West Nile. "That's what makes him so remarkable. He is still extraordinarily productive at the age of ninety." Dr. Darsie, who had worked at the Florida lab for almost a decade, listened to the testimonial without comment.

"How many scientific papers have you published since you got here?" Day asked

"Twenty-seven."

"How many papers have you published during your career?"

"One hundred and thirty-five."

"Do you remember the first?"

"Of course I do. The first was in 1949 on the genus Anopheles. I have three other papers on the griddle right now."

His colleague laughed with delight.

"He's a legend in the field of medical entomology," Day continued. "All the taxonomy questions at the lab go to him. To be productive at his age . . ."

"Please don't talk about age."

The mosquito man had wavy white hair, a white mustache, and a white goatee that made him look like the Kentucky Colonel—if only Col. Harland Sanders had been on a diet that excluded fried chicken. He was slender and pale, with a mind sharper than proboscis. His hearing remained acute enough to detect a mosquito's whine during one of his daily saunters. "I am relatively healthy," he told me crisply. "Every morning I walk three times around the campus. That's how I get a mile in."

When mosquitoes bit, he refused to give them the satisfaction of a swat. "If you are exposed to mosquito bites long enough, you become immune to the effects of the saliva, which the mosquitoes inject into your skin, which causes the itching," he said. "I don't even feel a bite anymore."

There were 3,084 known species of mosquitoes in the world. In the United States, Darsie knew of 174 species. Not all mosquitoes are biters. Mosquitoes that bite are females. They require a meal of blood to manufacture eggs. Darsie first became part of the mosquito food chain in Scottsdale, Pennsylvania, where he grew up. His mother was a homemaker and his dad was a coal mine engineer, but even as a child Darsie had a passion for insects. He was a science whiz in high school, majored in biology at Bethany College in West Virginia, and earned his master's at the University of Pittsburgh. Drafted into the air force, he spent the next four years in Florida.

"Ever hear of Buckingham Air Force Base?" he asked. He shook his head at my negative reply. "You must not know your history! It was in Fort Myers." Fort Myers during the 1940s had been an excellent place to experience voracious mosquitoes, though Darsie was hardly a mosquito man then. While serving in the medical corps, another soldier, a college professor, encouraged him to pursue a doctorate in applied science. After the war, Darsie finished his studies at Cornell.

He had stalked mosquitoes from Delaware ("*Aedes sollicitans* is an awful nuisance") to Katmandu ("For every one hundred mosquitoes I dissected, I found three with malaria parasites"). He learned early to wear long pants, a long-sleeved shirt, socks, and a hat. When night fell, he was always secure in his tent, flaps closed, safe from mosquitoes. He has never contracted a mosquito-transmitted disease. "Only time I was sick was when I crawled in a cave to study insect parasites on the island of Barbuda in the Caribbean and developed histoplasmosis. You don't know what histoplasmosis is? It is a disease you get from breathing powdered bat droppings. I was sick for quite a while."

He had studied mosquitoes at sea level. "In the Philippines, it was *Anopheles minimus* that can transmit malaria. By the way, you do know that you should italicize the genus and species, don't you?" He had studied mosquitoes in the Himalayas. "The highest I ever found mosquitoes was 12,000 feet. *Culex vagans*. What I admire about mosquitoes is their sheer adaptability. Why were they there? How had they gotten there? In Nepal, up in the mountains, they don't have old tires lying around for mosquitoes to lay eggs in like we have in this country. But they had ponds to water their yaks. Somehow the mosquitoes had gotten up there, and they were reproducing."

Darsie was married and had adult children. When I asked about them, he told me, "For personal reasons, I prefer to keep the family out of the story." He allowed that he enjoyed Broadway musicals, the old-fashioned ones, and admitted some expertise on sacred music. For a half century, he had sung in the church choir.

The choir of mosquitoes one hears whining around the ears at dusk is not singing. The sound is produced by the beating of wings. Even Darsie couldn't identify a mosquito by its whine. But if he could catch it and study it under a magnifying glass, he was in business. After a fruitful career with the Centers for Disease Control, the Agency for International Development, the University of South Carolina, and the International Center for Public Health, Darsie returned to Florida in 1996.

Florida had seventy-two known species of mosquitoes. The two most dangerous, known to transmit encephalitis and West Nile, were *Culex nigripalpus* and *Culex quinquefasciatus*. Few people become ill, but occasionally somebody dies. Mosquito-control employees from all over the country regularly visited the entomology lab in Florida to take a class with Darsie, who taught them to know their enemy.

The most fearsome mosquito in Florida, in terms of aggravation, was *Ochlerotatus taeniorhynchus*, also known as the salt marsh mosquito. In the Everglades in June, among the mangrove forests, some people claim that a swarm can blot out the sun. Everglades park rangers often wear special clothing, complete with head nets, during summer. Salt marsh mosquitoes are active and obnoxious throughout south Florida, but they were not known to transmit disease.

Darsie's lab was a big, modern building hidden among the oaks near the Indian River. His office was crammed with neat stacks of papers and boxes containing mounted mosquito specimens. Sometimes, as he peered through a microscope, he made sketches. What looked like a strange doodle to me turned out to be the breathing tube of a mosquito larva.

Sometimes he reared larvae for further study. To keep them alive, he had learned to feed them. He figured out the menu by their appearance. Predatory larvae, with their fearsome jaws and grabbing hooks, received liver powder and lacto-albumin. His book was filled with sketches and text about everything he had learned so far. The previous version of the book had been published in 1981. Information changed, and it needed an update. Even as his new book was hot off the press, Darsie continued to collect information for the next edition. He acknowledged that he might not live long enough to see it in print, but he was sure his science would endure.

On the day I visited, he was working on a paper with an entomologist who had been collecting mosquitoes at Grand Canyon National Park. "We are trying to identify species that might transmit West Nile," Darsie said. "We have identified seven species that have never been collected at Grand Canyon before."

Did he know how many species were found at Grand Canyon in all?

"Are you kidding? Of course I do! There are thirty-two species of mosquitoes that we know of at the Grand Canyon. They are mostly found in the lower elevations. If you don't want to be bitten, stay at the North Rim."

June 17, 2005

37

ANNA MARIA ISLAND

Old Jack Gray

If I hadn't been looking for Jack Gray, everything would have seemed normal at the old City Pier when I visited. Schools of nervous sardines swam frantically about the pilings, pursued from above by terns and below by mackerel. An armada of anglers, mostly elderly men, cast their lines with hope and fanfare when they weren't arguing about who caught what and when and what is the best lure for pompano. But Old Jack Gray was nowhere in sight.

I had met him a few months before, after a hurricane battered the ninety-six-year-old pier near Bradenton. I saw Gray, eighty-nine at the time, as the human embodiment of the worm-eaten structure. He had been fishing from the pier since 1946 and had no plans of stopping despite diabetes and bad lungs from smoking too many cigarettes and blood as tired as his dilapidated legs. Like the pier, he endured. When the sun rose each morning, both of them were still standing.

When I talked to him that first time, and wrote a story based on our interview, the irrepressible widower was pleased enough to buy two dozen copies of the newspaper for distribution to relatives and neighbors. On Jacaranda Street, where he long had been an institution, he was the helpful guy who looked after things without being asked, the fellow who gave all the widows mackerel fillets or bags of ripe papayas or onions from his garden, in return, perhaps, for a home-cooked meatloaf or a freshly baked apple pie.

Six weeks after our first meeting, he rose at his customary time, 4 a.m., and drove to the pier. He ate bacon and eggs at the pier restaurant and went fishing for two hours. Back home, he took a nap. He woke up feeling ill. A neighbor took him to the hospital, where doctors diagnosed a heart attack. For a few days, it was touch and go in intensive care, and neighbors back on Jacaranda, and his cronies over at the pier, held their collective breath. Pelicans can't talk, but if they could, they probably would have been whispering about the old coot, too.

Jack Gray, tough old cobb, survived. He moved to a rehab center and felt better by the day. Neighbors began their daily visits, and his pals at the pier arrived to tell him what was biting. But on Thanksgiving Day, his heart stopped again. Transported to the hospital, he never woke up. He passed away three days later, on November 30.

His champagne-colored Toyota Camry was still in the driveway when I arrived to pay my respects a few days later. An American flag flew from the antenna; his battered fishing tackle waited in the trunk. His niece, seventy-eight-year-old Dorothy Wickenheiser of Redington Shores, was tidying up the house, preparing it for sale, wondering what she was going to do with her uncle's fishing tackle, especially those jigs filling up cigar boxes in the utility room. In the backyard, Gray's new crop of onions had emerged from the soil. Now he wouldn't be there to tend them.

"Hard to imagine he's gone," the niece said.

Up and down the block, it was the same.

"I'm still talking to him in spirit," said sixty-nine-year-old Edna Tiemann, one of those widows who baked pies for Jack. "I keep thinking he's fishing in heaven."

He had always told friends and family that he didn't want a fuss made when his time came. But there was a small fuss anyway. His friends gathered at the end of the pier and scattered his ashes on the water near the pilings. Maybe those ashes would fuel the food chain that fed the mackerel and the pompano.

"Now small fowls flew screaming over the yet yawning gulf," wrote Melville in another century after another death. "A sullen white surf beat against its steep sides; then all collapsed, and the great shroud of the sea rolled on as it rolled five thousand years ago."

December 16, 2004

38

WEEKI WACHEE

Picture Man Tells His Story

Bob Hinton was talking to a cop. He always seemed to be talking to a cop. He was always talking, talking, talking. You didn't want to invite him to a Quaker meeting.

"Hey!" He was talking to a cop. "Hey! How are you? How are you? You know me, don't ya? Sure, you do. Yeah! YEAH! I think we met at that car crash in Homosassa." The cop, parked along State Road 50 in Hernando County, managed a weak smile. "Hey! Hey! How old do you think I am? What do you think? I'm seventy-five years old. I'M seventy-five DAMN YEARS OLD! Can you believe it? HEY! Most people my age, it's like 'Let's go to Wal-Mart' or 'Just let me lie on the couch.' I'M NOT GOING TO WAL-MART. I DON'T REST ON THE COUCH. Am I telling the truth?"

Cop smiled.

"I have more energy than people half my age. AM I RIGHT OR WRONG?"

In the early years of the twenty-first century, Bob Hinton was known to every cop, every firefighter, and every ambulance driver in eight west central Florida counties. Sometimes, when they arrived at a terrible auto accident, a flood, or a fire, Bob was waiting with his little video camera and many things to say.

He shot freelance video for almost every television station in the Tampa Bay area market. He shot video for the police and for schools. He was a video-taking fool.

The alligator under a car? Yes, that was Bob's footage on TV. The pine tree that fell on a mobile home after a twister? Bob drove his trusty Pontiac over miles of rain-slicked road to get the money shot.

"He's our guy up there," Keith Bunce, managing editor at WTVT–Ch. 13 in Tampa, once told me. "Nothing happens that he hasn't heard about. He reads the paper thoroughly, he's got his police scanner on, and he's out the door, ready to work, day or night."

No retirement for him. He liked working. Every time a TV station used his film, he made fifty bucks. He invested his fifty bucks in equipment or gasoline for the Pontiac.

"What do you think of my car? Huh? Pretty nice. Except for these scratches. Know how I got 'em? Hail. HAIL WAS COMING DOWN LAST WEEK SO HARD I SHOT VIDEO THROUGH THE WINDSHIELD. But even with the scratches, the car looks good. How many miles you think I got on it? HOW MANY?"

I thought as quickly as I could. Car looked new. Maybe 30,000 miles?

"I have 118,000 miles on it. Go ahead. Check the mileage. Hey. HEY! HOW OLD YOU THINK THE CAR IS?"

Bob's voice carried. Cops turned around.

"IT'S ONLY THREE YEARS OLD!"

Bob was hanging around the cops because a couple of guys had drowned in a Hernando County pond. Bob had footage on all the TV stations. TV wanted more. The cops said they wouldn't let Bob or anybody else except family and divers into the area again. Bob didn't argue, but he stayed anyway in case they changed their minds. Maybe his talking would wear them down. I decided to hang around with him.

"The cops love me. That's because I come from a family of policemen. My dad, he was a coal miner and a policeman in a mining town in Ohio. Every weekend he got his nose busted breaking up a bar fight between coal miners. TOUGH PEOPLE, COAL MINERS! I tried it myself for two weeks. These coal miners, they'd get drunk, and my father would need a nightstick. Next day they'd be friends again."

Another deputy pulled up. Waved to Bob.

"HEY! I KNOW YOU!" Bob called out. Then quieter: "Yep, yep. He knows me. They like me, the police. Want to know why? I NEVER SHOOT PICTURES OF DEAD BODIES! Not even if it's covered by a blanket. I'll shoot the car, I'll shoot the plane crash, I'll shoot the lake where the kid drowned, but I ain't taking no picture of a body. You know, the relatives don't want to see a picture of their dead husband or cousin or whatever. Some TV cameramen, that's all they want, a dead body. Not me, buddy. NOT ME!"

Bob Hinton spent eight years in the air force during the Korean War. He came home disabled in ways that are invisible. He will talk about everything except what happened to him in the war. "Even my wife don't know everything. I DON'T TALK ABOUT WHAT HAPPENED!"

As Bob talked and I listened, his wife, Louise, called him on his cell phone to remind him of something. "Yes, yes, I'll remember," he said sheepishly. A fatal accident or a plane crash—it didn't matter where Bob was, Louise could track down her unsung hero with a reminder to bring home a loaf of bread or a bottle of 7-Up. "We've been married twenty-seven years, and she still keeps track," he said.

Of course, she worried about her husband, who was recovering from prostate cancer. "I HATED IT!" he shouted at the woods. "I hated being in the hospital around all those old men who were scared and just talked and talked and talked about their health. Man, you got to be upbeat. AM I RIGHT OR WRONG?"

He looked as healthy as a chain-smoker could look, a little gaunt but without a hacking cough. He had an angular face and ear lobes that were losing the war to gravity. He hid his head under an ABC Action News ball cap.

After Korea, Bob moved to Florida and bought and sold antiques for decades. In 1990, he acquired his first video camera. Eventually the novelty of making birthday party and vacation videos wore thin. Soon he was patrolling Florida roads looking for disasters. Some cops were sure an accident wasn't a real accident unless Bob documented it.

Sometimes he edited accident videos into the high school prom videos he also shot. Those documentaries were shown in driver-education classes. He wanted students to know what could happen on the drive home from the prom if they were drunk or careless.

"It ain't fun what I do sometimes. YOU HEAR ME? IT AIN'T FUN. I've heard things I don't want to remember. A girl screaming as her car caught fire and she knew she was going to die. OH, MY LORD! I DON'T WANT TO REMEMBER THAT."

For a few minutes, thinking about tragedy, Bob got quiet.

"Hey, I'm a shy man," he announced after a short silence. "YES, I AM! But I want to show you something. No, I better not. Okay. I will. Come over here."

We walked over to the Pontiac. On the back seat lay a stack of papers. The papers told the story of Bob. They included testimonials from cops and American Legion commanders and TV station producers about his work. There was a testimonial from Rep. Ginny Brown-Waite, praising Bob in the *Congressional Record*. "Bob follows a passion," Brown told fellow lawmakers in Washington. "His greatest pleasure is giving to others."

Bob said he had other papers worth reading at home and jumped into his car. I followed him through the Hernando countryside to a Charmwood Avenue address. He and Louise lived in a pretty yellow ranch house in Spring Hill. In the backyard they maintained a graveyard for their late dogs.

Many of Bob's testimonials were in scrapbooks, but some were stored on the computer. Bob wasn't a computer person, but Louise was, which meant he had to involve her in his quest. Bob asked Louise to retrieve the computer testimonials. Grumbling, she started looking. In the meantime, he talked about the life and times of Bob Hinton.

"BOB, YOU'RE BRAGGING TOO MUCH!" Louise bellowed from the computer.

"No, I'm not, sweetheart," he protested meekly. "This fellow here wants to hear about me, is all."

"YOU'RE SHOWING OFF! AND TELL ME, WHEN ARE YOU BRINGING THE CLOTHES TO THE CLEANER?"

July 11, 2004

39

ST. PETERSBURG

Mother's Nature

I grabbed my cell phone and called my kids, told them their grand-mother didn't have long. Better get over here fast. They stood with me in the emergency room and looked helpless. The priest arrived and gave my mother the last rites. She looked up and blinked. I wasn't sure she understood that her love of strong drink had brought her here.

They had trouble finding a vein. I didn't think they would find one, but they did. Next they inserted a catheter. She kept asking to go to the bathroom. "Mom," I shouted into her ear. "You really don't have to go to the bathroom. They put a tube in you. It just feels like you have to go."

She said, "I have to go to the bathroom."

She was eighty-four and nearing the end at St. Anthony's Hospital in St. Petersburg. I thought back on everything I knew about her life as a little girl, her life with my dad, my relationship with her, how she took me countless times to *Pinocchio*, how she read Golden Books to me at bedtime, how she took joy in my writings as a little boy.

I thought of the good times and the bad, the laughter, the alcohol—especially the alcohol—and how she nurtured her grandchildren. I thought about her cigarettes and hidden bottles of wine, her wonderful childlike curiosity about everything, the funny faces she always made, the impossibly heavy purse she toted no matter what, the *National Enquirer* always folded neatly on her reading table. She was a small woman, barely five feet tall, but she looked even tinier on the big emergency room bed.

Bink! Bink! Bink!

The heart monitor was the sound track for her last day on Earth.

Beatrice Mary Grace O'Donnell. Courtesy of Jeff Klinkenberg.

My mother wasn't a mother from a Hallmark card. A tough Irish broad, Beatrice Mary Grace O'Donnell could swear, drink, smoke, and tell tall tales with the best of them. I was always grateful she never lived within walking distance of the dog track.

She was very funny, but also very sad. A high school dropout, she could do the *New York Times* crossword puzzle. As a kid I learned to duck when she got mad, though usually not quickly enough. She hit me with her hands, shoes, kitchen spoons, and, at least once, a seed pod from a poinciana tree.

She loved to talk, but even more liked to listen. You could spend hours with her and realize that for all the conversation, and all the joking, you didn't learn much about her. You were drawn to her warmth, but at some point, if you got too close, she might cut you off. She was one of the most colorful people I have known, and also among the most secretive. Fifty-four years I knew her without understanding her.

I can't tell you what she thought. I can only tell you what I know.

When I was a kid, she was the only mother on the block who routinely invited members of Jehovah's Witnesses into the house to argue religion. My mother was a staunch, rosary-saying Roman Catholic who believed that the Catholic Church was the one true church. I guess she thought it was her obligation to convert Jehovah's Witnesses before they converted her.

Mostly I think she was bored and lonely. She loved excitement. As a young woman, she was a knockout—Vivien Leigh as Scarlett O'Hara— and was used to being the center of attention. But Saturday mornings could be slow. If she had to buy a *Watchtower* to get a little conversation, so be it.

I would listen, mortified, as my mother and another religious zealot went nose to nose for an hour or two, both of them laying rhetorical traps, neither giving an inch, both secure in the knowledge that only one of them was bound for heaven.

I thought only Catholics got into heaven, and not many of those, because it was too easy to sin. I was taught that forgetting to say your prayers at night was a venial sin. Killing somebody was a mortal sin. If I believed the Dominican nuns who were my teachers, masturbating certainly was a mortal sin, and that worried me especially. Lying was somewhere in between. Same with taking the Lord's name in vain. My mother swore like a sailor.

If I dillydallied in the bathroom, or took my time getting dressed for school, or procrastinated about a decision, I could always count on my mother to set me straight.

"Shit or get off the pot!"

On Sunday, we'd sit together in a pew at St. Rose of Lima, a church always staffed by Irish priests. My mother, though born in America, was Irish all the way. After Mass, she would address the Irish priest as if she had just stepped off the boat from the Emerald Isle herself. I think she thought her fake Irish brogue would endear her to the good fathers. On the walk home, my mother and I sometimes took a shortcut through the woods on 107th Street in Miami Shores.

"You coming?" my mother would call, firing up a Pall Mall.

"Coming!" I'd shout back as I looked for garter snakes.

When I was pokey my mother roared, "Shit or get off the pot!"

She was born on August 10, 1919, in Chicago, in the home of Josephine and Matthew O'Donnell. They were second-generation Americans from Baltimore. I know little about my grandmother, but I've heard stories of Grandpa Mac. A troubled kid, he was raised at St. Mary's Industrial School, the same institution that housed George Herman Ruth, later known as the Babe.

Grandpa Mac drove a truck after he got out, married my grandmother, and then, according to family stories, murdered a man in a drunken rage. He fled to Chicago to avoid justice.

He was a wife beater and a drunk. When my mother was a little girl, he took her with him from tavern to tavern because she was pretty and precocious. She'd dance on the bar, inspiring Mac's cronies to buy him another round. One time I asked if her dad had ever hurt her. "He was the devil," she said.

He was a bootlegger for a while, but got caught and lost his car. When he had a job, he would blow his paycheck on whiskey and the horses and take off. My mother and her three siblings would end up in an orphanage while their mother worked as a maid. Then, bad news: Daddy would come home.

My mother told me once about her favorite Christmas, when a kind-hearted neighbor dressed as St. Nick dropped by with bags of candies for the kids. They were their only gifts the Christmas of 1926.

I think my mother's difficult childhood was why she never cozied up to people who had money; as far as I know, she never voted for a Republican in her life. In the 2000 presidential election, she cast her ballot for Ralph Nader. "He has spirit," she said. She valued spirit.

In eighth grade, a nun sent her to the blackboard as punishment for talking in class. As the nun addressed the other students, my mother made funny faces behind her. Eventually, my mother pulled a banana from her pocket, unpeeled it dramatically, and put the peel on the nun's headpiece. As the nun talked to the class, the peel waved in derision.

My mother got slapped silly, but I would like to believe she thought a little slap was worth it.

My mother met my father, Ernie Klinkenberg, in 1939. She sold candy and popcorn at a neighborhood movie theater. My dad was twenty-two, a piano player who dreamed of becoming the next Carmen Cavallaro. He wrote a song for her, "Candy Girl." I can remember hearing him play it when I was a boy, but I have forgotten the melody and the lyrics.

They married on November 19, 1941. He spent the war in London, Paris, and in the Philippines. They moved from Chicago to Miami in 1951, when I was two. He thought it was going to be easy finding music gigs, but he was wrong. He spent twenty-five years as the chief steward at the Fontainebleau Hotel in Miami Beach. The Cuban dishwashers and kitchen help called him "Mister Ernie" and encouraged him to play the piano whenever one was rolled into a nightclub or ballroom. One time he got to play Liberace's ivory piano in the Poodle Room.

My dad was a calming influence on my mother probably because they were opposites. She liked arguing; he refused to fight and went fishing. She hated the heat and humidity of a Florida summer; it didn't seem to matter to him that we were the last family on the block without air-conditioning.

My mother told me we were poor. I remember the time she sent me to Schwartz's Grocery to pick up a few things, and I lost the change on the way home. After she whacked me with a kitchen spoon, we knelt and prayed to St. Anthony, the patron saint of lost items. She grabbed my hand and dragged me down the street. We found the lost cash in the grass in front of the Philbrick Funeral Home.

Sometimes she fell into terrible funks. I remember annoying her on a Sunday drive when I was about six. She reached back, snatched my favorite cap from my head, and flung it out the window. As I wailed, my dad pulled off the road and retrieved the cap while my mother sobbed.

Mostly my parents laughed together, over slapstick stuff and bathroom humor. A roach that flew across the room and landed on my father's chest was the funniest thing she had ever seen. Another time, on one of those Sunday drives, a wasp glided through the window and stung my dad through his pants. Years later, my mother laughed so hard at the memory her upper plate flew across the kitchen. I remember being shocked; I never knew she had lost her teeth because of childhood malnutrition.

My mother was vain. She was sure neighborhood men were secretly in love with her. During the day, she dressed casually, and I have this memory of her hair always held in place by bobby pins. But when she and my dad went out, she gussied up.

She loved hats. In old photographs, she is often wearing something with polka dots and feathers. Even in tropical Miami, she'd wear hats to church when other ladies got by with simple handkerchiefs on their heads. In the sun, she'd wear bonnets or ridiculously huge straw hats like Mexican dancers might wear. On the top shelf of her closet, stacked like UFOs, were her colorful hat boxes. Even now, I have a hat fetish. If you see somebody ambling down Central Avenue wearing a beret, you can thank my mother. Also, if you know who has my baseball cards, let me know. When I was in college, my mother sold my collection for movie money.

My mother loved the Pink Panther movies. She liked anything slapstick. She liked a good steak, a baked potato, and spinach. She disliked fish, yellow squash, and carrots. She was a fan of *Concentration* and *What's My Line?* and the *Mike Douglas Show*. She hardly drank back then, maybe a glass of Mogen David on a special occasion. She smoked like a fiend, but always dismissed questions about it with an impatient "mind your own business."

She never smoked in front of her grandchildren when they were little. She'd smoke in the bathroom and think nobody knew. Everybody knew. The smoke would disperse through the air-conditioning vents. One time she picked up a can of air freshener and gave it a blast to hide the smoke. The air freshener was actually a can of Raid. Years later, suffering from emphysema, she always denied smoking when I took her to the doctor for her hacking smoker's cough.

She had taken up smoking when she was barely a teenager. When I was a kid, the house always smelled of stale cigarettes. I was a particularly sullen youth; my mother experienced a difficult menopause. To drive her mad I shared nothing of my life with her. I caught her going through my wallet and dresser drawer. If I was talking to a girl on the telephone, my mother would find an excuse to be in the room. We had no lock in the bathroom, which made being a teenage boy somewhat harrowing.

"What are you doing in there for so long?" she'd yell through the door. "Are you having a BM?"

Ernie Klinkenberg and the author, Jeff Klinkenberg, at the age of five, Key West, 1954. Photo by Beatrice Klinkenberg.

"No, Ma."

"So what's going on? You committing a mortal sin?"

My mother hated the idea of her sons growing up. She loathed long hair and the Beatles and boys who didn't tell their mothers everything, where they were going and what they had been doing. The night before I left home for the University of Florida, she wept.

"Are you sure you want to go?" she asked.

I was sure.

"You're not smart enough," she declared. "You'll fail."

It was the only time in my life I ever heard my father admonish her.

"Shut up, Bea."

He died from the complications of leukemia in 1982. For the longest time, my mother refused to leave South Florida and to move up to St. Petersburg. I couldn't imagine her living independently, but she thrived. She made new friends, learned how to balance a checkbook, and how to drive a car well enough to go to Mass and Winn-Dixie.

She was not a good driver, hitting the gas sometimes when she meant to hit the brakes. She drove through two garage doors, that I know of, and after she moved to St. Petersburg she became the terror of her new apartment complex parking lot. Every time she turned the key the hedges, bricks, and Detroit steel began sweating profusely.

She was drinking a lot by then. She was eighty, tired, confused, and sad. Many of her old friends had died. She missed my brother, who had moved to Canada. I had divorced and remarried, much to her regret. She didn't always keep a happy face, but she never blamed anybody or complained as far as I know. Nor did she admit she had a drinking problem. Even after the bad falls and emergency room trips, she denied drinking more than a glass of wine with dinner. Sometimes she forgot to eat dinner.

"Bea, you're killing yourself," one doctor told her. On the way home, minutes after the doctor warned her about drinking, she asked me to stop for a bottle of wine. I said no and left her in the truck while I ran into the pharmacy to fill her prescription. I was gone five minutes, but that was time enough for her to buy two jugs at the supermarket next door. Fortunately, I had a bag of sparkling grape juice in the truck. When I dropped her off at home, I substituted the grape juice for the wine. I left the wine next to a Dumpster frequented by homeless people. The wine probably didn't do them any good either.

My brother stopped drinking alcohol in 1988. Afraid of the family curse, I stopped in 2002. My mother continued. I moved her into an assisted-living facility, and for a while, it was just what the doctor ordered. She made lots of friends and was the queen of Boggle and other word games. She was also sure the handsome young recreation director wanted to marry her.

"He's my eye candy," she declared.

From the emergency room they moved my mother to a regular room. During the night her kidneys failed, and they wheeled her into intensive care. For the last time her family gathered around her.

My brother called from Canada. She heard him say his good-byes over a speaker phone. She seemed to be in no pain, though she kicked her size 4 feet under the sheet. A nurse explained that my mother might require kidney dialysis for the rest of her life. Doctors huddled; they worried about brain damage. I told them to make her comfortable.

We were ready for the end. I held her hand. One by one her grandchildren and my wife kissed her cheeks and said their weeping goodbyes. She was tough, my mother; her heartbeat stayed strong for hours. I told her it was okay to go, that her job was done. I told her it was time to join my father in heaven.

At 5 p.m. on January 30, 2004, she drew breath for the last time. I reached over and closed her eyelids and kissed her brow and laid my head across her breasts. Beatrice Mary Grace O'Donnell Klinkenberg, flesh-and-blood gal extraordinaire, was finished with this life once and for all.

My brother flew in from Canada. We threw an old-fashioned Irish wake at my house. We played Irish music, laughed at old photos, and told Bea stories. My brother remembered the time he took her to a Bruce Springsteen concert in the Orange Bowl in Miami. She was sixty-four then, probably the oldest person in the joint, but she stood on her chair and screamed like a bobby-soxer at a Sinatra concert. Afterward, she told my brother: "That was the most fun I've ever seen people have who weren't screwing." My brother failed to ask the logical follow-up question.

My dad's ashes had been buried at Bay Pines National Cemetery in Pinellas County years before. We had my mother cremated, too. The funeral director asked if we wanted to buy an urn. My brother and I had a better idea.

We drove to Beall's, her favorite department store, and bought a garish hat box at a 20 percent discount.

We buried her ashes, next to my dad, in that hat box.

May 9, 2004

THE FLORIDA HISTORY AND CULTURE SERIES
Edited by Raymond Arsenault and Gary R. Mormino

Al Burt's Florida: Snowbirds, Sand Castles, and Self-Rising Crackers, by Al Burt (1997)

Black Miami in the Twentieth Century, by Marvin Dunn (1997)

Gladesmen: Gator Hunters, Moonshiners, and Skiffers, by Glen Simmons and Laura Ogden (1998)

"Come to My Sunland": Letters of Julia Daniels Moseley from the Florida Frontier, 1882-1886, edited by Julia Winifred Moseley and Betty Powers Crislip (1998)

The Enduring Seminoles: From Alligator Wrestling to Ecotourism, by Patsy West (1998; first paperback edition, 2008)

Government in the Sunshine State: Florida Since Statehood, by David R. Colburn and Lance deHaven-Smith (1999)

The Everglades: An Environmental History, by David McCally (1999; first paperback edition, 2001)

Beechers, Stowes, and Yankee Strangers: The Transformation of Florida, by John T. Foster Jr. and Sarah Whitmer Foster (1999)

The Tropic of Cracker, by Al Burt (1999)

Balancing Evils Judiciously: The Proslavery Writings of Zephaniah Kingsley, edited and annotated by Daniel W. Stowell (1999)

Hitler's Soldiers in the Sunshine State: German POWs in Florida, by Robert D. Billinger Jr. (2000)

Cassadaga: The South's Oldest Spiritualist Community, edited by John J. Guthrie, Phillip Charles Lucas, and Gary Monroe (2000)

Claude Pepper and Ed Ball: Politics, Purpose, and Power, by Tracy E. Danese (2000)

Pensacola during the Civil War: A Thorn in the Side of the Confederacy, by George F. Pearce (2000)

Castles in the Sand: The Life and Times of Carl Graham Fisher, by Mark S. Foster (2000)

Miami, U.S.A., by Helen Muir (2000)

Politics and Growth in Twentieth-Century Tampa, by Robert Kerstein (2001)

The Invisible Empire: The Ku Klux Klan in Florida, by Michael Newton (2001)

The Wide Brim: Early Poems and Ponderings of Marjory Stoneman Douglas, edited by Jack E. Davis (2002)

The Architecture of Leisure: The Florida Resort Hotels of Henry Flagler and Henry Plant, by Susan R. Braden (2002)

Florida's Space Coast: The Impact of NASA on the Sunshine State, by William Barnaby Faherty, S.J. (2002)

In the Eye of Hurricane Andrew, by Eugene F. Provenzo Jr. and Asterie Baker Provenzo (2002)

Florida's Farmworkers in the Twenty-first Century, text by Nano Riley and photographs by Davida Johns (2003)

Making Waves: Female Activists in Twentieth-Century Florida, edited by Jack E. Davis and Kari Frederickson (2003)

Orange Journalism: Voices from Florida Newspapers, by Julian M. Pleasants (2003)

The Stranahans of Ft. Lauderdale: A Pioneer Family of New River, by Harry A. Kersey Jr. (2003)

Death in the Everglades: The Murder of Guy Bradley, America's First Martyr to Environmentalism, by Stuart B. McIver (2003)

Jacksonville: The Consolidation Story, from Civil Rights to the Jaguars, by James B. Crooks (2004)

The Seminole Wars: America's Longest Indian Conflict, by John and Mary Lou Missall (2004)

The Mosquito Wars: A History of Mosquito Control in Florida, by Gordon Patterson (2004)

Seasons of Real Florida, by Jeff Klinkenberg (2004; first paperback edition, 2009)

Land of Sunshine, State of Dreams: A Social History of Modern Florida, by Gary R. Mormino (2005; first paperback edition, 2008)

Paradise Lost? The Environmental History of Florida, edited by Jack E. Davis and Raymond Arsenault (2005)

Frolicking Bears, Wet Vultures, and Other Oddities: A New York City Journalist in Nineteenth-Century Florida, edited by Jerald T. Milanich (2005)

Waters Less Traveled: Exploring Florida's Big Bend Coast, by Doug Alderson (2005)

Saving South Beach, by M. Barron Stofik (2005)

Losing It All to Sprawl: How Progress Ate My Cracker Landscape, by Bill Belleville (2006; first paperback edition, 2010)

Voices of the Apalachicola, compiled and edited by Faith Eidse (2006)

Floridian of His Century: The Courage of Governor LeRoy Collins, by Martin A. Dyckman (2006)

America's Fortress: A History of Fort Jefferson, Dry Tortugas, Florida, by Thomas Reid (2006)

Weeki Wachee, City of Mermaids: A History of One of Florida's Oldest Roadside Attractions, by Lu Vickers (2007)

City of Intrigue, Nest of Revolution: A Documentary History of Key West in the Nineteenth Century, by Consuelo E. Stebbins (2007)

The New Deal in South Florida: Design, Policy, and Community Building, 1933–1940, edited by John A. Stuart and John F. Stack Jr. (2008)

Pilgrim in the Land of Alligators: More Stories about Real Florida, by Jeff Klinkenberg (2008; first paperback edition, 2011)

A Most Disorderly Court: Scandal and Reform in the Florida Judiciary, by Martin A. Dyckman (2008)

A Journey into Florida Railroad History, by Gregg M. Turner (2008)

Sandspurs: Notes from a Coastal Columnist, by Mark Lane (2008)

Paving Paradise: Florida's Vanishing Wetlands and the Failure of No Net Loss, by Craig Pittman and Matthew Waite (2009; first paperback edition, 2010)

Embry-Riddle at War: Aviation Training during World War II, by Stephen G. Craft (2009)

The Columbia Restaurant: Celebrating a Century of History, Culture, and Cuisine, by Andrew T. Huse, with recipes and memories from Richard Gonzmart and the Columbia restaurant family (2009)

Ditch of Dreams: The Cross Florida Barge Canal and the Struggle for Florida's Future, by Steven Noll and David Tegeder (2009)

Manatee Insanity: Inside the War over Florida's Most Famous Endangered Species, by Craig Pittman (2010)

Frank Lloyd Wright's Florida Southern College, by Dale Allen Gyure (2010)

Sunshine Paradise: A History of Florida Tourism, by Tracy J. Revels (2011)